THE THEORY
AND PRACTICE
OF WAR

The Theory and Practice of War

EDITED BY MICHAEL HOWARD

INDIANA UNIVERSITY PRESS
BLOOMINGTON

Copyright © 1965 by Cassell & Co. Ltd.

First published in the United States of America in 1966 by
Frederick A. Praeger, Inc.

Indiana University Press editions published by arrangement with
Frederick A. Praeger, Inc. First Indiana printing, 1975

Manufactured in the United States of America

Library of Congress Cataloging in Publication Data

Howard, Michael Eliot, 1922–   ed.
The theory and practice of war.

CONTENTS: Howard, M. Jomini and the classical
tradition in military thought.—Paret, P. Clausewitz
and the nineteenth century.—Craig, G. A. Command
and staff problems in the Austrian Army, 1740–1866.—
[etc.]
1.   Military art and science—Addresses, essays,
lectures.   2.   War—Addresses, essays, lectures.
3.   Liddell Hart, Sir Basil Henry, 1895–1970.
I.   Liddell Hart, Sir Basil Henry, 1895–1970.   II.   Title.
U19.H75   1975   355'.008   74-20502

ISBN 0-253-35950-3
ISBN 0-253-20177-2 pbk.

2 3 4 5 6 7 85 84 83

Contents

Foreword

IT is not our purpose in this volume to attempt any definitive assessment of the contribution which Liddell Hart has made to military history and theory, or to the events of his own time. For a thinker who is still so active such an attempt would be incomplete and premature. We have tried only to provide for him a worthy *Festschrift*: a collection of essays presented on his seventieth birthday to a great teacher by a group of his pupils, disciples, admirers and friends.

This group has been limited by considerations of space alone. Many such volumes might have been filled by contributions from the scholars, statesmen, historians and political thinkers who gladly acknowledge their debt to Liddell Hart, and the selection of those who should be invited to contribute has not been easy. It has been based on two considerations. The first was that the contributions should be grouped around a single broad, central theme: the development of strategic and tactical theory in the West from its origins in the eighteenth century until our own day, and the interaction of this theory with the actual practice of and preparation for war by soldiers and statesmen. The second was to make the contributors as representative as possible of the different categories and generations of thinkers whose work has been influenced by Liddell Hart: not only his distinguished contemporaries and that younger generation of senior officers who have had the opportunity of exercising command in war, but an even younger group of soldiers and scholars, some of them still in their twenties, whom Liddell Hart has devoted so much of the past two decades to helping and advising, and through whose work his teaching may well endure in its most lasting form.

The absence of any contribution from Germany, the land where Liddell Hart's ideas achieved such spectacular if sinister success, is a matter of keen editorial regret. Such a contribution was originally planned by one of the most distinguished of living German military historians, Dr Hans-Adolf Jacobsen, but ill-health forced him at the last moment to abandon it. His place was taken at very short notice by Captain Robert O'Neill of the Australian Army; to whom the editor owes a major debt of gratitude not only for the excellence of his essay but for the astonishing speed with which he produced it.

My thanks are due to Gerald Duckworth and Co. Ltd. for permission to quote from Major-General J. F. C. Fuller's *War and Western Civilization: 1832-1932: A Study of War as a Political Instrument and the Expression of Mass Democracy* (1932).

Michael Howard

Part 1

§1§

Jomini and the Classical Tradition in Military Thought

MICHAEL HOWARD

It is universally agreed upon, that no art or science is more difficult, than that of war; yet by an unaccountable contradiction of the human mind, those who embrace this profession take little or no pains to study it. They seem to think, that the knowledge of a few insignificant and useless trifles constitutes a great officer. This opinion is so general, that little or nothing is taught at present in any army whatsoever. The continual changes and variety of motions, evolutions, etc., which the soldiers are taught, prove evidently, they are founded on mere caprice. This art, like all others, is founded on certain and fixed principles, which are by their nature invariable; the application of them can only be varied: but they are themselves constant.

WITH these words Henry Humphrey Evans Lloyd began, in 1766, his *History of the Late War in Germany*.[1] It can almost be said that he opened also a new age in the history of military thought.

By the middle of the eighteenth century students of every aspect of human knowledge had almost completed their slow emancipation from the authority of traditional concepts handed down, usually through the medium of the Church, from classical antiquity. The tide of rational enquiry and scientific method which had begun to creep in in the days of Bacon and Galileo and had been brought to a stand in the seventeenth century, as rival orthodoxies divided Europe in their struggle for dominance, was now coming in in full flood, washing round and past those bastions of orthodoxy, the churches and the universities, bringing with it a new attitude, not only towards the phenomena of the universe, but to the organization and activities of man himself. The laws by which the universe operated and by which men regulated their societies could no longer be attributed to the dictates of an omnipotent Deity transmitted through an ecclesiastical corporation whose authority was enforced, sometimes with sadistic enthusiasm, by the secular authorities. But that some such laws must exist was self-evident to a society which had learned, after two centuries of near-anarchy, to value order as the prime social virtue. Newton had revealed them in the natural world—laws of a new kind, arising out of the properties of the matter composing the universe and not imposed on it by external or prescriptive authority. These laws created a pattern of behaviour uniform throughout the world, and by observing a part one could deduce the principles which operated the whole.

But was man not equally part of this universe? Were his activities not equally regulated by fundamental principles arising out of his nature and needs, deducible by observation and universally valid? So thought Montesquieu, whose great work on *L'Esprit des Lois* appeared in 1748 and opened with the precise but revolutionary definition: 'Laws, in their most general signification, are the necessary relations arising from the nature of things.'[2] So thought the authors of the great *Encyclopædia*, at once a manifesto and a *vade-mecum* of the new age, which began to appear in 1750. Education, penology, law, political economy, agriculture, the applied sciences, in all these fields pioneers were working, by the middle years of the century, to establish universally valid principles which would replace unthinking adherence to traditional patterns of behaviour as a guide to action.

One human activity, however, still awaited its Montesquieu, its Newton. Lloyd was not alone in observing that the practice of war was unique in remaining at the mercy of traditional prejudices. Voltaire had observed sardonically that 'The Art of War is like that of medicine, murderous and conjectural',[3] but did nothing to improve the situation. Marshal de Saxe opened his *Reveries de l'Art de la Guerre* with the much-quoted observation 'Every Science has Principles and Rules, only that of War has none';[4] but although his study is packed with wit and wisdom, no principles emerge. Guibert's *Essai Général de Tactique* (1772) opened with a similar plea, but his own work, with its confused and scintillating mixture of political insight and technical minutiae, is the last place to look for them. But Lloyd did more than wring his hands over the lack of any clear scientific thinking about military activity. He tried to do some himself.

In his Preface to the *History of the Late War in Germany*, Lloyd in fact attempted a preliminary sketch for a fuller study of military affairs which appeared fifteen years later in 1781, under

6

the title *Military Memoirs*. In this he pointed out that there were two parts to the art of war, a mechanical part which could be learned, and the application of it which could not. As with poetry and rhetoric, it was not enough to know the rules if one did not possess the talent. He pointed out also that war was not a matter of simple mechanics, for the forces involved were human ones, susceptible to moral pressures and instinctive weaknesses. He therefore devoted quite as much attention to questions of leadership and morale as he did to those of logistics, tactics, and the general conduct of operations. Finally, his discussion of the relationship of government policy and military operations showed, fifty years before the publication of Clausewitz's *Vom Kriege*, a firm understanding of the place of war as an instrument of policy, and the manner in which political considerations affected its conduct.

One can of course always find pioneers before the pioneers; and one can usually find obscure contemporaries whose work paralleled that of the thinkers to whom posterity has given the credit for new inventions. In the writings of the Marquis de Savorgnano in the sixteenth century and those of Montecucculi in the seventeenth we find a systematic analysis of the conduct of war far transcending the accumulation of factual and didactic detail which characterized most of the writers of their time.[5] In the work of Lloyd's contemporary, the Netherlander Colonel Nochern von Schorn, a substantial section is devoted to strategy, which is there defined as the art of commanding armies and conducting operations.[6] But there was in Lloyd's work a succinctness of expression and an economy of style which gave him a far greater influence than his more verbose contemporaries and predecessors; the more so, perhaps, because his conclusions were so entirely in harmony with the general pattern of eighteenth-century thinking. He did indeed deal intelligently with those moral aspects of war which were to be so much emphasized in the nineteenth century, and the political, which occupy us in the twentieth; but it was in mathematics and topography, those most exact of sciences, that he saw the true bases of the art of war. A firm grasp of these, he maintained, would always enable the

7

commander so to manœuvre his army as to attain his objective; and the objective would normally be the occupation of territory which would be of political value. If manœuvre failed, battle might be necessary; but Lloyd considered, as had Saxe before him, that an able general should be able to attain his objective without fighting one. Further, in reducing operations of war to an exact science, Lloyd laid the foundations of the vocabulary of strategic analysis which is still in current use. He coined the phrase 'line of operations' to describe the path by which an army moved from its starting-point to its ultimate destination; and armed with it he laid down certain elementary strategic principles. The line should be as short and as direct as possible. Its protection against the enemy should be a prime consideration in all strategic planning; the harassing of the enemy line of operations should be another. The line must lead to some really essential objective, and the selection of the correct line of operations might well determine the outcome of the campaign.

Two distinct schools of military thinkers can thus trace their ancestry to Lloyd. There were those who tried to follow him in establishing firm principles of strategy based on quantifiable geographical and logistic data; and there was the school which stressed primarily the moral and political aspects of war which made it impossible to treat its conduct as an exact science. Outstanding as an exemplar of the first school was Heinrich von Bülow, whose *Geist des neueren Kriegssystem* was published in 1799. Bülow added further terms to the strategic vocabulary. The destination of the army he defined as its *Objekt*. The magazine or depot from which it set out he termed its *Subjekt*; and the line linking the *Subjekts* on which the army depended he called its *Basis*. The concept of the *Subjekt* did not outlive its creator, but the terms 'objective' and 'base', together with Lloyd's 'lines of operations', moulded military thinking until our own day. But if in this sense Bülow fruitfully developed the ideas of Lloyd, in another he took them to lengths of rococo absurdity. He considered that all military operations could be conceived of in terms of a triangle, with its apex at the army's 'objective' and the other two corners at the outer edges of its 'base'. The angle at the apex,

8

he laid down, should be at least ninety degrees if the operation was to be carried out with safety. Anything less would make the line of operations unduly vulnerable to attack. Armed with this ready reckoner, and basing on it yet more abstruse geometrical calculations, a commander could prepare his operations with the maximum prospect of success.

This extreme formalism, which left the movements of the enemy army out of account altogether, was rejected by the overwhelming majority of Bülow's contemporaries and successors. It is remarkable, indeed, that such a work could be published three years after the first Napoleonic campaign in Italy of 1796. Perhaps Bülow should be seen as the last interpreter of eighteenth-century warfare and eighteenth-century rationalism, at a moment when such rationalism, civil and military, was being swept aside by the *Sturm und Drang* of the revolutionary era. It was Bülow's contemporary Georg von Berenhorst whose *Betrachtungen über die Kriegskunst* (1797) heralded the revolution in military thinking which was to match the revolution in warfare. Bülow followed Lloyd in the 'classical' school of military theorists who sought in the chaos of war for clear, consistent, interdependent principles as a guide to understanding and action. Berenhorst was the standard-bearer of the romantics. How could there, he demanded, be any 'principles of war'? Before the invention of firearms it might have been legitimate to speak of them; but modern weapons introduced so great an element of the contingent, the uncertain, the accidental, the unknown, that to attempt scientific analysis was a waste of a sensible man's time. Great captains like Frederick the Great owed their success not to any system that could be copied by others, not to any grasp of 'principles', but to energy, to genius, and to luck. The artificiality of the Frederician 'system' (which he compared unfavourably and inaccurately with the alleged naturalness and simplicity of the American tactics in the War of Independence), indeed the whole institution of standing armies with their drill and their uniforms, had had its day. To military affairs, in fact, Berenhorst brought a Rousseauite, a Wordsworthian demand for 'simplicity, naturalness, clarity and truth'.[7]

9

The nineteenth century thus opened with two extreme statements of opposing views in a dialectic whose resolution should be the ambition of every serious military theorist. Bülow and Berenhorst were soon to be displaced by two very much abler and more influential thinkers. The eighteenth-century tradition of precise operational analysis, based on logistical needs and topographical limitations, was to be transmitted to the armies of Europe and North America by General Antoine Henri Jomini (1779–1869); while the emphasis on war as the realm of the uncertain and unpredictable, a matching not so much of intelligence as of will, personality, and moral fibre, was to inspire the work of General Carl Maria von Clausewitz (1780–1831) and his yet more influential successors—Moltke, Foch, and the generals of the first World War.

Both Jomini and Clausewitz were far too experienced as soldiers and wise as thinkers to underrate the arguments of the opposing school of thought. In defining the relationship of the theory of war to its practice they wrote in much the same terms.

Of all the theories on the art of war [wrote Jomini][8] the only reasonable one is that which, based on the study of military history, lays down a certain number of regulating principles but leaves the greater part of the general conduct of a war to natural genius, without binding it with dogmatic rules. On the contrary, nothing is more likely to kill this natural genius and allow error to triumph than these pedantic theories, based on the false notion that war is a positive science and that all its operations can be reduced to infallible calculations. Yet the metaphysical and sceptical publications of certain writers succeed no better in persuading us that no rules of war exist, for their writings do absolutely nothing to disprove the maxims based on the most brilliant feats of modern war and justified even by the analyses of those who think they are disproving them.

As a general rule [admitted Clausewitz],[9] whenever an *activity* is for the most part occupied with the same object over and over again, with the same ends and means, although there may be trifling alterations and a corresponding number of varieties of combination, such things are capable of becoming a subject of study for the reasoning faculties. But such study is just the most essential part of every *theory*, and has a peculiar title to that name. . . . If theory investigates the subjects which constitute war; if it separates more distinctly that which at first sight seems amalgamated; if it explains fully the property of the means; if it shows their probable effects; if it makes evident the nature of objects; if it brings to bear all over the field of War the light of essentially critical investigation—then it has fulfilled the chief duty of its province. It becomes then a guide to him who wishes to make himself acquainted with war from books. . . . It should educate the mind of the future leader in War, or rather guide him in his self-instruction, but not accompany him to the field of battle.

But this acknowledgement of common ground was little more than a salute between two duellists. Each attacked the ideas of the other by implication, if not specifically. Clausewitz gave short shrift to Jomini's basic principles: 'To see the whole secret of the Art of War in the formula, *in a certain time, at a certain point, to bring up superior masses*—was a restriction overruled by the force of realities.'[10] Jomini loftily countered: 'If M. le général Clausewitz had been as often as I have myself in a position to ask these questions and see them answered, he would not have so many doubts about the effectiveness of theories of war based on principles, for theories alone can guide us to such solutions.' Indeed in the whole of Clausewitz's 'scholarly labyrinth', he maintained, he had been unable to find anything except 'a small number of illuminating ideas and noteworthy articles'.[11]

Jomini's taunt was, of course, quite uncalled for. He may have seen more action than had Clausewitz, but not very much more. Clausewitz had weathered the opening campaigns of the Revolutionary Wars in 1792–95 as a young ensign, and the concluding ones in Germany and at Waterloo as Chief of Staff to an Army Corps; but his service had had long interruptions with the eleven-year peace between Prussia and France after 1795, and the six years from his captivity as prisoner of war after the Jena campaign in 1806 to his enlistment with the Czar's armies in 1812. Jomini, having studied Bonaparte's early campaigns from his native Switzerland, had succeeded in exploiting the general disorder of the Napoleonic armies by getting himself attached to Marshal Ney's headquarters in the campaigns of Ulm in 1805, Jena in 1806, Eylau in 1807, and Spain in 1808, rising to the position of Chief of Staff while still retaining his Swiss nationality.

11

He served in the Russian campaign as military governor, first of Vilna and then of Smolensk, and rejoined Ney for the campaign in Germany of 1813. A series of flaming personal rows such as had characterized his entire military service (he resigned altogether some fifteen times) led to his crossing to the allied camp in time for the battle of Leipzig and the subsequent invasion of France in 1814. His opportunities for observing Napoleonic warfare at first hand were thus almost unrivalled; and he was able in his subsequent writings to put them to good effect.[12]

Jomini began to write in 1803. The study of the campaigns of Frederick the Great and of the young Bonaparte had revealed to him, he believed, precisely those fundamental Newtonian principles of strategy for which eighteenth-century theorists had sought in vain. These consisted, first, 'in directing the mass of one's forces successively on to the decisive points in the theatre of war, and so far as possible against the communications of the enemy without disrupting one's own'; secondly, 'in manœuvring so as to engage this concentration of forces only against fractions of the enemy's strength'; thirdly, on the battlefield, to concentrate the bulk of one's forces at the decisive point, or against the section of the enemy line which one wished to overwhelm; and finally to ensure not only that one's forces were concentrated at the decisive point, 'but that they [were] sent forward with vigour and concentration, so as to produce a simultaneous result'.[13]

One has only to compare Jomini's work with that of any of his predecessors—always with the exception of Lloyd—to appreciate the clarity of his insight. He did indeed have some claim to be the Newton for whom the military world had waited for so long. As for his own contributions to the Napoleonic campaigns, since he devoted the rest of a long life to touching up his image for posterity, retailing to credulous disciples how his advice alone had saved Ney and others from repeated disaster and how their ignoring it had consistently led to failure, it is difficult to distinguish truth from auto-hagiography. There is certainly enough independent evidence to indicate that he really did understand Napoleon's mind well enough to anticipate the movements of the French army both in the Marengo campaign of 1800 and the

Jena campaign of 1806, and that his analytic abilities awoke the respect of Napoleon himself.[14] Yet even the most respectful accounts of Jomini's career cannot conceal his weaknesses; and any contribution that he may have made to the success of French arms must have been counterbalanced by an intellectual arrogance and an inability to co-operate with his colleagues which would have made his presence at a busy headquarters almost intolerable. Jomini attributed the coolness which increasingly surrounded him, and his failure to achieve more brilliant successes, to the personal malice of Berthier, Napoleon's Chief of Staff; but even if such an element was present, it is not difficult to sympathize with the attitude of Berthier, wrestling with the multifarious problems of a huge and swiftly moving army, towards the dogmatic over-simplifications of the young Swiss theorist.[15] Armies, to quote Lloyd once more, are composed of *men*: great corporations whose functioning is limited not only by the frictions engendered by administrative shortcomings, natural hazards, inadequate information and human fear, but by rivalries, ambitions and an institutional inertia which it requires great qualities of character to overcome. These factors had—and have—to be understood if they are to be mastered; and it was Clausewitz, not Jomini, who rightly emphasized how essential such knowledge of human weakness must be to those who would conduct war.

It is understandable that the reputation of Jomini should have been increasingly overshadowed by that of his great rival. The Clausewitzian emphasis on *will* accorded well with the romanticism of the mid-nineteenth century. His emphasis on the Battle fitted the Social-Darwinian ideas which became current towards the century's close; while in our own day his reiterated emphasis on war as a political act is particularly relevant to the problems of a nuclear age. Yet in practice the influence of Jomini has been no less than that of Clausewitz; for it is in Jominian rather than in Clausewitzian terms that soldiers are trained to think. His *Précis de l'Art de la Guerre*, first publised in 1837, brought together in lucid and compact form the lessons he had scattered throughout his earlier works on the campaigns of Frederick and Napoleon,[16] and it is doubtful whether a more methodical and comprehensive

13

guide to the mechanics of military operations has ever been written. Military academies teaching the complicated craft of war would find Clausewitz a bewildering guide for busy young officers; but Jomini's *Précis* provided a ready-made outline for the staff-courses which the development of nineteenth-century warfare was making increasingly necessary for the armies of Europe and North America. Jomini personally shaped the syllabus of the new Military Academy founded in St Petersburg by Nicholas I;[17] his ideas, particularly as transmitted through Sir Edward Bruce Hamley's monumental *Operations of War*, provided the starting-point for such British officers as were prepared to interest them-selves in *la grande guerre*; one can trace his categories in the work of many French theorists such as Derrécagaix and Pierron; while as for the United States, according to one authority, 'It has been said with good reason that many a Civil War general went into battle with a sword in one hand and Jomini's *Summary of the Art of War* in the other . . . Jomini's writings were the means by which Napoleonic techniques were transfused into the military thought of the Civil War, which was so important in the develop-ment of basic patterns of modern battlefield procedure.'[18]

The *Précis* was, in short, the greatest military text-book of the nineteenth century. It can still be studied with profit, and not by soldiers alone. Like Clausewitz—perhaps indeed in imitation of him—Jomini understood that war was an instrument of policy, and varied in its nature according to the degree of national feeling or interest involved. His first chapter is devoted to this question of *politique de guerre*, the various kinds of war in which a nation can engage: ideological, economic, popular; to defend the balance of power, to assist allies, to assert or defend rights; with all the different demands they each made. In his second chapter he dealt with *politique militaire*, or domestic questions of military policy; and on all these matters, so relevant to our own times, his comments are particularly interesting. How does one preserve the *morale* of an army in peacetime? How does one ensure an adequate expenditure on defence? How should one organize recruitment and reserves? How should wars be financed? Above all, in the absence of a sovereign such as Napoleon or Frederick, who could command his own armies, what arrangements should be made for command? A sovereign who lacked military ability should, insisted Jomini, keep well away from his armies, where his presence could only do harm. He would embarrass the field commander, and 'if the army was outflanked, cut off from its communications and compelled to cut its way out, what sad consequences would result from the presence of the monarch at headquarters!'[19] In 1870 they certainly did. Rather, command should be given to 'a man of experience and courage, bold in battle and unshakeable in danger', with, as chief of staff, 'a man of great ability, straightforward and loyal, with whom the Supreme Commander can live in harmony';[20] the exact pattern, in fact, of high command as it was to develop in the twentieth century.

The actual conduct of war Jomini divided into Strategy, Grand Tactics (the conduct of battles), Logistics, Engineering (narrowly defined as siege warfare) and Minor Tactics. About the last two he had little to say, and his comments on Grand Tactics are significant primarily in a Napoleonic context. It was his writings on logistics and on strategy which were to have a more lasting relevance. Under 'logistics', which he defined as *l'Art Pratique de mouvoir les armées*, he included all the responsibilities of the General Staff. They comprised the preparation of all material of war; the drawing up of orders for alternative contingencies; the ordering of all troop movements; the collection of intelligence; the organization of supply and transport; the establishment of camps, depots and magazines; the organization of medical and signal services; and the provision of reinforcements to the front line. His stress on this branch of warfare reflected his experiences in the Napoleonic wars. Napoleonic operations, he wrote, 'depended on clever strategic calculations, but their execution was undoubtedly a masterpiece of logistics'.[21] Allowing for the complicating factor introduced by rail transport, Jomini's analysis remained valid as a basis for a manual of staff duties until the outbreak of the first World War.

It was in the field of strategy, however, that the famous Jominian 'principles' operated. Strategy he defined, indeed, as 'the art of directing the greater part of the forces of an army on to the most important point of a theatre of war, or of a zone of operations. Tactics is the art of putting them into action at the moment and at the decisive point of a battlefield on which the decisive *choc* must occur'.[22] From this mandatory principle, all strategic calculations flowed. The decisive point must be discerned, and a line of operations chosen leading to it from the army's base. 'The great art of choosing these lines of operations', he insisted, 'consists in making oneself master of the enemy lines of communication without compromising one's own.'[23] The choice of a line of operations thus depended as much on the dispositions of the enemy as it did on the lie of the land. Various combinations of lines were possible—concentric, eccentric, interior, exterior—according to circumstances. Possible also were various kinds of 'decisive point'. One might aim at the enemy flank and thence at his line of retreat. One might try to break through a weakly held centre. One might advance successively from point to point as had Bonaparte in 1796. And much of the skill in choosing one's line of operations lay in spreading them over as wide a front as possible, so that the enemy could not anticipate where one proposed to concentrate for the decisive blow.[24]

All these observations were simple, practical, and kept down to earth by frequent reference to the campaigns of Napoleon and of Frederick the Great. Unfortunately Jomini's analytic *penchant* led him farther into the field of abstract reasoning than his practical experience of war should have permitted him to venture. It may be legitimate, but it is also dangerous, for a theorist to think of a theatre of war in terms of a 'chessboard'. Round the fairly simple conceptual framework of 'bases' and 'lines of operations' which he had inherited from Lloyd and Bülow, Jomini embroidered a complex pattern of strategic lines, strategic points, objective points, strategic positions, strategic fronts, operational fronts, pivots of operations, pivots of manœuvre, zones of operations and lines of communication, each defined with the precision of a medieval schoolman and fitted into a general synthesis in a manner calculated to baffle the simple and fascinate the worst sort of intellectual soldier. It is not far-fetched to see the influence of this aspect of Jomini's thinking in the ponderous and pedantic conceptions of Halleck during the early years of the American Civil War.

This cumbrous analytic vocabulary is the more unfortunate since it obscures what was perhaps the most important legacy which Jomini left to future military thinkers. Like Clausewitz—indeed like anyone who had lived through those tremendous Napoleonic decades—he rejected the eighteenth-century belief, shared by Saxe and Lloyd, that campaigns could be won without battles. He did not labour the point as did Clausewitz; but in all his strategic analyses the objective of operations is always the enemy army, and all geographical objectives were means to that end, without intrinsic value of their own. On the other hand, unlike Clausewitz and his disciples, unlike, in particular, Moltke, he saw the battle in a broader context than that of a straightforward and massive conflict of forces, a 'bloody and destructive measuring of the strength of forces physical and moral' with whoever has the greater amount of both left at the end being the conqueror.[25] For Jomini it mattered *where* the battle was fought, and *how* the battle was fought. It could be delivered in advantageous or disadvantageous circumstances. It could lead to decisive or indecisive results, depending on the relative position of the respective lines of operation. Above all its conduct, no less than the calculations leading to its engagement, was a matter of skill as well as of resolution—of selecting the decisive moment, and the decisive point, for launching one's reserves, of orchestrating flanking threats with frontal attack. Jomini had seen enough battles to know how difficult this could be. 'Battles', he admitted, 'often escape all scientific control and provide us with essentially dramatic acts, in which personal qualities, moral inspirations and a thousand other causes sometimes play the leading part . . . in short, everything that can be termed the poetry and metaphysics of war will always influence their results.'[26] Nevertheless, a sound grasp of elementary principles would always provide a guide through the confusion, and make victory depend no less on wise judgement than on simple resolution and on chance.

This Jominian concept of the battle as intrinsic to operations yet subject to intelligent control was to be eclipsed by the doctrine, which Moltke and others read into Clausewitz, that the opposing army should be an objective which one attacked in the strongest possible force, relying upon greater numbers or greater moral strength to see one through. Moltke defined his strategy for 1870 as being simply 'to seek out the main forces of the enemy and attack them wherever we find them'.[27] The French Army's Plan XVII in 1914 was equally unsubtle. The Schlieffen Plan itself was certainly a manœuvre in true Napoleonic style, aiming as it did at crushing the enemy's flank, seizing his lines of communication and forcing him to battle under circumstances where a defeat would be decisive. Without such a rapid decision Schlieffen had foreseen that the weapons and the military institutions of the twentieth century could only produce bankruptcy and deadlock. So, in a way, had Jomini himself, three-quarters of a century earlier. The Napoleonic campaigns had shown, he pointed out in 1837, that 'distance no longer protects a country from invasion, and States who wish to insure against it need a good system of fortresses and defensive lines, a good system of reserves and military institutions, in short a sound military policy. That is why peoples everywhere are organizing themselves into militias to serve as reserves to the active forces, which will raise the strength of armies to an increasingly formidable level; and the greater the numbers in armies the more necessary will be a system of rapid operations and prompt decisions.'[28]

But the failure of the Schlieffen plan showed that the application of Jomini's principles to an age of mass armies backed by railways and armed with twentieth-century firearms presented technical difficulties which no one yet knew how to overcome. The classical principles of war seemed irrelevant to the requirements of trench-warfare. The 'romantic' qualities of moral strength and endurance came, for four long years, into their own. But out of that most tragic of conflicts, in which the Clausewitzian Battle acquired a frightful, Moloch-like existence of its own unrelated to strategic or political objectives, the new techniques were born which made it possible to think once more in terms of movement and manœuvre, of battle as an instrument and not an end, of generalship as an intelligent activity requiring skill and subtlety as well as moral resolution and logistical expertise, of war as the servant of policy and not its master. It was time, in fact, for a revival of classical military thinking; and that revival came in England, with the work of J. F. C. Fuller and B. H. Liddell Hart. It was appropriate that the cycle should recommence in the country where, with the writings of Lloyd a century and a half earlier, it had originally begun.

NOTES

1. *The History of the Late War in Germany between the King of Prussia and the Empress of Germany and her Allies.* By a General Officer (London 1766), i, Preface, p. 5.
2. Baron de Montesquieu, tr. Thomas Nugent, *The Spirit of the Laws* (New York 1949), p. 1.
3. Quoted by J. F. C. Fuller in *The Foundations of the Science of War* (London 1925), p. 19.
4. *Les Reveries . . . de l'art de la Guerre de Maurice Comte de Saxe* (Berlin and Potsdam 1763), i. p. iii.
5. Mario Savorgnano, *Arte militare terreste e maritima* (Venice 1599). *Memorie del General Principe di Montecucculi* (ed. Heinrich von Huyssen, Cologne 1704).
6. *Idées raisonnées sur un système général et suivi de toutes les connaissances militaires . . .* (Nuremberg 1783). See Max Jähns, *Geschichte der Kriegswissenschaften, vornehmlich in Deutschland* (Munich 1891), III, 1,775.
7. Jähns, op. cit., III, 2,130.
8. Baron de Jomini, *Précis de l'Art de la Guerre* (Brussels 1841), i. 12. Hereinafter cited as *Précis*.
9. Carl Maria von Clausewitz, tr. Col. J. J. Graham, *On War* (London 1949), vol. i. 107–108.
10. Op. cit., i. 98.
11. *Précis*, pp. 10, 195.
12. Ferdinand Lecomte, *Le Général Jomini, sa vie et ses écrits* (Paris 1869), *passim.*
13. *Précis*, p. 53.
14. See, e.g. de Montholon, *Mémoires pour servir à l'histoire de France sous Napoléon* (Paris 1823), I, and Gourgaud, *Sainte-Hélène, journal inédit* (Paris 1889). But see also E. Carrias, *La Pensée militaire allemande* (1948) for a more critical view.

15. John R. Elting, 'Jomini: Disciple of Napoleon', *Military Affairs*, xxvii (Spring 1964).
16. Most of Jomini's histories are comprised in his *Traité des grandes opérations militaires* (8 vols., 1804–10) and his *Histoire critique des guerres de la Révolution* (15 vols., 1816–24).
17. Lecomte, op. cit., p. 238.
18. Lt.-Col. J. D. Hittle, *Jomini and his Summary of the Art of War* (Harrisburg, Pa. 1947), p. 2.
19. *Précis*, p. 43.
20. Ibid., p. 46.
21. Ibid., p. 190.
22. Ibid., p. 228.
23. Ibid., p. 61.
24. Ibid., pp. 106–107.
25. *On War*, i. 246.
26. *Précis*, p. 227.
27. *Moltkes Militärische Korrespondenz aus den Dienstschriften des Krieges 1870–71* (Berlin 1896), p. 120.
28. *Précis*, p. 105.

§2§

Clausewitz and the Nineteenth Century

PETER PARET

O RIGINALITY and independence of mind are rarely comfortable characteristics, either for their possessor or for his fellow men. The new is difficult to achieve and to welcome. Yet within the compact majority that guards our taboos the innovator can count on subversive support, which changes hostility to enthusiasm and then to matter-of-fact acceptance of what has come to seem obvious. The stages of this process are often obscure. Sometimes an historic thunderclap bears out the prophet; often confirmation must wait for decades. Often, too, the original idea changes in the course of being put to work. Under the pressure of events it takes on forms never intended or imagined by its creator. With an efficiency that never ceases to be impressive, each generation chooses those features of an idea that seem immediately useful, while disregarding or even falsifying the total intellectual concept from which they stem.

Clausewitz's theories underwent such a process of selection and transformation during the nineteenth century. His political essays, which with one or two exceptions did not begin to appear in print until the late 1870's, could not contribute to the first impact of his thought. Most of his writings on military topics, however, became widely known soon after his death, with the publication, between 1832 and 1837, of an edition of *Posthumous Works* in ten volumes, the first three of which contained *On War*. It must be admitted that the German military public quickly sensed the exceptional intellectual effort represented by these historical and theoretical studies, the attribute 'classic' was not slow in coming; a decade after publication the arguments that *On War* presented already formed the subject of a work of popularization—an undeniable if dangerous accolade.[1] *On War* was translated into Dutch in 1846; several years later a French version followed; by the time Colonel J. J. Graham published his English translation in 1873, Clausewitz was considered throughout the Western world as Germany's most significant writer on war. But neither the campaigns nor the theories of the period make it readily apparent why men thought so highly of his work. A comparison of the critical literature with the original texts frequently shows the blur of minds not meeting each other, and even those contemporaries who felt convinced that their interpretations had caught the substance of the matter sometimes seemed at a loss to understand how the great reputation had arisen. 'There is something strange about Clausewitz's influence', the military historian Max Jähns wrote towards the end of the century, 'it is almost mystical in nature; his writings, too, never completed and published only after his death, have actually been read far less widely than one might suppose, and yet his opinions have spread throughout the entire [German] army and have proved immeasurably fruitful.'[2]

But what were these opinions which Jähns thought lay at the root of Moltke's strategic concepts and which the great military names of the Wilhelmine era from Schlieffen on never ceased to praise?[3] There is no sign that the century considered Clausewitz important for his speculations on war as a political and social phenomenon, or for such formulations as the distinction between total and limited war; certainly not for his most original achievement: subjecting the problems of armed conflict between nations to the dialectical analysis of German idealistic philosophy. These characteristics were indeed noted; but the interest of serving officers and commentators centred on different, and subordinate, aspects of his work. Here the military theorist shared a common fate with other figures of Germany's classical age, men who for a brief period had in their thoughts and writings combined a universality of outlook with an awareness of the specific, a sensitivity for the uniqueness of individuals and cultures. Such poets as Goethe and Hölderlin were never more crassly misconstrued than in the decades that preceded and followed on the founding of the second German Reich. And how much easier was it to go wrong when one descended from the realms of literature and philosophy to that area of activity which Gerhard Ritter argues should be termed the craft rather than the art of war.

Clausewitz's life coincided with one of the great turning-points in the history of warfare. In 1793, as a thirteen-year-old Prussian ensign, he participated in its opening phase, the attempt of the monarchical coalition to destroy the new régime in Paris. During the following decade, in a Brandenburg garrison and then as a student at the Berlin War Academy, he observed the new dynamism of the French nation and of her military tool as it developed, became institutionalized, and extended its power across Europe. His earliest surviving essay, written a year before Austerlitz, demonstrates the sureness with which he already grasped the essentials of Napoleonic strategy.[4] In the October campaign of 1806 he was captured. After his return from imprisonment in Soissons he joined the men who strove to remake Prussia's military institutions in the revolutionary mould. From 1812 to 1815 he fought against his French preceptors. Then came fifteen years of reflection and writing, followed in 1831 by a final tour of duty in the field, necessitated by the uprising of Polish nationalists —a type of conflict based, not on reasons of state, but on irrational, psychological motives, whose growing significance he had repeatedly predicted in his manuscripts.

Clausewitz was far from the first, even in the Prussian Army, to understand that a revolution in warfare had broken out beyond the Rhine. Numerous officers in the 1790's speculated on the reasons for the Republican victories, and their reports, discussions, and proposals, which filled the military periodicals, show that few among them failed to recognize some aspect of the explanation. But too often their views were fragmented, clouded by theoretical preconceptions and social prejudice, and their partial insights dissipated themselves in the dozens of minor administrative and tactical changes with which the Prussian Army experimented in the last years before the catastrophe of Jena. Among those who saw more clearly was Scharnhorst, the man who introduced the young Clausewitz to the systematic study of war and later, in the years of reform, came to rely on him as a close assistant. Scharnhorst did not formulate his inquiry into the unexpected setback of the monarchical armies in exclusively military terms. The reasons for the defeat of the Allied Powers, he wrote in 1797, 'must be deeply enmeshed in their internal conditions and in those of the French nation'—and he added that he was referring to psychological as well as to physical factors.[5] His analysis, ranging from the political motives of the opposing governments to the comparative effectiveness of their infantry's company organization and tactics, remains one of the best surveys of the War of the First Coalition. But Scharnhorst had no wish to proceed from studies of particular battles and campaigns to a philosophic investigation of war as such. He was a practical reformer, remarkably unaffected by the propagandists of either the old or the new orders, who wrote to persuade the statesmen and soldiers of Europe that without changes in strategy, administration and drill their armies would never succeed in countering the French threat. Clausewitz, notwithstanding an eventful career and a strong feeling for the technical minutiae of his profession, was of a more pronounced theoretical bent. His external circumstances also differed from those of the older man. He wrote the works of his maturity when the Emperor had been defeated, and it was no longer necessary to pattern one's arguments according to the ideological and political requirements of the moment. The time had come to draw the balance of the Napoleonic experience, to determine how indicative it was of war in general, and to demolish finally the methodical strategy of the *ancien régime*, and of those writers who carried its systematic approach over into the new age and attempted to catch war's boundlessness and violence in their refurbished nets of 'scientific principles'.

The combative posture of *On War* can scarcely be overlooked. During the second half of the century readers nevertheless tended to regard the book as though it had been written in a vacuum— their obligatory references to technological change since the author's day barely curbing their eagerness to apply his text to their own problems. The kind of distortion created by tearing the work from the soil that had nurtured it is exemplified by the exegesis commonly placed on Clausewitz's thesis of the importance of superior numbers. Proponents of the nation in arms, the war ministers and general staffs of continental Europe before 1914, gave an absolute value to these arguments, as did later unfriendly critics, with their condemnation of the author as a prophet of brute strength, whose thought had provided an intellectual cover for the stolid blood-letting of the first World War. The pressures of the age were strong indeed to blind readers to a position that the author had stated with the utmost clarity. He was concerned, Clausewitz wrote, to combat 'a strange idea that haunted the heads of some critics, according to which there was a certain size of an army that was the best, a standard size, beyond which additional forces were burdensome rather than useful'.[6] The theories of these writers—Clausewitz names Montalembert, Tempelhoff, and Massenbach among others— were based on their knowledge of the contemporary command and supply systems. Once these changed with the development of railways, of all-weather highways, the introduction of an effective staff, or simply—and more significantly—with the growth of a new attitude towards fighting on the part of commanders and troops, the concept of an ideal army-size lost any validity it might ever have possessed. It was unnecessary, however, to wait for the inventions of the future; logical analysis, which could not admit of limitations to the extent of violence or to the degree of energy called upon, showed up the hollowness of such mathematically established laws of warfare even more convincingly. The strong accents employed by Clausewitz in his debate with the rationalist literature of the preceding century suited the purpose—they were neither intended nor adequate to serve as maxims.

The campaigns of Frederick, of the French Revolution, of Napoleon, together with the inability of the theorists to span this diversity, gave Clausewitz the material on which to build his arguments. But his aim was to create a work of permanent utility. In this quest he was helped by the nature of warfare of the time. The absolutist system had maintained its military institutions in social and professional isolation and had generally employed them to support a carefully circumscribed policy. The 1790's destroyed these barriers. 'War again became a matter for the people as a whole, took on an entirely different nature, or rather approached more nearly to its true nature, its absolute perfection. The potentials that were mobilized had no apparent limits, instead these disappeared in the energy and enthusiasm of governments and their subjects. . . . War, freed from every bond of convention, had again broken loose in all its elemental fury.'[7] With these words Clausewitz foretold the future as much as he described the present. In the campaigns in which he himself had fought he recognized the forces that were to mark the use of war in the intercourse of nations during the next one-and-a-half centuries; but he had the advantage of seeing these forces at an early stage of development. The political revolution of Europe had scarcely begun, and it was not yet intensified by the revolution in technology. Clausewitz could speculate on war with a mind unencumbered by the innovations in armaments and by the ideological excesses that confused later generations. If the essential components of modern war already existed, complexities had not yet accumulated to an extent that inhibited universal analysis.

Naming the great lines of this analysis is sufficient to suggest the gulf that lies between much of Clausewitz's thought and the attitudes towards war that dominated the second half of the nineteenth century. Clausewitz proceeded from the belief that even operational problems could not be mastered from an exclusively military point of view. Not that a battalion should be committed according to political considerations; but the battalion's purpose, its doctrine and organization, derived from sources that rested in society, politics, technology. War, Clausewitz wrote, is not an isolated area of human activity, but rather an extension of policy in different form. War is an expression of political life, shaped by the social, material, and psychological qualities of each generation. It is an act of force, undertaken to bring about changes in the opponent's policy, and its ultimate objective must be the destruction of his will and of his means to resist. Violence has the tendency to accelerate. However, the concept of total violence, which provides the necessary point of reference in the analytic process, is modified in reality by political interests, material and psychological strengths, and by the imponderables of life. Politics govern the purpose of fighting, the means employed, the goals to be attained. Together these factors determine the character of each particular war: a nation may fight for its existence, or the political purpose and military goal are limited, with a consequent diminution of the energies mobilized. As reality modifies the ideal of total violence, so accidents and emotion, the frictions of life, interfere with the execution of plans, whether these apply to squadrons or an army: action in war is movement in a resistant medium. Theory and practice should be cognizant of one another, but it is erroneous to expect them to coincide. Theory must take into account the infinite diversity of actual war and avoid the restrictive character that pertains to any synthesis. Its task is not to produce a guide for action, but to help educate judgement and to provide ideal standards with which to measure and evaluate the forms that war assumes in reality.

The parts of Clausewitz's argument best understood in the second half of the century were the limitations he placed on the role of theory, and his complementary discussion of the imponderables of war. This expressed analytically the Prussian doctrine of his day, as it had evolved out of the wreckage of the manœuvre strategy of the post-Frederican age and then proved itself during the War of Liberation. Several related factors were accommodated: the growing size of the forces available; their increased mobility, rendered possible by more flexible administration and more encompassing sources of supply; the new significance of battle; the necessarily higher degree of operational initiative granted subordinate commanders. The doctrine's effectiveness depended on a common strategic purpose and firm co-ordination by the supreme leadership. To assure both was the function of the General Staff, which came to combine in unique fashion the duties of education and planning with the powers of command. In the development of this organization Clausewitz assumed a special place, both as soldier and writer, and with its triumphs of 1866 and 1870 his fame became world-wide, though many of the Staff's responses to the problems of war in an age of materialism and aggressive nationalism no longer were in agreement with his thoughts. He had become a symbol: the scholarly officer who vanquished the *beau sabreur*. In Germany his stature was further increased by a transfigured view of the early years of the century. During his lifetime Clausewitz had been far from popular; his radicalism had been feared and as a result his career, though respectable, had not been brilliant and was personally disappointing. Now, in the Wilhelmine Reich, he became honoured as the intellectual witness of the Reform Era, the theoretician counterpart of the great charismatic leaders—the Blüchers and Yorcks—and his books received the same patriotic attention that was devoted to the analysis of their campaigns. Clausewitz's universalistic outlook, however, as well as his philosophic idealism, his successors preferred to regard as conventions of his generation, as intellectual and stylistic mannerisms, rather than as central qualities of his work. They could do little else, since the emphasis Clausewitz placed on the relations between politics and war—a permanent interaction in which the political factor dominated—ran directly counter to the main movement of continental military thought. It was in keeping with this trend that when the German edition of *On War* was first reprinted, in the 1850's, the editor obscured, if he did not completely reverse, the passage favouring the supremacy of civilian over military leadership even in times of war.[8] The same exclusive professionalism, steadily extending its writ despite opposition in government and in the Army itself, led from Moltke's conflict with Bismarck concerning the shelling of Paris to that fatal over-valuation of the purely technical which found its most complete expression in the Schlieffen Plan.[9]

On War did contain sections that Wilhelmine—and Victorian—readers found more in accord with their inclinations. It was characteristic of Clausewitz that his speculations never strayed far from the touchstone of real life; when the thread of logic ran too fine he severed it. 'As many plants bear fruits only if their stems do not shoot too high,' he wrote, 'so in the practical arts the leaves and blossoms of theory must not be allowed to grow too high, but must be kept close to experience—their proper soil.'[10] Strategic and operational analyses illustrated the real war, and on their basis Clausewitz developed what may be termed a second category of propositions: the reciprocal relationship between attack and defence; the concept of the culminating point; the theses that the attack weakens as it progresses, and that it is the

30

weaker form of war with the more positive aim, while the defence is the stronger form with the more negative aim. Though in varying degree these and other arguments were suggestive of factors that might obtain in all conflicts, they necessarily reflected the specific conditions of the Napoleonic era far more immediately than did Clausewitz's thoughts on the basic nature of war. But just as his readers ignored the dialogue with other analysts in which the author of *On War* was engaged, so they made light of the historical context and the methodological functions of these propositions. His readers agreed with Clausewitz that theory should not aim for omniscience, and indeed went far beyond him in claiming that it could never be as essential as practical experience, and yet they continued to search theory for recipes of action. Essentially it was a Jominian rather than a Clausewitzian attitude that dominated military thinking, and in the intensely empirical atmosphere of the times, *On War* could hardly avoid being considered as a kind of operational manual.

The result was a jumble of misunderstandings from which the interpretation of Clausewitz was to suffer far into the present century. The extent to which this confusion affected military policy can only be guessed at; some observers, at least, thought it was possible to point to direct consequences, the German General Staff officer, for example, who wrote a few years before the first World War that the shortcomings of Prussian strategic reconnaissance in the Königgrätz campaign was largely due to the fact that 'in the teachings of General von Clausewitz, who until 1866 was considered to be the first and foremost authority on everything pertaining to war, reconnaissance was barely discussed'.[11] The failure of *On War* to address itself specifically to practical problems was repeatedly noted and deplored, and some critics, such as General von Scherff, came to the depressing conclusion that, after all, Clausewitz analysed mainly those nebulous features of war that could never be taught at all.

There were exceptions to this intellectual confusion, among soldiers as well as among scholars, but their thought had little immediate effect. Most significantly, Marx and Engels found in Clausewitz's pages a gratifying professional confirmation for their view that armies and wars 'reflect the relationship between factors of production and the structure of society', and that the form each war assumed was determined by the character of the powers engaged. Their contemporary, Wilhelm Rüstow, a Prussian lieutenant of liberal convictions who ended his military career as Garibaldi's Chief of Staff, applied Clausewitz's historical analyses to his studies of European military institutions, attempting, though often with inadequate knowledge, to trace the reciprocal workings of tactics, strategy, political theory, and policy.[12] Rüstow strongly influenced a greater historian, Hans Delbrück, whose major work fulfilled the promise of its magisterial title, *History of the Art of War in the Framework of Political History.* The bearing which scholarly investigation of the past may have upon contemporary defence policy has rarely been made more evident than by Delbrück's 'rediscovery'—to use his own term— of Clausewitz's argument that effective strategy need not be based on a war *à outrance,* but could also make use of limited means and goals. For decades the Great General Staff and its allies in the German academic community disputed this thesis on historical as well as as operational grounds.[13] The practical implications of their opposition did not become clear until 1914. Among German professional soldiers it was General von Caemmerer above all others who sought to persuade his fellow officers of the value of abstract thought for the study of modern war. In England during the same period Colonel G. F. R. Henderson blended Clausewitzian concepts with the pragmatism of the Imperial soldier in a number of essays on war, strategy, and military criticism that have retained their freshness to the present.[14]

The key that enabled such disparate minds to read Clausewitz's works in something of their author's spirit was their understanding of a fact that had always been self-evident to all but the narrowest specialist: war transcends the purely military. Awareness of the influence that policy and politics exert on operations did not, of course, imply a similarity of political views. Nor did it necessarily mean agreement with the political tendencies that might be discerned in *On War* and in the campaign histories. These, to be sure, were little more than hinted at. In developing his theories, Clausewitz, on the whole, took rational political leadership for granted: 'We assume that policy combines and reconciles all concerns of internal administration, including those of humanity . . . policy, after all, is nothing in itself but simply the representative of all these interests towards other states. That policy may take a wrong direction, that it may serve the ambition, the personal interests or the vanity of rulers, has no bearing here . . . here we can consider policy only as the representative of all interests of society.'[15] In theoretical passages and in numerous historical references he pointed to the reciprocal ties between the civilian and military spheres; but rarely did he express a judgement on the wisdom of the policies involved.

His political opinions were expressed more openly in letters and in those manuscripts that had not been incorporated in his *Works*. A reading of these pieces reveals a paradox. The century that was familiar with Clausewitz's military theories and found them difficult to accept, in some respects acted in harmony with Clausewitz's political views, which on the whole had remained unknown.

Clausewitz's essays on political topics, and his papers and letters that dealt with military questions from a largely political point of view, did not begin to appear in print until late in the century. The earliest to be published, in 1858, was an article on the social and political implications of the militia to the Prussian state. 1869 saw the appearance of the third volume of Pertz's Gneisenau biography, which contained the memorandum Clausewitz had written in 1812 to justify those officers, including himself, who were resigning their commissions rather than serve under French command against Russia. In his biography of Clausewitz, published in 1878, Schwartz printed an extensive correspondence as well as several manuscripts on political themes. Ten years later the Historical Section of the General Staff at last felt free to release Clausewitz's study of Prussia in 1806, after some of the author's indignant comments on men and events had already been quoted by historians. Further letters and manuscripts were published during and after the first World War.[16]

Clausewitz's political writings are not only scattered through the historical and periodical literature, they are also fragmented in content and approach. The pieces were occasional, motivated by specific events—the Carlsbad Decrees, the French Revolution of 1830, the Polish Insurrection. Though his appreciation of its political nature was fundamental to his study of war, the political attitudes that underpinned Clausewitz's military theories were not in themselves developed into a system. The political basis for his inquiries was formed neither by a theory of international relations nor by a belief in the rightness of a particular political and social order, but rather by a number of insights into the nature of power. Their unifying element was a concern for political efficiency. From the first essay on strategy by the twenty-four-year-old to an analysis of the European national community sketched out a few months before his death, his writings show a steady fascination with the energies that could be created by combining the determined exploitation of a country's social and economic resources with an aggressive, or at least positive, foreign policy.

The French Revolution had taught him that a state's greatest source of political energy could be its people. This force, restrained when society was parcelled into mutually exclusive compartments of rank and profession, could be released by giving each individual scope to develop, by creating within him a sense of loyalty to the state, an identity of interests with its leaders, so that he would freely expend his energy for its sake. The state, Clausewitz put it, should breathe life into the individual human force.

Together with his recognition of the energy resting in the population—and his willingness to exploit it even if this meant social change—went an appreciation of the role that psychological forces could play in the internal and external affairs of the state. Statesmen who ignored the political significance of passion, of the irrational, whether in governments, generals, or peoples, ran the risk of misinterpreting the modern world. It has frequently been remarked how difficult it was for Metternich to recognize that Napoleon might pursue a course of action that obviously conflicted with the interests of France. Clausewitz never fell into this error. He expected the Emperor to obey his demon, whatever the consequences. But neither did he overlook the eventual accretion of power that might result from a conflict of personal and national interests. Napoleon's adventure of the 100 days was hopeless and costly, and yet it put the needed crown on a legend that was to influence the later course of French history. Similarly, the stand Frederick the Great took against a European alliance added to the Germans' fund of moral, and thus political, energies; but only in the rarest of circumstances would an absolutist system permit its people to draw on this balance. As the right to make policy was limited to the few, so participation in carrying out state policy was restricted: that is to say, war was isolated from the people as a professional rather than a national activity, its character largely shaped by the employment of mercenaries and by conventions limiting the extent and intensity of violence. The soldiers themselves were drilled to suppress all emotion and initiative, until, in the clichés of the period, they resembled clockwork figures and mechanical puppets. The release of popular energy through the French Revolution made them obsolete. Clausewitz would not deny that the republican spirit was less than universal, that the *levée en masse* remained an ideal, that the revolutionary armies suffered far more from desertion than their professional opponents, who fought not for principles but for a few cents a day; but the extent to which the ideal was actually fulfilled seemed less significant to him than the new possibility that men—if they wished—could now make the cause of the state their own.

There could be no assurance, Clausewitz wrote towards the end of his life, that the years between 1789 and the battle of Waterloo would set the pattern for the future. A profound separation of governments and peoples might again come about. 'But', he continued, 'the reader will agree with us when we say that once barriers are torn down they are not so easily set up again.'[17] The high potential of military and political energy in the peoples of Europe was an incontrovertible fact to him, and both during the Napoleonic era and in the calmer years that followed he argued that governments and societies acted contrary to their interests if they attempted to ignore or repress the strongest sources of power at their disposal.

Power, to Clausewitz, was the essence of politics, as violence was the essence of war. Consequently he favoured those internal conditions that rendered the state strongest in its external relations. For that reason too, the need for broadening the political base seemed to him to remain urgent in Prussia even after the victory over Napoleon. If the Crown was unwilling to grant a constitution, he wrote to Gneisenau in 1816, it might at least relinquish some of its absolute power to the most distinguished men in the state.[18] He ridiculed the fear of revolution, particularly when it was advanced as an argument against militias or national guards. From its inception he had been one of the most determined supporters of the *Landwehr*, not so much for its purely operational value, but because such formations assured the people a greater role in the military establishment, and thus strengthened the entire fabric of the state. 'Prussia', he wrote at the height of the liberal persecutions, 'needs to arm the entire population so that it can withstand the two giants that will always threaten it from East and West. Should the state fear its own people more. . . ?'[19] It was one of the minor ironies of the period that when Metternich at the Congress of Aix-la-Chapelle persuaded the Prussian representatives of the subversive threat posed to the state by students, journalists and civil servants, Clausewitz was the officer in charge of security arrangements for the meeting.

But if he scoffed at the danger of revolt and pressed for constitutional guarantees it was not for his own ideological reasons. He was as scornful of the romantic patriotism of the professors and students, with their book-burnings and longings for the medieval empire, as he was of Metternich and the other Austrian 'drillmasters of the human spirit', as he once called them. He suspected the academics' sense of political realism, and he feared the aid they gave the Prussian reactionaries, who used their exaltations as an excuse for frustrating every move towards a more efficient division of authority. Decisive for Clausewitz was the extent to which the power of the state could be mobilized for the purpose of its foreign relations. So long as it did not block or stunt popular energy, a nation's form of government and the character of its social structure were matters of secondary importance.

Clausewitz was as ready to appreciate the special qualities of a people or a state, their peculiar historical configurations, as he was free of ideological preconceptions. His objectivity, however, was not a reflection of indifference, and he had to fight to achieve it. As a young man, soon after his release from French internment, he had written an essay *Die Deutschen und die Franzosen*, which contrasted the cruel and boastful French with the affectionate, honest and loyal Germans. But this arrogant confrontation of national character, whose language betrayed the influence of Mme de Staël and the Schlegel brothers, was not simply a compensation for his imprisonment; he wrote primarily to persuade the German people that it had no cause to fear a renewed war with the French. The essay was a call for political mobilization, akin to such pamphlets as Heinrich von Kleist's *German Catechism*, and Clausewitz's attitude soon changed. By the time he returned to France as a conqueror his emotional nationalism had given way to a degree of calm that he found lacking in nearly everyone else in the Prussian camp. A typical passage in a letter to his wife of July 1815 criticized the Prussian military leaders for wanting to blow up the *Pont de Iéna* and for being rude to Louis XVIII, thus making themselves unpopular with the people and the new régime alike. The English will emerge best from the occupation, he added, 'because they seem not to have come here in our spirit of passionate revenge'.[20] He was not carried away by the nationalistic exclusiveness that was emerging from an earlier German love for the fatherland, though he was willing to exploit its popular appeal.

Relations between the states were in his eyes too serious a matter to befog with emotion or moral argument. When, a few months before his death, in two articles he was unable to get accepted for publication, he surveyed the condition of Europe after the revolutions of 1830, he did so largely from the point of view that was coming to be known as *Realpolitik*.[21] Prussia's interests and the international equilibrium, he argued, did not favour national self-determination in Italy and Poland, and no considerations of history or of diplomatic or ethical commitment, persuasive as these might be, could be allowed to alter this conclusion. But if he rejected the 'position of seemingly supranational interests', his analysis of the Prussian situation was equally free of moral cant. Nothing was more alien to him than to justify by specious moral claims a policy that he judged to be essential for the interests of the state. When he was twenty-eight he had written that he found Machiavelli a highly instructive author, particularly in his discussion of the relations between governments, and had added, 'the only point on which Machiavelli can be faulted is that with a certain indecency he called things by their right name'.[22] The power that the state was and could become, he recognized, as he recognized the state's role in the development of the individual; but he did not impute an inherent moral value to the existence of any particular nation, or to its rise to greater power.

This suggests the limits of agreement between Clausewitz's political concepts and the attitudes that dominated the Wilhelmine age. If his views on politics foreshadowed the future, they did so imperfectly and partially. Few statesmen could achieve his independence of judgement; fewer still would consider foreign affairs as the measure of all things. Throughout the century the diplomatic and military posture of every nation was weakened by antagonisms between the classes and between its rulers and large groups of the ruled. And yet, nations were learning to mould their societies for the purposes of competition and conflict with unheard-of efficiency, and were using power in a way ever more in keeping with Clausewitz's almost mechanistic evaluation of force—though Clausewitz had never masked his opinions with the idealization of national and class egotism which now lent an increasingly strident note to politics and war. As his political writings became known they too were misconstrued and falsified. His recognition of the significance of social energies and his understanding of the workings of state power were incorporated in the intellectual arsenal of the period; their ethical postulates, which in practical terms stood for limited aims in foreign affairs and a sharing of responsibilities and duties within society, were ignored. Today the delusions and disasters of nationalism may finally be behind us. At least the controlled, rational use of political and military force has become a universally understood need of our times. No longer engaged in the old battles, we can evaluate Clausewitz with greater objectivity than could his immediate successors. Both as the theorist of war and as an interpreter of Europe entering the modern age, Clausewitz has come to mean more to this century than he did to his own.

NOTES

1. Karl Eduard von Pönitz, *Militärische Briefe eines Verstorbenen* (Adorf 1845). The following year Pönitz published a critique of conditions in the Prussian Army under the title *Militärische Briefe eines Lebenden an seinen Freund Clausewitz im Olymp* (Leipzig 1846), which attacked the Guards mystique, discrimination against Jews, inhumane treatment of the common soldier, the proliferation of medals, and other facets 'unsuited to a progressive military institution'.
2. Max Jähns, *Geschichte der Kriegswissenschaften* (Leipzig 1891), III, pp. 2,852–2,853.
3. See Schlieffen's introduction to the 5th edition of *Vom Kriege* (Berlin 1905), and the announcement by the publishers, Ferdinand Dümmler, of the 6th edition in 1910, with statements by, among others, the younger Moltke and the later Field-Marshals von Woyrsch and von der Goltz.
4. *Strategie aus dem Jahr 1804* (ed. Eberhard Kessel, Hamburg 1937). The author also predicts, p. 42, that 'if Bonaparte should once reach Poland, he would be easier to defeat than in Italy, and in Russia I should consider his destruction as assured'.
5. 'Entwicklung der allgemeinen Ursachen des Glücks der Franzosen in dem Revolutionskriege', in *Militärische Schriften von Scharnhorst* (ed. Colmar von der Goltz., Dresden 1891), p. 195.
6. Carl von Clausewitz, *On War*, Book III, chap. viii.
7. Ibid., Book VIII, chap. iii b.
8. Ibid., Book V II, chap. vi b. The faulty version, which, incidentally, became the basis for all English translations, was not corrected until A. W. Bode's edition of *Vom Kriege* appeared in 1935.
9. That even in the 1890's, and later, senior German officers could still take a sophisticated view of the problems of grand strategy is exemplified by Schlichting and Caemmerer. The former, who

retired in 1896 as Commanding General, XIV Corps, was a pronounced critic of Schlieffen's 'mechanization of the spirit'. His military and political attitudes have been carefully analysed in Sigfrid Mette's work, *Vom Geist Deutscher Feldherrn* (Zürich 1938), pp. 163–220. Caemmerer, one of the youngest lieutenant-generals in the Army, wrote a number of important books on strategy and military history after his early retirement, among them the basic *Die Entwicklung der strategischen Wissenschaften in 19. Jahrhundert* (Berlin 1904). Discussing the relationship between politics and war in his excellent study, *Clausewitz* (Berlin 1905), p. 105, he argued that 'in resolving the highest problems of war no one may exclude the other from participation, neither the statesman the general *nor the general the statesman* [italics in the original]. And therefore the great strategist of our Wars of Unification, whom we all honour and love for his exceptional qualities of mind and character, was in error before Paris when he rejected the attempts at reconciliation of the leading statesman, and permitted the problem to grow into a conflict involving the monarch. That he was also concretely in the wrong has been proved by the military–technical investigation of the incident. . . .'

10. *On War*, Preface of the author.
11. Wilhelm Foerster in his edition of Prince Frederick Charles' memoirs, *Prinz Friedrich Karl von Preussen: Denkwürdigkeiten aus seinem Leben* (Stuttgart–Leipzig 1910), II, 27.
12. An example of Rüstow's work at its best is his interpretation of Frederician linear tactics as the supreme military reflection of the absolutist system in his *Geschichte der Infanterie* (Nordhausen 1864), II, 223–275.
13. Delbrück included an account of the conflict in the 4th volume of his *Geschichte der Kriegskunst im Rahmen der politischen Geschichte* (Berlin 1920), pp. 439–444.
14. See especially the articles written for the *Encyclopædia Britannica*, and subsequently reprinted in the volume *The Science of War* (London 1905). Recently Jay Luvaas has published a selection of Henderson's pieces under the title, *The Civil War: A Soldier's View* (Chicago 1958).
15. *On War*, Book VIII, chap. vi b.
16. 'Unsere Kriegsverfassung', *Zeitschrift für Kunst, Wissenschaft und Geschichte des Krieges* (1858), Nr. 7; Georg Pertz and Hans Delbrück, *Das Leben des Feldmarschalls Grafen Neithardt von Gneisenau* (Berlin 1864–80), 5 vols.; Karl Schwartz, *Leben des Generals Carl von Clausewitz* (Berlin 1878), 2 vols.; *Nachrichten über Preussen in seiner grossen Katastrophe*, Nr. 10 of *Kriegsgeschichtliche Einzelschriften herausgegeben vom Grossen Generalstabe*

(Berlin 1888). Particularly to be noted among later publications is the correspondence between Clausewitz and his wife edited by Karl Linnebach, *Karl und Marie von Clausewitz* (Berlin 1916); selected papers edited by Hans Rothfels, *Carl von Clausewitz: Politische Schriften und Briefe* (Munich 1922); and 'Zwei Briefe des Generals von Clausewitz: Gedanken zur Abwehr', special number of the *Kriegswissenschaftliche Rundschau* (March 1937).

17. *On War*, Book VIII, chap. iii b.
18. Letter of 12th October 1816, Pertz-Delbrück, V, 152.
19. 'Unsere Kriegsverfassung', reprinted in Rothfels, p. 153.
20. Letter of 12th July 1815, printed in Schwartz, II, 161–164. See also the entry in his diary of the same date, ibid., II, 158–161.
21. 'Die Verhältnisse Europas seit der Teilung Polens', Rothfels, pp. 222–29; and 'Zurückfuhrung der vielen politischen Fragen, welche Deutschland beschäftigen, auf die unserer Gesamtexistenz', ibid., pp. 229–38.
22. 'Historisch-politische Aufzeichnungen', ibid., pp. 51–67; see in particular p. 64.

§ 3 §

Command and Staff Problems in the Austrian Army 1740-1866

GORDON A. CRAIG

O N 18th June 1857 the Austrian army celebrated the hundredth anniversary of the founding of the Order of Maria Theresa, that association of officers who had been awarded the right of membership for actions of personal initiative which had contributed significantly to victories for Austrian arms. The Chancellor of the Order was old Prince Metternich, and he lavished upon the arrangements the same care that he had given to the organization of the Congress of Vienna in 1814. At the commemorative banquet at Schönbrunn, which was attended by representatives of all the regiments of the Army, Emperor Francis Joseph was presented with a bullet from the field of Kolin, set in gold and accompanied by a plaque which was engraved with the names of Field-Marshall Daun and all the other soldiers who had won the first Maria Theresa Crosses on the day of that victory over Frederick of Prussia. Later, against the background of the Gloriette, there were *tableaux* depicting scenes from the history of the army since Maria Theresa's day, speeches by court actors in honour of those who had died in battle for the Habsburg cause, and a dramatic portrayal of an episode from the battle of Aspern. The day's festivities ended with a performance of Schiller's play, *Wallenstein's Camp*.[1]

It is melancholy to reflect upon how quickly this proud tribute to Austria's military greatness was followed by the humiliating defeats that robbed the Habsburg monarchy of its influence and possessions in Italy and Germany and handed it over to an uncertain future. For this precipitate fall from glory, which stunned contemporary Europe,[2] various reasons have been given, notably, the Empire's lack of national unity and the unreliability of some of its subject nationalities, its grave weaknesses in financial resources and administration, and the deficiencies in weaponry that resulted from inadequate military expenditure.[3] These factors were undeniably important. It is the contention of this paper, however, that the defeats of 1859 and 1866 were equally influenced by serious problems of civil–military relations and unresolved

45

differences of attitude with respect to the art of war which were rooted in the very past celebrated by Metternich's theatrical set-piece in 1857.

I

It was entirely appropriate that the celebration should have included a play about Wallenstein, for although that enigmatic figure had met his death at Eger more than a century before Maria Theresa came to the throne, his influence lived on in her army and that of her successors. It was, indeed, from the remnants of the mercenary force raised and trained by Wallenstein that Austria's first standing army was created, when Emperor Ferdinand III commissioned nine foot regiments and ten regiments of horse at the close of the religious wars.[4] In the eighteenth century some of those same regiments fought against Frederick on Bohemian battlefields where Wallenstein's army had manœuvred; and a century later the Hessen Cuirassiers who distinguished themselves at Skalitz and Langenhof could claim legitimate descent from the Pappenheimers mentioned in Schiller's play, and at least three other regiments had a similar ancestry.[5] In Wallenstein's castle at Gitschin, the capital of that Duchy of Friedland which Ferdinand II created for his Captain-General after the Battle of the White Mountain, Emperor Francis II spent five weeks in 1813; and it was there that Metternich, Nesselrode and Wilhelm von Humboldt held some of the negotiations that preceded Austria's adhesion to the Grand Alliance against Napoleon.[6] Thus, Wallenstein had at least a tenuous connection with the subsequent victories of the armies led by Schwarzenberg and Radetzky. Gitschin was also the scene of a day-long fight between an Austro-Saxon force and the Prussian First Army in June 1866, a battle which might have been won if it had not been for failures of communications with the Supreme Command in the rear.[7]

But Wallenstein's influence upon the Austrian army assumed other forms than these, and more unfortunate ones. After all, the most memorable thing about the *Friedländer* was that he had been an ambitious man and possibly a treasonable one; and the obscurity of his motives had led the same emperor who had rewarded him with a duchy for his victories to divest him of power and, possibly, to encourage his assassination. Performances of Schiller were not needed to keep this memory alive. It is not too much to say that there was always a kind of Wallenstein complex in Vienna, which created grave civil–military problems and troubled command relationships in the army throughout the modern period.

It is striking that there was hardly a ruler or a chief minister after Maria Theresa's time who was not in some measure suspicious of outstanding field commanders. The great Empress was perhaps exceptional in this respect because, unlike most of her successors, she was capable of gratitude. She never forgot that Daun's victory at Kolin had marked a major turning-point in Austria's fortunes, and she remained loyal to the Field-Marshal long after her ministers and allies had begun to clamour for his recall on the grounds that his excessive circumspection stood in the way of complete victory over Frederick. Daun repaid his Empress's support by working indefatigably to modernize and make an efficient fighting force out of an army that had in 1740 been a disorganized welter of units without leadership, armament or training; and he left to his successor Lacy a basically sound organization and a fighting force that was generally considered to be as good as Prussia's.[8]

The two most gifted field commanders in the period that stretched between the Seven Years War and the creation of the alliance of 1813 had less happy relations with their sovereigns. Laudon, the victor at Olmütz and Kunersdorf and Glatz, was a better strategist than Daun and infinitely more offensive-minded. He also, however, enjoyed a popularity greater than any Austrian commander since Eugene of Savoy. This hardly ingratiated him with Joseph II, who found no employment for the Field-Marshal's talents. Laudon was relegated to a retirement that lasted almost a quarter of a century, until in 1789, a year before he died, he was hurriedly summoned to extricate the Emperor from the complications of a badly planned war against the Turks and displayed his old mastery, for the last time, by capturing the stronghold of Belgrade.[9]

Worse was the treatment meted out to the man who is sometimes called Austria's greatest *Feldherr* after the time of Eugene. In all of his campaigns Archduke Charles had to contend with the suspicion of his brother, Francis II, and the open hostility of the Emperor's ministers, who did not hesitate to question his strategy or even his direction of operations. In 1793, for instance, when the young Archduke, in what was virtually his baptism of fire, drove the French revolutionary army of Dumouriez out of the Austrian province of Belgium, these initial victories were vitiated by the persistent refusal of the Emperor, acting on the advice of his minister Thugut, either to strengthen the Austrian forces in the west or to use diplomatic means to secure a more effective alliance with Prussia. When French pressure was renewed at the beginning of 1794, Charles was denied the overall command that his previous victories justified; and the Austrian army of the west, badly led, was smashed by Jourdan at Fleurus.[10] Two years later, when the critical situation on the Rhine made it impossible to deny Charles supreme command, Thugut arranged to have a tool of his own, Lieutenant-Field-Marshal Count Bellegarde, appointed as his deputy and, through him, interfered with the operations against the enemy. Despite the resultant annoyance and confusion, Charles fought a masterful double campaign against Jourdan and Moreau, defeating them separately and forcing their armies back across the Rhine.[11] But even this did not stop ministerial incursions into the operational field or reduce the suspicions with which Charles was regarded in Vienna.

The Archduke made enemies in the capital partly because he did not restrict his activities to the military sphere. With great conviction, he held that a nation's foreign policy must be determined on the basis of a proper assessment of its resources, and particularly of its military strength and potential. In the Austrian case, this precept was often flouted. Increasingly in 1796 and 1797 Charles felt that the government was seeking to achieve objectives that were beyond the reach of an army whose vigour and spirit had been worn down by incessant campaigning; and he did not hesitate to travel to Vienna to press his case. These occasional forays were resented and feared by ministers who, for their part, never had any compunction about meddling in Charles' own sphere of competence, and they also aroused the indignation of his brother. In 1797, when the Archduke came to the capital in his capacity as commander on the Italian front, and warned that peace should be sought because troop morale was at the breaking-point, he was, as he said ruefully, simply 'hunted out of Vienna'.[12] The young Bonaparte subsequently proved that all of Charles' fears were justified, but this won him no credit. After the Government had been forced to submit to the peace of Leoben, Charles was relieved of his post in Italy and sent to Mannheim in disgrace, to take up command of the Rhine Army once more but with strict orders to remain at his new headquarters unless given specific authorization to leave it.[13]

Charles' position did not improve with the passage of time. During the War of the Second Coalition, incessant ministerial interference brought him to the point of resignation, a step which he reconsidered only after the Emperor accused him of insubordination. Once more he won smashing victories in the field, this time over Masséna in Switzerland, but once more they were thrown away by politically inspired changes in the allied command structure, which allowed the French to recover.

The complete lack of co-ordination between political and military strategy that resulted from all this brought Austria to the nadir of its fortunes at Marengo in 1800. At long last Thugut was forced from office, and there was a popular demand for a grant of greater authority to the one Austrian soldier who seemed to be capable of beating the French in the open field. To this feeling the Emperor yielded: Charles was appointed President of the Supreme War Council in January 1801 and six months later was made War and Naval Minister as well. With the whole military establishment unified in his person, he was now in the position to carry through reforms he had long believed essential. But this opportunity was of limited duration. For a brief period Charles was permitted to effect changes in disciplinary codes and training, in recruitment and staff work; but in 1805 the Emperor undid the very basis of these reforms by destroying the newly created unity of the military system, re-establishing the *Hofkriegsrat* as a separate body, and depriving Charles of any influence over it. He even undermined the Archduke's authority in the Army Command by dismissing his chief aides and saddling him with a Quartermaster whose views were diametrically opposed to his own, a General Mack, who Francis believed had military gifts as great as his brother's. These demoralizing changes coincided with the outbreak of the war of 1805, during which Charles was sent to the Italian front, too far away to prevent Mack's crushing defeat at Austerlitz, which destroyed everything that had been accomplished since the beginning of the century.

After 1805 Charles took up the task of reform once more,[14] successfully enough to prepare the army for the great effort of 1809 and for the first clear defeat of Napoleon in battle, the Austrian victory at Aspern. But if Aspern was the height of Charles' career, it was also its end, not merely because it was followed by Wagram, but because there was to be no future employment for him. Despite his great services to the state, there was no disposition to appoint him to supreme command again. When the great hour of liberation struck in 1813, neither the Emperor nor his chief minister Metternich wanted him, and the latter said, 'We need a commander who makes war, not one who is a politician. The Archduke wants to be Minister of Foreign Affairs as well, and that is not compatible with the functions of a commander.'[15]

The supreme command in the campaign that led to Leipzig, and eventually to Napoleon's abdication, fell, therefore, not to Charles but to Field-Marshal Karl Philip Prince Schwarzenberg, a competent but not inspiring *Feldherr*, whose system of command Clausewitz (perhaps a biased observer) described as 'hesitant and lacking determination'.[16] Schwarzenberg was too circumspect to dabble in politics and too dull to acquire a popular following large enough to worry the politicians in Vienna. Even so, he was not entirely spared the kind of interference that had plagued his predecessor. In September 1813 his Chief of Staff, Radetzky, urged him to impress upon the Emperor the necessity, not only of increased material support, but also of less court interference in the sphere of strategical planning. 'Every operational plan which we have so far proposed', he wrote, 'has been greeted with opposition as soon as we spoke of putting it into effect. Everybody has something to say in the way of criticism, but no one ever tries to put forward a better proposal.'[17] In December 1813 the momentum of the Austrian drive towards France slowed when the Emperor and his aides objected to the army's crossing the Rhine. When Radetzky pressed for a continuation of the offensive, Francis said jokingly that it looked as if he would have in the end either to imprison or to behead him because of his operational ideas, and one of the Emperor's councillors asked spitefully, 'Are you trying to be smarter than Prince Eugene?'[18]

Differences between generals and politicians are not uncommon in wartime, and it would be difficult to find a nation whose history was entirely free of civil–military conflict. The striking feature of the Austrian case, however, is the fact that such conflict was so continuous that it became a kind of law of Austrian politics. Even in the great crisis of 1848–49, when the fate of the dynasty depended on the vigour and skill of its soldiers, the court and the politicians found time to indulge their now traditional suspicion of outstanding military talent; and the new Emperor Francis Joseph joined them in this exercise. On 13th February 1849, during the Hungarian campaign of Field-Marshal Windischgrätz, the *Wiener Zeitung* reported a rumour that the Emperor intended to honour the commander by making him Duke of Friedland. This evocation of Wallenstein's name, with what seemed to the Emperor to be an implication that he would himself become a mere tool in the arms of the military, annoyed Francis Joseph and made him responsive to those politicians and soldiers who wanted to pull Windischgrätz down for reasons of their own. In April 1849, the Field-Marshal was recalled from Hungary, on the grounds that his campaign against the rebels had bogged down and that he had nothing further to offer but the unpleasant prospect of Russian intervention to save the Austrian cause. He was replaced by *Feldzeugmeister* Ludwig Freiherr von Welden, who had played an active part in the conspiracy against him and who had boasted of the ease with which he would dispose of the Hungarian troubles. As in the case of other such changes of command in Austrian history, the results were not happy. Welden's confidence evaporated within a month of his appointment, and he began to clamour, in almost panic-stricken tones, for the very course he had earlier described as unnecessary. In May Russian aid was solicited after all, and intervention followed.[19]

It has to be admitted that the soldiers often invited suspicion. Archduke Charles had had independent views about foreign policy which suggested to some an unwillingness to stay within his proper sphere. Windischgrätz, on the eve of his Hungarian campaign, had written a letter to the Emperor asking that no ministerial decisions on major issues be made without prior consultation with him, a request which Francis Joseph must surely have remembered when the Wallenstein article appeared in the *Wiener Zeitung*. Haynau, the Austrian commander in the mopping-up phase of the Hungarian revolution, was so arrogant in his exchanges with Vienna and so adamantly opposed to any form of ministerial control or even advice that he had to be recalled.[20]

There were enough incidents of this kind in the years of revolution to make the Emperor thoroughly distrustful of the commanding generals of his army, including the now revered Radetzky, whose headquarters—'*cette boutique de Vérone*', as Metternich called it—he came to regard as a centre of potential subversion.[21] This feeling persuaded him to go beyond the tactics of control used by his predecessors—ministerial interference with command matters, the practice of burdening commanders with deputies and aides whose views were incompatible with their own, and the like—and to concentrate all important matters of command, troop dispositions and movements, and personnel in his own hands. Since it was impractical to suppose that he could deal with all these matters personally, he established a Central Military Chancery to handle them and placed at its head his Adjutant-General, Karl Ludwig Count Grünne von Pinchard. The son of one of Archduke Charles' aides, Grünne was a man of natural wit, great energy and limitless vanity. His practical knowledge of the military art, however, was as exiguous as his confidence in his military judgement was great, and he almost automatically opposed those who knew more about soldiering than he did himself. Thus, he played a leading role in turning the Emperor against Windischgrätz, and he was always critical of the saviour of Austria's Italian provinces, whom he once described as 'that old ass Radetzky'. To place command matters completely in the hands of this political general—for that was the practical result of the Emperor's decision, and it remained so for the next ten years— could only be productive of trouble if another great crisis should arise. And Austria's history was never free of crisis for very long.[22]

II

The confusion and inefficiency that were caused in command relationships by what has here been called the Wallenstein complex were made worse as a result of attitudes and habits of mind within the officer corps itself which originated at least as far back as the battle of Kolin and its sequel. That battles are often won by personal initiative is true, and that willingness to assume responsibility should be inculcated in any army's officer corps is equally so; but the efficiency of a military machine depends nevertheless upon the maintenance of a delicate balance between freedom and subordination. There was no Austrian Kleist to dramatize the importance of the latter quality, and it was not among the values most highly honoured by the Order of Maria Theresa. At the risk of exaggeration, indeed, it may be suggested that the mystique of that order was largely responsible for the frequent instances of departure from and disobedience to orders by regimental, brigade and even corps commanders in Austrian campaigns. To win the Cross of Maria Theresa was the ambition of every officer and, since it could be won only by an act of individual bravery, a nice observance of orders often seemed inexpedient.

Imperceptibly this led the average Austrian officer to place a higher valuation upon individualism than upon system and—by extension—upon qualities of the spirit than upon those of the mind. In the Prussian army of the Old Dessauer's time and even later there had been a lot of expressed scorn for 'ink-splashers' and 'pedants',[23] but this was much diminished after the reforms of the Napoleonic period. In Austria, it continued at least as late as the disaster of 1866. Resistance to any systematic study of the business of war was fairly general outside of the technical branches of the service; and, with the higher charges of the army in the hands of great nobles who regarded war as a kind of blood sport, there was little pressure upon junior officers to change their attitude. When the future Field-Marshal Mollinary started his career as a cadet in the Sixteenth Infantry Regiment in Treviso in 1837, he served under a colonel who left all matters of education and training in the hands of an adjutant who was incompetent to deal with them. In consequence, 'nothing was done for the theoretical education or improvement of the officers and cadets. Nobody even bothered to see that the not inconsiderable number of them who had not mastered the verbal usages peculiar to the regiment were kept working at them.'[24] Conditions like these were, unfortunately, not confined to Treviso.

After 1848 there was a tendency in high places not merely to disregard learning but to distrust it. This at least was the Emperor's reaction to the defection of so many Italian and Hungarian officers during the year of revolution. Francis Joseph was soon declaring, in a marginal note on a reform proposal submitted to him, that the 'strength of the army lies not so much in educated officers as in loyal and gallant ones', adding that this should be borne in mind when command positions were filled in the future.[25] In practice, this attitude could only lead to discrimination against officers who were too conspicuously 'learned', and this was indeed the case during the years of Grünne's influence.

It is clear that the evolution in Austria of anything corresponding to a modern general staff system would be strongly influenced by these attitudes, for the general staff is supposed to be the seat of intelligence, the brain of the army. In the broadest sense, a general staff has two functions: 'first, the systematic and extensive collection in time of peace of specific information which may be important to the future conduct of operations or to proper preparation for future operations; and, second, intellectual preparation for the future conduct of operations either through systematic development of skill for the handling of contingently anticipated situations or through the elaboration of specific plans for war, or both'.[26] The second function generally includes the training of a corps of specifically designated staff officers who can serve at army, corps, brigade and division headquarters, and give appropriate information and advice to commanding officers. In Austria, the machinery for the accomplishment of these tasks was developed, but the results were none the less hardly impressive.

As in other countries, the Austrian general staff system had its origins in the eighteenth-century Quartermaster-General's Staff, an organization charged with the totality of arrangements necessary for the quartering of troops in the field. In Maria Theresa's time, a start was made towards widening the functions of this staff (which originally resembled an engineering corps) and adjusting them to the changing nature of war. Field-Marshal Daun was a man who regarded war as a 'comprehensive science' which had to be learned. In his view, a true commander had to have knowledge of tactics and weapons and maps, of the resources of his own and other countries, and of the technical problems of command, and he must, in addition, have some sense of strategical theory. 'Intelligence and strength are the only decisive things in warfare,' he told his royal mistress. 'Intelligence is the most important quality for officers, just as good morale is for the common soldier.' Believing this, Daun encouraged the Empress in her support of her new military schools at Wiener-Neustadt and bent his own energies towards such tasks as the improvement of cartographic work, the beginning of serious operational studies, and the introduction of yearly manœuvres for the army.[27]

The momentum which Daun gave to the development of a staff system was not maintained in the years that followed, although Joseph II showed some fleeting interest in the subject.[28] It was not until the Archduke Charles' reforms in the years 1800–1809 that new progress was made. Like Daun, Charles was insistent that good commanders were not born but made, and that the future of the Austrian state would depend to a significant degree upon the quality of its military education. Charles sought to systematize officer training so that it would be continuous from the level of

Subaltern all the way up to the rank of General. At the same time, he set about reorganizing the Quartermaster-General's Staff by removing from it all officers who had been serving as adjutants or administrators, and converting it into a body exclusively devoted to strategical and operational duties, the preparation of technical and cartographic studies, the accumulation of intelligence about foreign armies, and other modern staff functions. This systematization was carried farther after 1809, when Radetzky was Chief of the Quartermaster-General's Staff. In 1810 this body was reorganized to provide separate sections for cartography, intelligence and communications, war archives, general staff corps (service with army and divisional commands), and service with legations and embassies abroad (the beginning of a system of military attachés).[29]

All this represented progress, although no more than was being made by other states in this period. In the years after 1815, unfortunately, while other countries (especially Prussia) continued to develop the efficiency and authority of their general staffs, the reverse was true in Austria.

One reason for this was that the Chief of the Quartermaster-General's Staff occupied a relatively modest position in the military hierarchy. Archduke Charles had hoped to make the holder of this position the Supreme War Council's chief adviser for all operational and strategical matters, and an imperial decree of 1809 had actually defined the Chief's position in those terms. But he was never given enough rank to hold his own with the department chiefs (*Hofkriegsräte*) in the Supreme War Council, and his influence was always checked by military bureaucrats who, Radetzky once said, knew about as much 'of the army, its spirit and its needs as they do about the Sultan's Divan'.[30] Another reason was financial. As early as 1820, the Emperor felt it necessary to order that in the autumn manœuvres of that year no costly experiments (the throwing of bridges across the Danube and the like) be attempted and that observers pay their own expenses. Similar curtailments were made all through the period before 1848, and other economies hampered the development of staff training. Financial stringency also played a part in the failure to expand the General Staff Corps, with the result that, when the revolution burst upon the empire, there were only eleven trained general staff officers available for service with the army in Italy, which at that time comprised some 70,000 men.[31]

But more important than these things was the widespread disregard of the importance of learning as a military virtue, which diminished the prestige of staff work even in the eyes of some of those who became staff officers. In 1811 Radetzky had said (with perhaps a premonition of what was to happen) that vigilance would have to be exercised lest general staff work become 'a fertile ground for lucky mushrooms' (*Glückspilze*, careerists) and lest 'a glib tongue, a good seat on a horse, and a good supply of technical terms be considered sufficient to qualify a man for staff service'.[32] When the later Chief of General Staff Beck was assigned as a lieutenant to the Operations Bureau of the *chef* of the Vienna Army Command in 1851, he found conditions that justified Radetzky's fears. With a few exceptions, all of the officers on the staff were 'happy idlers, who either had names that showed they belonged to the high nobility or possessed powerful protectors'. Among them was the son of the horse-dealer who took care of the commanding general's stable. A year later, when Beck qualified for admission to the War College, he discovered that that organization, in the very first year of its existence, was adapting itself to prevailing values. The emphasis was on rote learning, and horsemanship played an excessive role in the curriculum.[33]

After Emperor Francis Joseph had established his Military Chancery in 1849 and given his full confidence to Count Grünne, the reduction of the influence of the general staff and of staff officers in general became a matter of formal policy. Grünne made the newly established Adjutants Corps the executive agency for his directives and, on army and divisional staffs, adjutants who reported directly to him usurped functions that had once been performed by members of the General Staff Corps. Mollinary, who watched this system operating in Italy in 1849 and saw the Emperor's Adjutant-General Schönhals do everything in his power to disrupt the work and countermand the directives of

Radetzky's brilliant *chef*, Heinrich Freiherr von Hess, admitted that the adjutants were generally talented, energetic and patriotic men, but added that they were unschooled in the art of war and, perhaps for that very reason, resented the staff officers, who were.[34] After the suppression of the revolutionary disorders, Grünne saw to it that Hess, who had been made Chief of the Quartermaster-General's Staff, was not only by-passed, even in strategical matters, but publicly humiliated as well; and, since Hess was not the kind of man who fought back, the influence of his staff reached bottom in the 1850's.[35] Deprived of authority, money and prestige, there was little it could do to keep alive the important truth that war is a complicated business which can be mastered only by intelligence and application.

The effects of this were noticed by at least one sapient foreign observer. In 1854, the Prussian military attaché, Prince Kraft zu Hohenlohe-Ingelfingen, an artillery officer whose batteries were to help blast Austrian troops off the height of Chlum on 3rd July 1866, observed the annual manœuvres of the Austrian army. All branches of the service, he noted, were suffering from grave deficiencies of training and equipment, and 'the exercises of combined arms demonstrated that the unit leadership, as well as the overall command, was in a childish condition, which surprised me'.[36] The following year saw no improvement. The manœuvres were badly planned and executed, and, since there were no critiques, seemed rather pointless. After one day's exercises, Hohenlohe met the Austrian artillery general, Bauer von Bauernfeld, riding slowly back to quarters and asked him why he seemed so glum. Bauer answered, '*G'lernt hob i nix!* (I haven't learned anything!)'.[37]

Unfortunately for Austria, it was not in manœuvres alone that the results of this deliberate flight from intelligence were perceptible.

III

On the eve of the Italian war of 1859, there was a flaring up of that civil–military incompatibility that had prevented proper co-ordination between force and diplomacy in the days of the Archduke Charles. Relations between the military chiefs and the ministry of Count Buol-Schauenstein had deteriorated rapidly during the Crimean War, for in that conflict Buol had worked energetically for intervention on the side of the Western Powers, while the soldiers (including Grünne, who for once found himself on the side of Windischgrätz and Hess) stood either for neutrality or for loyalty to the old Russian alliance. In an audience with the Emperor after the Paris Conference of 1856, the Austrian ambassador to Paris, Count Hübner, accused the soldiers of being directly responsible for Austria's present isolation. They had made intimations of assistance to Russia which the Government had never intended, and by doing so they had increased Russia's resentment, while discrediting the Government in the eyes of the English and the French. Dabbling in politics, said Hübner violently, had become a military disease, and he went on to cite examples from the year 1849. The Emperor, on the whole, seemed to agree with him.[38]

The diplomats got their own back in 1859, by disregarding military considerations entirely in the planning of national policy. In his dealings with the Italian and French Governments, Buol used tactics that were calculated to make war inevitable, while at the same time he refused to admit to his colleagues that the situation was serious enough to justify the soldiers' demands for an urgent and comprehensive armaments programme. In meetings of the Emperor's advisers, he persistently denied that France was serious about supporting the Piedmontese Government in any hostilities that might ensue; and he dropped broad hints about prospective Austrian alliances with Prussia, the German states, and even Great Britain. He agreed that the Archduke Albert, the son of Archduke Charles and a distinguished soldier in his own right, should go to Berlin and try to win a Prussian promise of aid in the event of French intervention, but then undercut this mission by despatching an ultimatum to Piedmont without informing Albert that he intended to do so. Finally, having created a situation in which war in the most unfavourable conditions was inevitable—Hess had persistently warned that an ultimatum would invite disaster, and he was right —Buol washed his hands of the whole business. At a meeting of the ministers on 27th April 1859, Grünne pointed out that the soldiers had a right to know who exactly were their enemies, what precisely were their objectives, and who specifically might come to their assistance, and he asked fretfully what had become of all of Buol's fine promises. The minister answered blandly that negotiations were continuing but that he regarded the situation as similar to that which had obtained when Maria Theresa came to the throne. In any case, he added, 'the answers to the questions posed by His Majesty's Adjutant-General no longer lie in the diplomatic sphere; full responsibility for giving the decisive answers lies now with the military'.[39]

The damage done by this classic case of faulty civil–military co-ordination was now compounded by military maladroitness arising from the intellectual slackness of the last half century. This is not the place for a detailed account of the Italian campaign of 1859;[40] but a few items from the sorry record are worth noting. The Austrian army marched into Italy without an adequate supply system, or accurate intelligence of enemy strength and capabilities, or even reliable maps to guide its movements. Thanks to Grünne, it was led not by Hess, who knew Italy, where he had served as Radetzky's *chef* in 1849, but by Franz Count Gyulai, a court favourite who had so little confidence in his own abilities that his cautious fumbling ruined troop morale before he had made real contact with the enemy. At the same time, he was deaf to the advice of others and was soon on such bad terms with his Chief of Staff, Kuhn, that they corresponded only in writing. Conditions at Gyulai's headquarters were so confused that one commander said that the spectacle turned his stomach. There was no clear chain of command, and unit commanders were constantly receiving contradictory orders from two or more higher officers and continually having to recall their troops from one pointless mission in order to despatch them on another equally so. Because of this sort of thing, what slim chance there had been of defeating the Italians separately before the French came up in strength was lost, and by the beginning of June Gyulai's forces were in full retreat across the Ticino. Magenta was fought on the 4th June 1859 and led to new withdrawals so precipitate that headquarters lost all control over the subordinate commands.[41]

Gyulai was relieved of his post on 18th June, and the Emperor assumed personal command of the army, with Hess at his side— but with Grünne there too, and all of Grünne's staff. This change-over did not improve the situation, since it soon transpired that all orders issued by Hess had to be verified by Grünne's Chancery before being forwarded. Mollinary, who visited headquarters at this time, records a scene that sums up everything that was wrong with the direction of the war. When the army high command departed from Villafranca, it did so in a long row of handsome carriages, the Emperor and an aide leading the procession, followed by the archdukes, then the Adjutant-General, then the other generals assigned to the Military Chancery, and then the swarm of wing adjutants. At the very end of the line came an ordinary *Postkalesche*, drawn by two unprepossessing horses: transportation for the Chief of the Quartermaster-General's Staff! Hess climbed in wearily and after a few moments said to Mollinary, 'You can have no conception of *how* I suffer!'[42]

IV

On 24th June, Solferino completed the discomfiture of the Austrian army and the discrediting of those who had brought it to this sorry pass. Buol had already been dismissed; Hess, worn out by age and disappointment, submitted his resignation; Grünne tried to shore up his position but came under such sharp attack from people like Hübner that the Emperor was forced to let him go. The Hofburg was suddenly filled with new faces. Rechberg, a careful diplomat of the Metternich school, took over Buol's functions. Lieutenant-Field-Marshal Franz Folliot de Crenneville, a soldier who knew infinitely more about war than Grünne had known, and who was a good, if occasionally over-critical, judge of men, assumed the post of First Adjutant-General. The whole military establishment was reorganized, what had been the Supreme War Council being transformed into a

Ministry of War and placed under the leadership of August Count Degenfeld-Schonburg, an energetic man who was determined to correct the weaknesses revealed in Italy. Finally, the most popular soldier since Radetzky and the hero of Solferino, *Feldzeugmeister* Ludwig August von Benedek, was made Chief of the Quarter-master-General's Staff.[43]

This change of order had the effect of reducing the civilian–military differences which had been productive of so much harm in the years from 1854 to 1859, for Rechberg got along rather well with the soldiers. Its effects upon the efficiency of the army were also marked, but mixed. There can be little doubt that the excellent performance of the Austrian artillery and cavalry in the war against Prussia, and particularly in the battle of Königgrätz, owed much to the vigour with which Degenfeld tackled problems of weaponry, supply and training in those arms. On the other hand, the War Minister was also at least partly responsible for drawing false conclusions from his observation of French tactics in 1859 and, as a result, for placing excessive emphasis upon shock tactics in Austrian training in an age in which battles were to be decided by fire power. This prejudice in favour of the bayonet, which was shared by the Emperor himself, was strengthened by the successes won by Austrian troops in Denmark in 1864, although these victories were gained, as shrewd Prussian observers noted, at excessive cost in lives.[44]

Leaving this aside, it is notable that in one vital area *no* improvement was made: namely, in the general staff system. No change could really be expected here unless someone with authority encouraged a general change of attitude towards the role of intelligence in war. Benedek, who perhaps possessed the necessary personal weight to accomplish this, was not sufficiently interested to try. For one thing, he did not have the time to do so: in addition to being Chief of the Quartermaster-General's Staff and head of the General Staff Corps, he held the post of Governor of Hungary until October 1860 and was then appointed commander of the Second Army in Italy. This meant that most of his staff work had to be carried on by deputies, first by General von Ramming and later, from 1861 to 1864, by Lieutenant-Field-

Marshal Nagy. This was hardly an arrangement designed to enhance the authority or prestige of the general staff.

But more important was the fact that Benedek—and this was true also of Archduke Albert, whose influence in the army, if not on the public, was as great as Benedek's[45]—was more interested in preserving what was often called 'the old army spirit' than he was in advancing the uses of intelligence and the skills associated with staff work. A member of the Order of Maria Theresa himself—he had won his cross at Curtatone in May 1848[46]—Benedek believed that wars were won by courage, discipline, and *élan,* and these were the qualities he sought to encourage in his peacetime commands. On the other hand, officers who sought to win his approbation by arranging operational exercises or writing tactical studies received no encouragement.[47] These things bored him. He was, as Chief of Staff Beck's biographer has written, 'an opponent of any kind of staff work done at the green table and, above all, of every kind of scholarly activity by soldiers'.[48]

Not even Benedek's most recent biographer has been able to point to much in the way of achievement during his term as Chief of the Quartermaster-General's Staff.[49] Some changes of procedure were introduced into the cartographic, historical and archival sections; the role of the staff in the programme of the *Kriegsschule* was broadened; and a railway section was established. To avoid the kind of friction that had existed at army and corps headquarters in 1859, the influence of the Adjutant's Corps was reduced, although it is worth noting that Benedek opposed this reform and that it was not complete. On the other hand, much was not done: the position of the Quartermaster-General's Staff remained ambiguous, as Benedek's successor pointed out in a memorandum in 1865; the relationship between its chief and the head of the Operations Section in the Ministry of War was never made clear; and he had no effective control over the selection of *chefs* for the different army corps.[50]

Most critical was the failure to impress the officer corps in general with a sense of the vital importance of a good staff system. None of the glamour that had been associated with the Prussian staff system since Scharnhorst's time attached itself to the

Austrian Quartermaster-General's Staff. It had, indeed, to a distressing degree, remained 'a fertile ground for *Glückspilze*', and this was widely known. When Beck was working in the cartographic section in these years, he was charged with the task of making a military geographical survey of central Germany, based on reports which were to be sent home by another staff officer working in Germany. This second officer, however, disappeared into the casinos of Bad Ems and, when Beck pleaded for material, told him to dig it out of Baedeker.[51] Nor was this sort of dry rot confined to the junior ranks. Henikstein was able to write in 1865, 'I ask myself whether it is not shameful that we have four *chefs* on army staffs at the present time who are completely incompetent.'[52]

When Henikstein became vocal about these deficiencies, the man who was to lead the Northern Army against Prussia in 1866 refused to take his friend's complaints seriously. Benedek had already advised his successor, when Henikstein insisted that he did not have the necessary talent to be chief of staff, that he worried too much. Let him take the job for a while. After all, if something important like a war should come along, he could always give it up and take command of a corps![53] This advice, which neatly expressed Benedek's unflattering opinion of the role of intelligence in war, explains why the Austrian staff system was almost as confused and ineffective in 1866 as it had been in 1859.

There is reason to believe that, after his fall from grace, Benedek began belatedly to doubt the validity of the philosophy of war which he had shared with the great majority of the officer corps of the Austrian army. 'How could we prevail against the Prussians?' he said sadly to a visitor. 'We have learned so little, and they are such a studious people.'[54]

NOTES

1. Egon Conte Corti, *Mensch und Herrscher: Wege und Schicksale Kaiser Franz Josephs I* (Graz, Wien 1952), pp. 190-191.
2. For examples of newspaper opinion after the defeat of 3rd July 1866, see Gordon A. Craig, *The Battle of Königgrätz: Prussia's*

Victory over Austria, 1866 (Philadelphia, Pa. 1964), pp. ix, x.

3. For emphasis upon the financial question and the inadequacy of military spending, see Oskar Regele, *Feldzeugmeister Benedek: Der Weg nach Königgrätz* (Wien 1960), especially pp. 108 ff., 290-384.

4. Edmund Glaise von Horstenau, 'Oesterreichs Wehrmacht im deutschen Schicksal', in *Oesterreich: Erbe und Sendung im deutschen Raum* (ed. Josef Nadler and H. Ritter von Srbik, Salzburg and Leipzig 1937), p. 207.

5. Alfons Freiherr von Wrede, *Geschichte des K. u. K. Mährischen Dragonerregiments Fr. Franz IV Groszherzog vom Mecklenburg Schwerin No. 6* (Brünn, n.d.), pp. 5, 560 ff.

6. *Wilhelm und Caroline von Humboldt in ihren Briefen* (ed. Anna von Sydow, IV, Berlin 1910), p. 40; Theodor Fontane, *Der deutsche Krieg von 1866* (2 vols., Berlin 1871-72), i., 205 f.

7. Craig, op. cit., pp. 74-78.

8. Friedrich Walter, 'Feldmarschall Leopold Joseph Graf Daun und Feldmarschall Gideon Ernst Freiherr von Laudon', in *Gestalter der Geschicke Oesterreichs* (ed. Hugo Hantsch, Innsbruck, Wien 1962), pp. 263, 274.

9. Ibid., p. 274.

10. H. Rössler, *Oesterreichs Kampf um Deutschlands Befreiung*, I (Hamburg 1940), 102-104.

11. Ibid., pp. 109-111.

12. Ibid., p. 112.

13. Ibid., pp. 112 f.

14. For details see Ludwig Jedlicka, 'Erzherzog Karl, der Sieger von Aspern', in Hantsch, op. cit., p. 319; R. Lorenz, 'Erzherzog Karl als Denker', in *Das Bild des Krieges im deutschen Denken* (ed. August Faust, I, Stuttgart and Berlin 1941), pp. 258 f.

15. Oskar Regele, *Feldmarschall Radetzky: Leben, Leistung, Erbe* (Wien 1957), p. 118.

16. Karl von Clausewitz, *Vom Kriege*, 16th ed. (ed. Werner Hahlweg, Bonn 1952), p. 222.

17. Regele, *Radetzky*, p. 137.

18. Ibid., p. 162.

19. Corti, op. cit., pp. 16-25.

20. Ibid., pp. 4 f., 57 f., 60.

21. Ibid., p. 172.

22. On Grünne, see, *inter alia*, Joseph Redlich, *Emperor Francis Joseph of Austria: A Biography* (New York 1929), pp. 43 ff., 91 f.; Edmund Glaise-Horstenau, *Franz Josephs Weggefährte* (Zurich, Wien 1930), pp. 37 ff.; Corti, op. cit., pp. 6 f., 27.

23. See Gordon A. Craig, *The Politics of the Prussian Army, 1640-1945* (Oxford 1955), p. 25.

24. Anton Freiherr von Mollinary, *Sechsundvierzigjahre im oester- reich-ungarischen Heere, 1833-1879* (Zurich 1905), i. 39.
25. Corti, op. cit., p. 27.
26. Dallas D. Irvine, 'The Origin of Capital Staffs', *Journal of Modern History*, x (1938), p. 165.
27. Walter in Hantsch, op. cit., pp. 263-265.
28. Ernst Benedikt, *Kaiser Joseph II, 1741-1790* (Wien, 2nd ed. 1947), p. 180.
29. On all this, see Jedlicka in Hantsch, op. cit., p. 319; Lorenz in Faust, op. cit., pp. 258 ff.; Regele, *Radetzky*, pp. 88, 398-401.
30. Mollinary, op. cit., i. 62 f.; Regele, *Radetzky*, pp. 397 f.
31. Regele, *Radetzky*, p. 226; Mollinary, op. cit., i. 118.
32. Regele, *Radetzky*, pp. 399 f.
33. Glaise-Horstenau, *Franz Josephs Weggefährte*, pp. 31 ff.
34. Mollinary, op. cit., i. 118 f.
35. Ibid., i. 250; Glaise-Horstenau, *Franz Josephs Weggefährte*, pp. 37-38.
36. Prinz Kraft zu Hohenlohe-Ingelfingen, *Aus meinem Leben* (4 vols., Berlin 1897-1907), i. 280 ff.
37. Ibid., p. 337.
38. Corti, op. cit., p. 172.
39. For Buol's policy, see ibid., pp. 212 ff., 220 f.; H. Ritter von Srbik, *Deutsche Einheit* (München 1935 et seq.), ii. 340 ff., 353.
40. See, *inter alia*, the accounts in W. von Willisen, *Die Feldzüge der Jahre 1859 und 1866* (Leipzig 1868), *Benedeks nachgelassene Papiere* (ed. Heinrich Friedjung, Leipzig 1901), and H. von Moltke, *Militärische Werke*, III (Berlin 1904). An interesting recent sketch is Anton Frhr. von Bechtolsheim, 'Vor 100 Jahren: Magenta', in *Wehrwissenschaftliche Rundschau*, ix (1959), 427-454.
41. Glaise-Horstenau, *Franz Josephs Weggefährte*, pp. 50-65; Corti, op. cit., pp. 221-233.
42. Mollinary, op. cit., ii. 44.
43. On Crenneville and Degenfeld, see H. Ritter von Srbik, *Aus Oesterreichs Vergangenheit* (Salzburg 1949), pp. 116-118. On Benedek, see *Benedeks nachgelassene Papiere*, pp. 1-250 *passim*, and especially 63, 134, 175, 183, 265; and Regele, *Benedek*, pp. 261-289.
44. On this subject, see Craig, *Königgrätz*, pp. 8-10; Hohenlohe-Ingelfingen, op. cit., iii. 105 f.; Srbik, *Aus Oesterreichs Ver- gangenheit*, p. 118.
45. Srbik, *Aus Oesterreichs Vergangenheit*, pp. 109 ff.
46. *Benedeks nachgelassene Papiere*, pp. 74 f.
47. Mollinary, op. cit., ii. 108.
48. Glaise-Horstenau, *Franz Josephs Weggefährte*, p. 71.
49. See Regele, *Benedek*, pp. 171 ff.

50. Eugen Frauenholz, 'Feldmarschalleutnant Alfred Freiherr von Henikstein im Jahre 1866', *Münchener Historische Abhandlungen*, 2. Reihe, 3. Heft, pp. 34 ff.
51. Glaise-Horstenau, *Franz Josephs Weggefährte*, p. 71.
52. Frauenholz, loc. cit.
53. Ibid.
54. *Benedeks nachgelassene Papiere*, p. 406.

§4§

European Military Thought and Doctrine, 1870-1914

JAY LUVAAS

THE Franco-Prussian War forms a watershed as significant to military as it is to diplomatic history. After 1870 the main currents in military thinking flowed from Berlin rather than Paris as German military doctrine and institutions, tactics and organization, and even bits of the language and uniforms were swept into the other armies and deposited. *Aufmarsch* and *Schwerpunkt* became as much a part of the informed soldier's working vocabulary as *echelon* and *l'arme blanche*. The German system of annual manœuvres and the famed General Staff found imitators everywhere, and sooner or later the size of the infantry company in neighbouring armies was increased to correspond to the German organization of 250 men that had served as the basic tactical unit in 1866 and 1870.[1] After the impressive and startling Prussian victories over Austria and France the major powers in Europe likewise adopted the German system of compulsory service and military territorial districts, and if Britain and the United States were slower than the others to remodel their institutions, it did not take either army long to replace the French *képi* with the Prussian *Pickelhaube*—a 'new look' reflecting the change in military thinking.

To wade through the flood of technical and theoretical literature that appeared after 1870 could easily consume the worst years of one's life. New professional journals gave soldiers everywhere an opportunity to air their views; new military schools stimulated the study of war in all phases and gave direction to theory and doctrine. Revised tactical manuals accompanied the ferment of discussion and tried in vain to march in step with technological change. Even military history, which to a writer like Napier, author of the *History of the War in the Peninsula*, meant narrative within the framework of accepted military maxims, now often became the captive of historical sections of the various General Staffs or else served as a vehicle to prove the validity or fallacy of some particular point of view.

Now that the waters have receded it is possible to detect the

71

main channels of military thought and doctrine during these years of transition, energetic exploration and compulsive preparation. The problems naturally varied somewhat from army to army: peripheral wars often aggravated situations which to the military world seemed unique, and the English-speaking nations never completely fell into the mainstream of continental military thought. Yet the developments in each country tended to move in the same general direction, for the basic problem—apart from questions of geography and national policy—was a common one: how to adjust to the changes forced upon society by the French Revolution and to capitalize upon the products of the Industrial Revolution, particularly in the fields of armament, transportation and communication. At first the solution seemed simple and obvious—imitate the Germans. But twenty years later the main course of instruction was still the German wars for unification, and the march of technology had quickened. It was at this point that many of the theorists foundered.

In the realm of strategy, the spirit of the new German doctrine found austere expression in the memoranda of the Chief of the General Staff, Count Helmuth von Moltke. In 1868–69 this studious warrior had written as follows.

> The operations plan for the offensive against France consists solely in seeking out the main enemy force and attacking it wherever it is found. The difficulty lies only in the execution of this simple plan with very large masses. . . . Our mobilization is prepared to the last detail. Six through railroads are available to transport the armies to the region between the Moselle and the Rhine. The timetables which determine the exact moment of departure and assembly for each unit are ready. . . . In possession of the river crossings, we should already assume the offensive a few days after (the fourteenth day of mobilization) with more than a double superiority in numbers.[2]

Here then is the formula by which Moltke would translate the doctrines of Clausewitz into action: seek out and destroy the enemy army with superior forces made available by the mobilization of the nation's manpower, meticulous peacetime planning, and the relatively well-developed system of German rail communications. No mention of the geometrical forms that dominated the earlier works by von Bülow and Jomini; none of the metaphysics that often clouded the theories of Willison and Clausewitz; and certainly no references to the time-worn shibboleths found in most writings on strategy. For strategy, according to Moltke, 'is a system of expedients' and not an abstract science. Its secrets were to be uncovered empirically rather than by rational thought, and Moltke rejected any idea of universal rules or systems that might deteriorate into dogma. Moltke thus reduced the whole problem to the limits of what could safely be calculated in advance. In 1870, as in 1866, every effort was to be made to bring three Prussian armies within supporting distance of one another, and once this was accomplished it did not much matter what the enemy attempted to do—superior numbers, if not more aggressive leadership and better tactics, would produce the victory, 'the decisive fact of war'.

Moltke's success meant that his ideas, which had evolved gradually as he laboured over successive military blueprints for German unification, soon became elevated into fundamental doctrine. (As recently as the battle of Königgrätz one Prussian divisional commander, upon receipt of an order signed by the Chief of Staff, had exclaimed: 'This seems all shipshape and proper, but who on earth is this General Moltke?')[3] In Germany Moltke's disciples spent the next forty years defining and elaborating upon the principles underlying his strategy and adapting them to the new conditions.

For the most part German military writers shared Moltke's aversion to rational dogmatism in their investigations of the anatomy of war. Verdy du Vernois, for example, insisted that war, like life itself, could not be reduced to rigid and immutable rules beyond those of birth and death. 'Always the special case decides; such a rule is correct in one case, inaccurate in another.' Blume was another who contended that 'strategy is an art' and that therefore 'as a result of its very essence it can not be a science'. 'It would be disregarding the nature of strategy to seek to transform it into a learned system exactly determined.' And Moltke's successor, Waldersee, likewise criticized the tendency of military treatises to lay down rules applicable to all circumstances.[4]

It was not to be expected, therefore, that German students of strategy in the years following 1870 would become addicted to method. Blume's 'concise but profound analysis' of strategy is typical in treating the subject 'more in the nature of speculation than of doctrine'. Stressing the offensive as the most effective form of conducting war, Blume's study of strategy published in 1882 is essentially an elaboration of Moltke's views, although neither this work nor its more lively offspring, Prince Kraft's *Letters on Strategy* (1887), drew upon Moltke's original papers, most of which were as yet unpublished. In this sense the complete significance of Moltke's doctrine could not be appreciated until after his retirement in 1888.[5]

An exponent of the inductive method, Prince Kraft devoted his series of conversational letters to a strategical analysis of the recent campaigns, where the details were 'sufficiently known' and which might yield enough general insight 'so that in similar cases if even the circumstances are not exactly the same we shall have a just basis for our decisions'. Disavowing any intention of establishing 'an absolute system of strategy', which to his mind was a quack cure-all, he none the less hoped that even if his readers should forget the dates and the details, they would still retain 'the true principles of strategy', which did nothing more than to provide a sense of direction. These were:

1. National policy must go hand in hand with strategy.
2. The hostile army is the first object of strategy.
3. One can never be too strong for a decisive battle.
4. One may not follow a fixed system, but must always rely on sound judgement.
5. To change strategical plans when not forced to by circumstances leads to disaster. . . .

Before accusing Prince Kraft of blind acceptance of the doctrines of Clausewitz and of failure to see beyond the wars of 1866 and 1870, it is necessary to take note of his purpose in writing. Convinced that 'abstract rules never apply in their entirety to any concrete case', his main concern was to explain to a younger generation of German officers how physical and intellectual forces had shaped strategy in modern war. He did not address his letters to the more remote future, because he recognized that even the basic concepts of war and peace, of policy and strategy, were apt to change.[6]

This pragmatic approach is characteristic of Germany's perhaps best-known military writer of the period. The principal aim of von der Goltz in writing *The Nation in Arms* in 1883 was 'to recall to strategy the attention which hitherto has been diverted almost exclusively to generalship in battle'. Clausewitz had written of war that was to be total and absolute; von der Goltz, who only a few years earlier had published a controversial study of *Leon Gambetta and his Armies* (1877) in which he had called attention to the *lévée en masse* introduced by the French after the initial disasters, attempted in rather general terms to explain the meaning of Clausewitz to the nation in arms. He offered nothing really new, no significant departure from Clausewitz or the methods of 1870, certainly no formula to be applied universally. He wrote 'for the present only', and like Prince Kraft he limited his observations 'to the military operations of our own time'. But writing for the mass army, von der Goltz suspected that fundamental changes in war and society lay beyond the horizon. 'The day will come when the present aspect of war will dissolve, when forms, customs, and opinions will again be altered. Looking forward into the future, we seem to feel the coming of a time when the armed millions of the present will have played out their part. A new Alexander will arise who, with a small body of well-equipped and skilled warriors, will drive the impotent hordes before him. . . .' But von der Goltz was interested in present realities, not visions of the future. 'Fancy', he wrote, 'lacks the model on which to sketch its lines', and the farthest that he could peer into the future was to distinguish 'the absolute necessity of a closer union between siege operations . . . and action in the open field, . . . more general use of entrenchments . . . [and] . . . heavy artillery, as of old, again accompanies armies in the field, in order to be at hand where the power of field-guns proves inadequate to break down resistance.'[7]

Most of what has been said about von der Goltz would apply also to the views of Bernhardi except that the latter, instead of regarding war 'as a continuation of policy by other means', seems almost to have considered it an end in itself. Influenced by Social Darwinism as well as the historical views of Treitschke, Bernhardi looked upon war as 'the greatest factor in the furtherance of culture and power', a 'biological necessity' which could be justified even on religious grounds because of the 'combative' attitudes in Christianity. But in his strategical thinking Bernhardi was cast from the same mould as his predecessors. He too rejected any thought of trying to press the campaigns of Napoleon or Moltke into a system; he believed, along with practically every German military writer since Clausewitz, that the offensive was the strongest form of waging war and that the sole aim of strategy was to bring about the decisive battle under the most favourable conditions. To a greater degree than the others Bernhardi seems to have been concerned about the impact of the mass army upon military operations. Quality, he insisted, should not give way to quantity; and *force*—by which he meant not only the size of an army but also its efficiency in terms of weapons, training, mobility and morale—must not be confused with *numbers*. Perhaps this concern was inevitable in a day when increasing attention was being devoted to problems of mobilization and strategical concentration, for as von der Goltz had observed a few years earlier, 'the difference between the great military powers is . . . almost reduced to one of hours'.[8]

German strategical thought finally came to rest in the master plan of Count Alfred von Schlieffen, Chief of the General Staff from 1891 to 1905. The details of the much-publicized Schlieffen Plan and the assumptions that lay behind it have been admirably treated in the recent study by Professor Ritter:[9] suffice it to state here that in so far as a technician can ever follow in the footsteps of a philosopher, Schlieffen continued in the tradition of Moltke. Yet there are important differences between the two. Schlieffen lacked Moltke's grasp of political factors and his objectives were not so limited. In 1866 and 1870 Moltke had only to push Austria and France out of German affairs, but Schlieffen had to cope with the probability of a general European war involving rival systems of alliances, each built upon the idea of the nation in arms. War had become absolute; victory now seemed to rest upon the speedy annihilation of the enemy. Whereas Moltke had used strategy as a *guide* and had allowed subordinate generals considerable initiative, Schlieffen tried to control his commanders more rigidly and to dictate the movements of the enemy by means of his master plan. While paying lip-service to Moltke's legacy of 'not one method, one remedy . . . but many',[10] Schlieffen himself was unable to resist the temptation of a single panacea for victory.

In France the lines of strategical thought are more difficult to delineate. Stunned and humiliated by the recent débácle, the first reaction of French soldiers was to blame inferior numbers and tardy mobilization for the defeat and hence to create a new-model army 'along lines roughly paralleling the German system of compulsory military service', with a modern general staff and all of the trimmings. This was accompanied by an intellectual reawakening of sorts as military writers fought again the battles of 1870. Some discovered that their army had lost as a result of passive leadership, inept administration and a lack of co-operation, which led indirectly to the establishment of the *École Militaire Supérieure* in 1878, a reform of the General Staff two years later, and a general increase of interest in all matters connected with military education. Others, concluding that the Germans had won because they had been the first to catch the drift of modern war, analysed the Prussian campaigns and attempted to understand Moltke's method of waging war. Ultimately their investigations brought them into contact with the theories of Clausewitz, which in turn led to a re-examination of the Napoleonic wars as the source of most of Clausewitz's ideas. One of the central themes in French military literature after 1870 turns on the question: did Moltke merely apply the principles of the great Napoleon to modern conditions of war, or did he through envelopment and concentration of his armies *during* battle—in contrast to Napoleon's system of uniting *before* battle—contribute something original in the evolution of strategy? To a patriotic French officer it often made a difference.

At first French writers on strategy followed the lead of their German contemporaries by revolting against the formalism and anatomical analysis of Jomini, for fifty years their instructor in Napoleonic methods. This can be seen in the early writings of General Lewal, organizer of the *École Militaire Supérieure*, a brilliant staff officer and a prolific and influential student of war. Writing in elaborate detail on all phases of war—mobilization, marches, reconnaissance, supply and combat—Lewal at first was reluctant even to admit the existence of strategy as such, and as the title of one of his later books, *The Strategy of Combat* (1895), plainly suggests, Lewal tried even to discard conventional terminology in thinking along functional lines. With battlefields now extending over many miles and armies swollen by hundreds of thousands, familiar definitions seemed to have lost their meaning. Nor was it enough merely to extend old rules to cover these new conditions. 'This is an error. It has occurred with profound modifications, and the extension will neither be manifested upon the whole nor in the same manner. The concentration of armies will take place in less time, and their distance at the beginning will diminish almost completely. . . . The unexpectancy of combat is inevitable, and in view of this fact he who invokes the memory of the glorious manœuvres that led to Marengo, Austerlitz and Jena is open to censure. . . . Now one arrives on the ground and one fights there: that is the war of the future.' According to this line of reasoning, strategy became in effect little more than mobilization, the initial phase of battle which Lewal predicted 'will be the beginning of an immense armed drama' lasting days and consuming ever-increasing numbers of men. No longer was there the time or room in which to manœuvre: the army must employ dense masses within a limited space, avoid gaps in the line and shun isolated operations by independent units.[11]

A more conventional treatment is found in Derrécagaix's *Modern War* (1885). Although cognizant of the changing nature of war, this author insisted that 'the principles of the past preserve all of their importance'. From the *Correspondence* and campaigns of Napoleon he deduced principles which he then used to measure the effectiveness of the Prussians in 1866 and 1870. His conclusion? That Napoleon's principles were still applicable; the Prussians owed their victories 'less to the genius of their leaders than to a sound application of the rules of the military art'. It was not strategic considerations so much as inadequate preparations for mobilization and a faulty system of tactics that led to the French defeat; there was no need, therefore, to scuttle valid principles in search for a phantom. One had only to study the Prussians' military system, emulate Moltke's simple and rapid mobilization, and understand the way in which the Prussian generals had applied established principles to modern war.[12]

Derrécagaix's work is typical of the period in several respects. His massive assembly of historical data to illustrate eternal principles was imitated and carried to extremes in the writings of General Pierron, whose *Strategy and Grand Tactics* (1887) had the appearance of a scientific treatise but in reality was little more than a juxtaposition of pertinent orders or extracts from other studies. Derrécagaix's assessment of Moltke as the gifted shadow of Napoleon was a popular theme in the works of Captain Gilbert and Generals Maillard and Bonnal, each of whom found much to criticize in what they understood (often mistakenly) of German doctrine. Indeed Bonnal, while imitating the German method of study by exhaustive probing into the history of selected campaigns, seemed almost to declare independence from the German influence. Admitting that the elements composing the Prussian Army in 1866 had been 'particularly sound', Bonnal found 'many false ideas' about strategy circulating among the high command. Had the Austrians only followed the simplest principles of Napoleon 'the throne of the Hohenzollerns would have been imperilled'. 'As it was, the Prussian troops . . . redeemed the mistakes of the superior leading by their energy, their intelligence, and their excellent military education.' Or, in the words of another who was trying to debase the German currency still in circulation, 'The soldier made good the blunders of the soothsayer, and the soothsayer gave the lesson to the soldier.' Moltke was dead and so, many hoped, was the spell his victories had cast upon an earlier generation.[13]

Bonnal and his school were instrumental in injecting an

offensive spirit into French strategic planning. Until 1884 it had been the intention of the French military leaders to retard any German advance through the use of forts while mobilizing methodically and assembling vast armies in the interior with which to strike any German units penetrating beyond the frontier. Beginning in 1887, however, French war plans called for more aggressive action along the frontiers, and after the alliance with Russia the French Army became committed to an offensive strategy. In 1898 the man entrusted with the task of devising the new Plan XIV was Bonnal, whose ideas thus had received official acceptance.

This spirit of the offensive drenched the writings of the most prominent and influential of all French theorists between the wars, the future Marshal Foch. So much has been written about Foch[14] that it is necessary here only to suggest his place in the development of French strategical doctrine. Like Ardant du Picq, whose writings had placed a new emphasis upon morale, Foch stressed the moral and psychological elements in war; like Lewal and Bonnal he tried to resist the German influence, although there is ample evidence from his writings that he leaned heavily upon Clausewitz and his basic assumptions do not differ from those of many of his German contemporaries. For Foch, claiming that there was 'no such thing as an *absolute* theory', felt that one had 'only to deal with *contingencies*'. He too believed in a short, violent war with battle being the main goal of strategy, but whereas most German theorists claimed that modern firepower had made the desired envelopment possible only on a strategical and not a tactical level, Foch contended that 'Tactical results are the only things that matter in war. . . . *No strategy can henceforth prevail over that which aims at ensuring tactical results, victory by fighting*.' His four principles—economy of forces, freedom of action, free disposal of forces and security—together imply movement, if not the free-swinging manœuvres of Napoleon, at least 'movement in order to *seek* battle . . . to *assemble* one's forces on the ground . . . to *carry out* the attack'.[15] In the hands of his enthusiastic disciples, Foch's faith in the offensive became in an exaggerated form the guiding impulse in the French plan of campaign adopted in 1913. More concerned with strategic deployment than with any specific manœuvre or operation as such, Plan XVII had only one fixed objective: 'Whatever the circumstances, it is the . . . intention to advance with all forces to the attack.'[16] Indiscretion, it would seem, had become the better part of valour.

Strategical thought in England and the United States was not tied to any specific situation and as a rule lacked originality. Indeed very little was written on the subject, and the foremost texts were culled from earlier works and reflected the geometrical approach of Jomini. Hamley, whose *Operations of War* (1866) in various editions endured as a text for half a century, assumed that the maxims of Jomini and the Archduke Charles were still valid after 1870. His revisions were in the portion dedicated to tactics, and even here he was years behind the times. Unlike most continental theorists, Hamley virtually ignored moral factors, and if neither Clausewitz nor Foch mentioned the sea, there is no indication that Hamley ever gave much thought to what the former had written about war. With one important exception: Captain John Bigelow's *Principles of Strategy* (1894) was also distilled from the works of earlier theorists. But from Sherman's March through Georgia, Bigelow seems to have developed a better concept of total war. At least he recognized what would happen when war was 'brought home to a hostile people'.[17]

There were other primers on strategy, but the only work with any claim to originality is Colonel C. E. Callwell's *Small Wars: Their Principles and Practice* (1896). This was one area where British soldiers exceeded all others in experience, and Callwell's attempt to discover the extent to which accepted principles must be modified to meet the conditions of colonial warfare filled a real need before the Boer War and was even translated and published in France, at that time Britain's foremost colonial rival. It speaks volumes for the vitality of British strategical thought during this period that among the two dozen and some titles listed in the War Office Library in 1912 under 'Colonial Warfare', this was the only book written by an Englishman! The main difficulty seems to have been that until the nation's political

81

leaders defined the role of the army and decided what priorities should go to Imperial Defence, Home Defence and the expeditionary force that after the turn of the century was being prepared for possible intervention on the Continent, British theorists and military planners had no choice but to grope in the dark. In Germany and France it was possible to anticipate every detail of mobilization beforehand and shape the strategy accordingly. In England, on the other hand, 'it is as useless to anticipate in what quarter of the globe our troops may be next employed as to guess at the tactics, the armament, and even the colour . . . of our next enemy'. Colonel G. F. R. Henderson and others ultimately reacted against the formalism of Hamley, the strategic pedagogue of the British Army, but although Henderson was able to portray something of 'the spirit of war. . . . Moral influences, [and] the effect of rapidity, surprise and secrecy' in his famous biography *Stonewall Jackson and the American Civil War* (1898), which he had written partially to serve as a treatise on war and to develop his own strategical concepts, neither he nor his fellow officers produced a really significant work on strategy. The best-informed minds either remained in the field of grand tactics or else, like Spenser Wilkinson and Colonel à Court Repington, became increasingly involved in military administration and organization.[18]

The tactical literature is more extensive, highly technical, and often difficult to grasp because of its complex forms and plodding devotion to detail. Manifestly, much of what has been said of strategical thought would apply more or less in the realm of tactics as well. The Germans did not reject abstract science in the one merely to adopt this method in the other, and in both fields French writers often placed a high premium on offensive spirit and will. It remains, then, only to suggest the general trends and to frame some of the pressing issues.

A tacit recognition of the increased powers of the defensive and a desire to seek greater dispersion in infantry formations was common among tacticians after 1870. Clausewitz had pointed to the natural advantages of the defensive—a fact often ignored by later disciples—and Moltke, even in his pre-war essays, repeatedly had mentioned the growing power modern weapons were giving to the defensive. Hence the emphasis upon envelopment in Moltke's writings, which ultimately reached such a point that he believed it no longer possible to achieve a tactical envelopment —the solution lay in the domain of strategy.[19]

The tendency towards dispersed order was foreshadowed in the new tactical manual adopted by the United States Army in 1867. The author, Major-General Emory Upton, learned from his experiences in the Civil War (which included a successful assault against a fortified Confederate beachhead at Rappahannock Station in 1863 and a break into the famed Mule Shoe at Spotsylvania a year later) the value of simplicity, flexibility and above all, skirmishing: 'In the skirmish drill, the officers . . . will constantly aim to impress each man with the idea of his individuality, and the responsibility rests upon him; they will see that the men economize their strength, preserve their presence of mind, husband their ammunition, and profit by all the advantages which the ground may offer for cover.'[20] Two years later Prussian authorities were startled by a pamphlet that rejected, on the basis of the 1866 campaign against Austria, both the column and the line in favour of 'the skirmish swarm', the 'only battle formation which can be effective'. The official defence of the company column, which presented four ranks to the enemy when the section of skirmishers (two ranks) was out, failed to settle the issue, and one of the first tactical studies to appear after 1870 reiterated the thesis that 'the frightful effects of our fire-arms necessitates dispersion'. In his *Tactical Deductions from the War of 1870-71*, Captain Boguslawski concluded: 'Great clouds of skirmishers and small tactical units, that is the form for infantry. . . . All idea of attacking with large compact masses, or of drawing them up in line to fire upon one another, is finally exploded. . . . The real secret of infantry fighting . . . now consists in so regulating and controlling the independent action of the individual soldier, and of the leaders of a tactical unit, as to facilitate . . . the direction of the fight, without losing the advantages of that same independent self-reliance. . . . The fighting formation for our infantry is that of a cloud of skirmishers.'[21]

A similar respect for firepower was shown in England by progressive soldiers like Major-General Sir Patrick MacDougall and young Lieutenant Frederick Maurice. The best mode of attack, according to MacDougall, was to throw out a strong line of skirmishers to attract the fire of the enemy, followed by the main line of battle which would attack by successive rushes. But even this, MacDougall warned, was no sure recipe for success: future campaigns 'will in all probability be decided by strategic rather than tactical manœuvring'. Maurice argued that assaulting troops must adopt flexible formations and make better use of ground. 'If an army is to retain *the power of attack* at all, it must nowadays attack in skirmishing order, with a proper system of supports and reserves.' Like most Germans, Maurice decided that flank attacks offered the best and in many cases the only real prospect of success, and he agreed with MacDougall that the best solution would be some combination of offensive strategy with defensive tactics.[22]

Although the years immediately following the Prussian victories witnessed experiments with what one authority describes as 'the most marvellous formations', the prevailing view favoured dispersion in one form or another. The French infantry regulations of 1875 'can be considered as the triumph of dispersed order'; the German regulations of 1876 did away with the old column of attack and gave increased attention to 'fighting in open order'; while British doctrine moved in the direction of 'four attenuated lines unprotected by skirmishers'. So carried away were some British reformers, in fact, that MacDougall once witnessed a battalion in manœuvres advancing in extended order against an 'enemy' occupying the same extent of front but in close order, therefore outnumbering the assailants by three to one.[23]

In the 1880's, owing largely to the difficulty of blending initiative with discipline in dispersed formations and of concentrating a sufficient volume of fire against the point under attack, attempts were made to stiffen the firing line. Following an earlier suggestion by Major von Scherff in *The New Tactics of Infantry* (1873), tacticians now began to think in terms of a firing line, support and reserve in the battle line, the whole to be reinforced by a second and sometimes even a third line. By building up the firing line and urging volley firing, it was hoped that attack formations would increase both the density and control of fire. They certainly increased the size of the target to be offered.

The *German Field Exercise* of 1888, stating that 'Every engagement intended to be of a decisive character will entail the occupation of the entire space available for deployment by a dense fighting line,' prescribed the following.

When the fighting line has arrived to within short range of the enemy, and, having been sufficiently reinforced, has paved the way for the assault by the highest attainable fire action, the bodies of troops echelonned in rear should be brought up to the foremost line without a halt, and together with it should deliver the final blow. The drums of all closed bodies commence beating from the moment that the advance to the assault can no longer be concealed from view. . . . In this most decisive moment of the attack there is only one watchword for a fighting line, and that is 'Forward! Forward! straight for the goal!' The beating of drums, the continuous sounding of the 'Rapid advance' by all the buglers, sets everybody . . . in motion, and with cheers the assaulting troops throw themselves upon the enemy.[24]

The French regulations of 1884 reveal a similar tendency—a thick battle line advancing 'head erect' without being preoccupied with losses; while the 1895 regulations carried the doctrine to almost criminal lengths.

As soon as the battalion has arrived within 400 metres of the enemy, bayonets are fixed, and individual fire . . . of the greatest intensity delivered. . . . The advance is made by successive rushes followed by a quick fire of short duration. The fighting line reinforced by the reserves, and if necessary by the battalion in second line, gradually reaches to within 150 or 200 metres of the enemy. At this distance magazine fire is commenced, and all available reserves . . . close up for the assault. At a signal from the Colonel the drums beat, and bugles sound the advance, and the entire line charges forward with cries of '*en avant, à la baïonette*'.[25]

Extract *la furie française* and this does not differ drastically from what British officers were taught in Clery's *Minor Tactics* and American officers read in Wagner's *Organization and Tactics*

(1894), the standard tactical texts in their respective armies. And Wagner, it is curious to note, was one of the few to call attention elsewhere to the value of intrenchments in the Civil War. But so then did Henderson, and at one time he too had professed belief in the efficacy of the frontal attack by successive lines of infantry.

Fortunately the defeats in South Africa forced a re-examination of British tactics and led to the adoption of a more realistic doctrine; although the emphasis was still on building up the fire line, 'the form was essentially elastic and adapted to the ground, with the definite objects of . . . utilizing such cover as was available, and presenting as difficult a target as possible to the enemy'.[26] Instead of seeking to learn from events in South Africa and Manchuria, French and German writers showed a marked tendency to judge events in the light of their own predilections. One has only to read General Langlois' *Enseignements de deux guerres récentes* to appreciate the extent to which the *Conseil Supérieur de la Guerre* remained impervious to criticisms growing out of the British experience against the Boers. The patronizing tone of the German General Staff official history of *The War in South Africa* (1906) reveals a similar attitude, while the triumph of the Japanese in Manchuria was regarded by German critics with much the same satisfaction as a teacher contemplating the achievement of a prize pupil. Whereas the British official history of the Russo-Japanese war had taken note of the value of hand grenades in trench-warfare, the effectiveness of the machine-gun, and the growing dependence upon earthworks, the first German infantry regulations issued after that war state that the use of ground is limited to the preservation of direction, and place fresh emphasis upon bayonet action: 'To attack is to carry a firing line as near as possible to the enemy. The assault with the *arme blanche* definitely seals his defeat.'[27] The French regulations of 1902, while taking greater recognition of firepower, continued to be dominated by the offensive spirit. Foch proclaimed that 'any improvement of fire-arms is ultimately bound to add strength to the offensive', and the new doctrine in 1913 asserted that 'the French Army, returning to its traditions, no longer knows any other law than the offensive. . . . All attacks are to be pushed to the extreme . . . to charge the enemy with the bayonet in order to destroy him. . . . This result can only be obtained at the price of bloody sacrifice. Any other conception ought to be rejected as contrary to the very nature of war.'[28] 'I believe in order that I may understand'—surely such faith is worthy of St Augustine.

The cavalry trotted down a parallel road. The first desire of most military writers after 1870 was to learn; only later did they succumb to the instinct to preserve. The basic issue was whether cavalry would continue to employ shock tactics, hurling itself at the enemy in dense formations in an effort to crush their forces by the sheer impact of the mounted charge, or whether cavalry would learn to utilize firepower. In England in the 1860's several writers, taking their cue from cavalry operations in the Civil War, preached a radical doctrine that cavalry had become mobile firepower, dependent upon the horse primarily as a means of locomotion, a view shared by most United States officers with recent experience in the Civil War or against the Indians (of the twelve squadrons sent with the expeditionary force to Cuba in 1898, only one was mounted).

In Germany the approach was more conservative. General Karl von Schmidt, who had learned in 1870-71 that it was 'indispensably necessary' at times for cavalry to fight dismounted, although he still preferred shock action for most occasions, used his influence as a member of the Cavalry Commission in 1874 to see that the new regulations issued the following year gave greater attention than before to dismounted tactics. In France, on the other hand, the regulations of 1876 prescribed shock tactics as 'essential conditions for success', although there were a few writers like Colonel Bonie who maintained that cavalry must be able to fight dismounted if it was to hold its place on the modern battlefield. 'Cavalry that cannot fight on foot as well as on horse', Bonie insisted, 'is backward cavalry, unequal to its mission and fatally dedicated to defeat.'[29]

In the 1880's there was a pronounced revival of faith in the power of shock tactics. Both the French regulations of 1882 and the German regulations of 1886 stressed the *arme blanche*. Probably the most important contribution in the realm of theory was Lewal's *Tactique des Renseignements* (1881), in which the French General developed the strategic possibilities of the cavalry division in gathering information, providing security and executing raids. Nevertheless Lewal, like von Schmidt, advocated dismounted tactics only when other means were inadequate to the occasion. In Germany the writings of Captain Hoenig and Prince Kraft fortified those who believed that cavalry still had an important function in battle. Recognizing that increased firepower had reduced cavalry to a position of 'equality' with the other arms, Prince Kraft in his *Letters on Cavalry* (1884) contended that soldiers were over-reacting to the change: 'Judging by the experience of war, I have . . . come to the conclusion that the part played by cavalry in offensive battle may yet, in spite of the extension of the sphere of the effect of fire on the other arms, be under certain circumstances of a most decisive character; but I consider the chances for cavalry in a defensive battle to be yet more favourable. . . . The cavalry masses can be posted close to the spot selected, and under cover, and be let loose at the right moment.'[30] Von der Goltz was another who insisted that cavalry 'will again play its role in deciding the day, as in former times. . . . German infantry has nothing to fear from the enemy's cavalry', he boasted: the problem was 'whether our cavalry will make itself feared by the enemy's infantry.'[31]

The Boer War brought the issue to a head. French and British regulations in 1904 provided for increased dismounted fighting, but it did not take long for the impressions formed in South Africa to fade. In France, where Foch was writing of cavalry squadrons suddenly appearing 'out of a cloud of dust or of smoke' to press home a charge, there was a general neglect of dismounted training; and in Germany Bernhardi read the new regulations and wrote two volumes in a fruitless effort to induce greater realism in cavalry doctrine. Convinced that cavalry must make greater use of firepower, Bernhardi pleaded with his fellow officers to 'be neither dazzled nor spellbound by the glamour of a past which can never be recalled.'[32]

But in England even Bernhardi was regarded in some circles as being too conservative. His admission that the 'old shock charge is dead' was not enough for Erskine Childers, who had fought against the Boers and was convinced that the *arme blanche* should be abolished in favour of mounted infantry. Unfortunately few cavalrymen then, or even after the war when they had to come to terms with the tank, were willing to be separated from their horses, and the *Cavalry Training Manual* of 1907 reaffirmed the doctrine that: 'The essence of the cavalry spirit lies in holding the balance correctly between firepower and shock action. . . . It must be accepted as a principle that the rifle, effective as it is, cannot replace the effect produced by the speed of the horse, the magnetism of the charge, and the terror of cold steel.'[33] Financed by cavalry officers serving at the time in England, the *Cavalry Journal* was founded in 1906 to perpetuate this point of view.

The formation and manœuvres of artillery were more simple and less controversial than was the case with the other arms. Prior to 1870 the concentration of fire characteristic of the Napoleonic battle often was neglected: during the Civil War the heavily wooded terrain, and faulty organization, worked against this principle, and in 1866 the Prussian artillery 'on almost every occasion', according to Prince Kraft, 'entered upon the scene far too late and with far too small a number of guns'.[34] But the Prussians learned and so, after 1870, did the other armies; to the point, in fact, where the employment of artillery in masses became the first article of faith. Prince Kraft's informative *Letters on Artillery* (1884) seems to have carried the greatest weight of any book written on the subject and survived even the technical changes in *matériel*, notably the quick-firing field-guns, improvement in shrapnel and the reintroduction of heavy siege guns. In general the role assigned to the artillery in battle was first to overcome the enemy guns in an immense artillery duel and then to render close and effective support to infantry in the attack. If there was a trend in artillery tactics it was towards an increase in the amount and calibre of the guns, which gradually transformed artillery from an auxiliary arm into the dominant weapon in battle. If indeed infantry remained the queen of battles, then no coronation was possible without a preponderance of artillery.

Space is lacking in which to discuss the other issues that caught the attention of military writers during these years or even to out-line the theories of those who rebelled against doctrine that was fast hardening into lines every bit as rigid and impenetrable as the trench systems of 1914-18. In every army the discussion of current problems was guided by a few intellectuals usually associated with the *Kriegsakademie,* the *École Militaire Supérieure,* the Staff College and other institutions maintained for the purpose of training the higher officers. In most cases the open search for solutions in the 1870's had narrowed to a solemn commitment to official doctrine by the turn of the century, a movement that can be traced in the drill manuals and even in the official histories prepared by the various general staffs. By about 1890 there was a pronounced trend away from the slavish imitation of German methods and organization in the armies of France, Russia and England, and the German Army itself seemed to be changing some-what in character.

For the first decade after 1870 perceptive students of war noted that the Prussians had owed their success as much to the quality of their leadership as to their organization and tactics, and the prevailing theme in many German treatises dealt with the basic problem of *Drill oder Erziehung*—how to reconcile individual initiative and originality with the necessary discipline at both the tactical and the strategical level. Most foreign officers under-estimated the importance of this issue and in time the Germans themselves lost much of the spirit that had guided the operations and manœuvres of 1870. Commenting on the German manœuvres of 1895, Henderson wrote that even the soldiers 'act like intelligent beings, who thoroughly understand their duty, and the fact speaks volumes for the way in which even the privates are taught to use their initiative, and for the excellence of the system of individual training'.[35] Yet in 1911 this same army made a quite different impression: Repington of *The Times* saw 'sullen-looking, half-cowed, and machine-made' soldiers attacking in 'a methodical and plodding manner', and on another occasion he wondered 'what has become of the great school of Moltke. . . . To those who have kept their finger on the pulse of foreign armies during recent years, the decadence of German military criticism comes by no

means as a surprise. Certain Western armies began to lose something of their fine point in the early 'nineties of the last century;
a long peace and the wearisome round of barrack-yard routine
produced their inevitable results.'[36] As any reader of *The Defence
of Duffer's Drift* (1904) could attest, the British Army that entered
the Boer War suffered from the same limitations.

The World War, for a time at least, brought military thought
and doctrine closer to reality than had been the case since the
1880's. What happened? Why did so few military thinkers
anticipate what the machine-gun and trench would do to war?
Perhaps, had the first battle of the Marne been a German victory,
they would have been much closer to the truth, but in surveying
the literature of the period, three quotations from prominent
writers on war seem to suggest what caused the distortion.

'Science, in a *Pickelhaube*, has taken possession of the field of
battle, and all who do not prostrate themselves before this idol of
the day are reactionaries, narrow-minded, and behind the age.'

'Wherever one looks one sees a clever idea degenerate into a
trick of the drill-ground.'

'It is well known that military history, when superficially studied,
will furnish arguments in support of any theory or opinion.'[37]

NOTES

1. This was the case within five years in Austria-Hungary, Russia,
   France and Italy. The United States Army went over to the larger
   company organization in 1901, the British Army went over in
   1913.
2. *Generalfeldmarschall Graf von Moltke, Ausgewählte Werke*. I.
   Feldherr und Kriegslehrmeister (Berlin 1925), pp. 79, 82.
3. Quoted in Walter Goerlitz, *History of the German General Staff,
   1657-1945* (New York 1953), pp. 87-88.
4. Verdy and Blume are quoted in Col. Eugène Carrias', *La Pensée
   militaire allemande* (Paris 1948), pp. 261-262.
5. Lt.-Gen. von Caemmerer, *The Development of Strategical
   Science during the 19th Century* (London 1905), pp. 95, 222-223;
   Spenser Wilkinson, *War and Policy* (New York 1900), p. 154;
   Carrias, *La Pensée militaire allemande*, pp. 270-271, 277, 291.

6. Gen. Prince Kraft zu Hohenlohe-Ingelfingen, *Letters on Strategy* (London 1897), i. 1-11, 101; ii. 1-3.

7. Von der Goltz, *The Nation in Arms: A Treatise on Modern Military Systems and the Conduct of War* (5th ed., London 1906), pp. vii, 1-8.

8. Friedrich von Bernhardi, *On War of Today* (London 1912), i. 44-60, 89; ii. 23-32, 402-404; von der Goltz, *The Conduct of War: A Short Treatise on its most important Branches and Guiding Rules* (London 1899), pp. 158-159.

9. See Gerhard Ritter, *The Schlieffen Plan: Critique of a Myth* (London 1958).

10. *Generalfeldmarschall Graf Alfred von Schlieffen, Gesammelte Schriften* (Berlin 1913), ii. 439-441.

11. Général Lewal, *Stratégie de combat* (Paris 1895), i. 3, 35; ii. 189. A brief critique of Lewal's theories is found in von Caemmerer, *Development of Strategical Science*, pp. 229-239.

12. Col. V. Derrécagaix, *Modern War* (Washington 1888), i. 22-23, 232, 290, 660; ii. 490.

13. Gen. H. Bonnal, *Sadowa: a Study* (London 1907), p. 22. Gen. Cardot is quoted in the excellent analysis of Carrias, *La Pensée militaire française* (Paris, n. d.), p. 290.

14. The best study of Foch's theory and practice of war is still Liddell Hart's *Foch: Man of Orleans* (London 1931) which, because of its critical attitude, was 'more or less banned' in France when the publisher, 'apparently under pressure from some higher quarter,' broke his contract on the ground that 'the book is too different' from the prevailing French view of the national hero. (Private information.)

15. Marshal Foch, *The Principles of War* (London 1918), pp. 8, 42-43, 45.

16. Plan XVII is contained in Brig.-Gen. J. E. Edmonds' *Military Operations in France and Belgium, 1914*, i. (London 1922), 444-449.

17. Quoted in Russell F. Weigley, *Towards an American Army: Military Thought from Washington to Marshall* (New York 1962), pp. 95-97.

18. G. F. R. Henderson, 'The War in South Africa', *Edinburgh Review*, cxci (1900), 251-252.

19. Moltke, *Ausgewählte Werke*, i. 321-322, 335, 356.

20. Emory Upton, *A New System of Infantry Tactics Double and Single Rank adapted to American Topography and Improved Fire-arms* (New York 1868), p. 98.

21. Capt. May, *On the Prussian Infantry, 1869* (London 1870), p. 40; Capt. A. von Boguslawski, *Tactical Deductions from the War of 1870-71* (London 1872), pp. 160-161. Col. Bronsart von Schellendorf, later to achieve recognition as the author of *The Duties of*

the General Staff, was the man picked to answer the arguments of Capt. May. See von Schellendorf, *Précis of a Retrospect on the Tactical Retrospect; and Reply to the Pamphlet on the Prussian Infantry of 1866* (London 1871).

22. Maj.-Gen. Sir Patrick MacDougall, *Modern Infantry Tactics* (London 1873), pp. 15-20, 26, 27; Lieut. F. Maurice, *The System of Field Manœuvres best adapted for enabling our Troops to meet a Continental Army* (Edinburgh 1872), pp. 26-31, 74-79.

23. Général Thoumas, *Les Transformations de l'armée française: Essais d'histoire et de critique sur l'état militaire de la France* (Paris 1887), ii. 460-461; Prince Kraft, *Letters on Infantry* (London 1892), pp. 50-54, 114; MacDougall, 'The Late Battles in the Soudan and Modern Tactics', *Blackwood's Edinburgh Magazine*, cxxxv (1884), 605-610.

24. Quoted in Col. Robert Home, *A Précis of Modern Tactics* (rev. ed., London 1892), pp. 37, 42.

25. Quoted in Maj.-Gen. J. F. C. Fuller, *War and Western Civilization: 1832-1932: A Study of War as a Political Instrument and the Expression of Mass Democracy* (London 1932), pp. 152-153.

26. Edmonds, *Military Operations in France and Belgium, 1914*, i. 9-10.

27. Maj. de Pardieu, *A Critical Study of German Tactics and of the New German Regulations* (Fort Leavenworth 1912), pp. 21-24; Capitaine Breveté Niessel, *Tendances actuelles de l'infanterie allemande* (Paris 1905), pp. 48, 57.

28. Quoted in Liddell Hart, *Foch*, p. 67.

29. Col. T. Bonie, *Étude sur le combat à pied de la cavalerie* (Paris 1877), pp. 36-37, 40-41, 165 ff.

30. Prince Kraft, *Letters on Cavalry* (London 1893), pp. 82-83.

31. Von der Goltz, *Nation in Arms*, pp. 316-321.

32. Bernhardi, *Cavalry in War and Peace* (London 1910), p. 367.

33. Quoted in Erskine Childers, *War and the Arme Blanche* (London 1910).

34. Prince Kraft, *Letters on Artillery* (2nd ed., London 1890), p. 6.

35. War Office, Intelligence Division, *Extracts from the Reports of various officers on the Manœuvres in Austria, Belgium, France, Germany* . . . (London 1896), p. 53.

36. Col. Charles à Court Repington, 'The German Army Manœuvres', *The Times*, 12th, 14th and 17th October; *The War in the Far East, 1904-1905* (London 1905), p. 335.

37. Gen. Dragomirov, quoted in Home, *Précis of Modern Tactics*, p. 17; Fritz Hoenig, *Inquiries concerning the Tactics of the Future* (4th ed., London 1899), p. 37; Bronsart von Schellendorf, quoted in Prince Kraft, *Letters on Artillery*, p. 108.

§5§

Doctrine and Training in the British Cavalry 1870-1914

BRIAN BOND

FROM the days of Frederick the Great and his dashing cavalry commander, Seydlitz, down to the ill-fated charge of Lord Cardigan's Light Brigade in 1854, there was no reason to question the effectiveness, particularly the psychological impact, of the *arme blanche*—the warhorse and 'cold steel' of lance and sabre—on the field of battle. Certainly there were numerous occasions —notably at Waterloo—when well-disciplined infantry proved impervious to the 'shock tactics' of the cavalry charge, but those were offset by many successful charges against demoralized infantry and artillery, sometimes completed by devastating pursuits.

The rash of European conflicts between 1859 and 1870 and, even more significantly, the American Civil War, suggested to all but the most tradition-bound soldiers that the cavalry's capabilities had undergone a profound and permanent change. Though the connection was only slowly realized and accepted, these campaigns showed that firepower had increased enormously and that cavalry, in so far as it applied shock tactics of knee-to-knee close-order charging, had suffered a corresponding eclipse. By 1871 the meagre achievements by cavalry shock tactics on the part of any of the belligerents in the recent wars had cast the arm's future role into the melting-pot. The cavalry's failure was variously attributed to adverse physical conditions, as was plausible in the case of much of the American terrain; or, more simply, to poor training and inept leadership, as was indeed true of the French cavalry in 1870. Among the few soldiers who did perceive that increased and ever-increasing firepower was the fundamental reason, were an Indian Army officer, Sir Henry Havelock, and a Canadian Militia Colonel, George Denison. Their basic perceptions may serve to set the technological background against which British cavalry organization and training developed, or failed to develop, in the half-century before the first World War.

In the pre-Crimean era, Havelock pointed out, cavalry had

successfully charged infantry basically because 'the clumsy, uncertain smooth-bored "Brown Bess" only admitted of being loaded, primed and fired about twice in a minute—and cavalry could cover the danger zone of 200 yards in about thirty seconds'. Now (he was writing in 1867) rifled arms had extended the danger zone to at least 800 or 1,000 yards, and in addition the new arms of precision were bringing careful attention to individual marksmanship. Havelock's criticisms were directed not at cavalry as such, but against the cult of the *arme blanche* for, he argued, the Northern cavalry in the American Civil War had actually enhanced the cavalry's role by using the rifle as their main arm. They were ready to draw swords and charge on opportunity, but dismounted fire, combined with the mobility provided by the horse, were more effective tactics.

The notion that the rifle should become their principal arm and dismounted action habitual was anathema to European cavalry, and was made even less palatable by Havelock's caustic phrasing; he described, for example, 'the British lancer with his flag and pole' as 'a gorgeous anachronism borrowed from the Middle Ages'. Although Denison was also deeply impressed by the combination of fire and shock tactics in the American Civil War he was far less convinced than Havelock that traditional cavalry charges were now a thing of the past. He proposed to keep at least a quarter of the mounted force as 'real cavalry, armed as such, educated as such, and taught that nothing can withstand a well-executed charge. . . .'[1]

Despite differences of approach and emphasis, Havelock and Denison were at one in thinking that firepower would increasingly dominate the battlefield to the disadvantage of cavalry, and that the American Civil War provided the best practical examples of how cavalry could adapt themselves to the new conditions. On the latter point they were twenty years ahead of their time. For a variety of reasons the impact of the Civil War on British military thought was muffled, and its effects are hard to trace either in official doctrine or in such limited field training as then existed.[2] British military thinking was blinkered chiefly by the more or less subconscious assumption that only European wars really 'counted'. Thus by defeating France—the military paragon of Europe since Napoleonic days—Germany became the dominating influence on British official doctrine. Shock tactics remained the ideal of the German cavalry and it was in this aspect that the British cavalry found comfort when faced with the disturbing practices of trans-Atlantic horsemen.

Even with the wisdom of hindsight it would be a mistake to think that by 1871 the horse was an anachronism on the field of battle. Tactically it was still the chief means of mobility, while its strategical value in reconnaissance, raids and protective duties had recently been demonstrated, particularly in France in 1870, and was even likely to increase as armies and battle fronts both expanded. On the other hand the obstacles to the horse, such as automatic guns, barbed wire and entrenchments, though already ominous, had not yet given their full power to the defensive. Thus the problem, in the period before 1914, was not whether the cavalry should be abolished, but how far it should and could be adapted to face new conditions. In the strategic sphere the 'lessons' of war as affecting European cavalry seemed sufficiently clear as to be accepted by the British cavalry as a matter of pragmatic adjustment and development; an unsurprising response since the arm's importance was unquestionably increased. This was not the case in the tactical sphere, where the 'lessons' of war were far less obvious at the time and where changes which seemed moderate and reasonable to an outsider were fiercely resented by the cavalry, for whom the lance was 'a state of mind' and 'the charge' connoted not merely a tactical movement but a whole way of life. It was, therefore, on the closely related issues of armament, mounted and dismounted action, and the feasibility of the charge that the great cavalry controversy revolved.

A sketch of the British cavalry in the middle of these 'dark days' must first underline its small size in the Army as a whole. In 1870 there were only thirty-one cavalry regiments as against 144 infantry battalions (each roughly the equivalent of a cavalry regiment), and the number remained unchanged down to 1914. In 1889 it was calculated that there were in the Regular Army, including British troops in India and the reserves, 266,692 men, of which the cavalry and its reserves accounted for 21,922 or 8·2 per cent. The proportion of mounted men in the auxiliary forces was much smaller.[3] Fewness of numbers was emphasized by dispersion. The usual distribution was fourteen regiments in England, one in Scotland, six in Ireland and ten overseas, mostly in India.[4]

A combination of factors, however, gave the cavalry national as well as service prestige out of all proportion to its size. Over its real historical achievements there had accumulated an aura of glamour and romance, epitomized by the half-serious boast that the cavalry's role in battle was to add tone to what would otherwise be an unseemly brawl. This accumulation of past achievements was distilled into 'the cavalry spirit', an essence said to be found in no other corps and of practical value as a foil to unwelcome reforms. In addition, the traditional aristocratic tone of the corps was preserved by careful 'vetting' of officer candidates and by very high regimental expenses. Writing in 1906, Sir Evelyn Wood recalled that 'eight years ago most Commanding Officers recommended an annual allowance of from £500 to £600. Now, it is alleged, a very careful officer may join the cavalry at an initial expense of £400, and either hunt or play polo on an allowance of £300.'[5] These details are included not merely to add colour, but as essential factors in understanding the horror with which the cavalry regarded the loss of their traditional role, and the obduracy of their rear-guard action.

Although an elaborate cavalry organization existed on paper from the division and brigade down to regiment and squadron, most of the cavalryman's working life was spent in none of these formations but in the smallest unit of all, the troop. The main reason for this was the cavalry's social system, whose object was to ensure that officers spent a minimum of time on regimental duties and a maximum on hunting and other congenial pursuits. So much time was taken up with 'internal duties' that field training had to be crammed into two three-week periods. The 9th Lancers, for example, were supposed to attain proficiency in mounted and dismounted duties, scouting, reconnaissance, commands and signals in four days.[6] It was this 'Wellingtonian' state of affairs, still operative in the late 1870's, that had to be swept away before large-scale exercises could be of any value.

British cavalry was divided into three classes—heavy, medium and light—according to the size and weight of the horse and rider. The heavy class comprised the five regiments of the Household Cavalry and these did not serve abroad. There were thirteen medium regiments of Dragoons and Lancers and an equal number of light regiments, all Hussars. Dragoons and Hussars had carried muzzle-loading carbines (and some of them pistols also), as well as swords, long before the Crimean War, whereas the Lancers had carried only swords, lances and pistols. Breech-loading Snider carbines began to be issued soon after the Crimean War and were superseded in turn by the Martini-Henry (1878), Lee-Metford (1892) and, finally, Lee-Enfield (1901).[7] Carbines were adopted reluctantly, especially by the Lancers, one of whose regiments is reputed to have deposited its first issue on a manure heap.[8] Thus by 1880 all cavalrymen carried sword and carbine and the Lancers retained their own weapon in addition. Despite the frequent issue of new types of carbine, musketry was not taken seriously by the cavalry much before the late 1880's but was, on the contrary, held to be 'degradation and a bore', as was perhaps inevitable so long as the annual ammunition allowance was only forty rounds per man.[9]

In the first half of Victoria's reign military manœuvres were practically unheard of: the nearest equivalent was the Volunteer Force's Annual Field Day at Brighton, a spectacle of great popular appeal but of no military significance. These continued to receive the approbation of the Horse Guards until 1871, when a particularly incompetent display caused the supervising general to report to the Duke of Cambridge that until the men were better drilled and better officered they would be of greater danger than service to the state.[10] The first man to realize the importance of field training was probably the Prince Consort. When even the simplest manœuvres were regarded by many senior officers as 'the pedantic arcana of a secret guild' the Prince conceived the simple but at that time novel idea that opposing forces ought to man-œuvre against each other. An experimental 'battle' took place at

Cæsar's Camp, near Aldershot, in 1858, but then the Prince's untimely death delayed developments for a decade.[11]

Chief credit for the introduction of real manœuvres must go to Sir Hope Grant, who became Commander of the Aldershot District in 1870, though it must be said that the Duke of Cambridge also favoured the idea. Grant persuaded Cardwell to permit the considerable force of 30,000 regular and auxiliary troops to encamp in Berkshire in 1871.[12] At short notice the project was cancelled by the War Office, ostensibly because of the late harvest, but quite possibly because transport was lacking to convey more than 5,000 men from Aldershot.[13] Rather than abandon the scheme a 'battle' was hastily arranged near Aldershot.

The chief obstacle to large-scale manœuvres in 1871 and for the rest of the century was lack of land. Parliamentary parsimony meant that field training depended largely on the patriotism of a few great landowners, like Lord Wantage, and their co-operation was frequently foiled by the objection of non-residents holding the shooting rights.[14] A second obstacle to holding manœuvres was the defective organization of the Army under the Cardwell system. The linking of battalions from 1872 ensured that those at home were perennially engaged in training recruits for overseas drafts, while the local Army Commands were deficient in administrative essentials, such as transport, until after the South African war.[15]

In the political atmosphere of late Victorian England the efforts of even the keenest soldiers, like Sir Evelyn Wood, to simulate real war conditions were doomed to failure. When crops must be avoided, game preserves left undisturbed and constricting boundary lines rigidly respected, the cavalry had little alternative but to practise the charge. Even when a new temporary training area was acquired on Cannock Chase in 1873, the cavalry had got to know every inch of the ground as well as Aldershot long before the manœuvres ended.[16] Although combined training of all arms in the field only became possible after the purchase of part of Salisbury Plain by the War Office in 1898, a new era in cavalry training may be dated from 1889 when Sir Evelyn Wood took over the Aldershot Command. A great innovation took place in the following year when a Cavalry Division was encamped on the Berkshire

102

Downs and 'exercised in the duties of scouting and manœuvring'. The old parade ground movements—excepting the charge—were abandoned as it was realized that 'leaders cannot be found with heaven-born inspiration; it is experience alone, acquired in peace, that will enable them to use cavalry masses with effect in war'. From 1895, also, Sir Redvers Buller the Adjutant-General, with Sir John French as his assistant, was drawing up a new Cavalry Manual and reorganizing the cavalry at home into permanent brigades.[17]

In the numerous minor colonial campaigns between 1870 and 1898 the regular cavalry had few opportunities to distinguish itself, though such feats as Sir Drury Lowe's dash to Cairo after Wolseley's victory at Tel el Kebir in 1882 were much praised. The main reason, of course, was that most campaigns took place in terrain completely unsuited to the *arme blanche*, terrains such as the equatorial forests of West Africa or the mountains of Afghanistan. It was an indication of the *arme blanche*'s limitations that when the 9th Lancers joined Sir Frederick Roberts in the latter theatre in 1879, he at once transformed them into mounted riflemen, ordering them to carry carbines—as their principal weapon—slung on their backs, while their swords remained attached to the saddle.[18] Consequently irregular cavalry began to play an important part in colonial warfare.

The rise of irregular cavalry in the British service, under the various titles of Frontier Light Horse, Mounted Rifles or Mounted Infantry, may be illustrated from the career of Sir Redvers Buller, whose heyday as a fighting field commander fell between 1870 and 1885. As a major in the Kaffir war in the summer of 1878, Buller commanded a miscellaneous body of men called the Frontier Light Horse. Composed of British, Boers and aliens, this motley force reached a maximum of 900 men; its appearance was highly unmilitary and its tactics were improvised, with dismounted action an important feature. In the following year Buller, now a Lieutenant-Colonel, commanded 1,400 irregular horsemen in Sir Evelyn Wood's 'Flying Column' on the left flank in the Zulu war. Buller put his trust in the carbine and had no use for the sabre, saying 'he was sure that if his men had been so armed on Inlohbana [from which the British were driven on 28th March] they would never have got up the hill, and if they had would most certainly not have come off alive'.[19] Mounted infantry were used in 1881 against the Boers, and again in 1882 Sir Garnet Wolseley raised a mounted infantry column in Egypt by taking contingents of picked men from each infantry battalion. The commander of this column, Major (later Major-General Sir) Edward Hutton, became in the following decade the leading advocate of mounted infantry as a supplement to the regular cavalry.[20]

The actual achievements of irregular horsemen in relation to the other arms in these minor wars should not be exaggerated. They were important rather as practical evidence that in certain conditions horsemen trained to rely chiefly on the carbine and fighting on foot were more useful than cavalry steeped in *arme blanche* tactics. Moreover, these innovations were not the work of 'amateur soldiers'—the contemptuous kind of phrase sometimes used to discredit the mounted troops of the American Civil War—but of famous soldiers who were to dominate the British Army in the late 1880's and 1890's: Roberts, Wolseley, Wood and Buller.[21]

Thus while official cavalry doctrine at home still reflected continental fashions in giving pride of place to shock tactics, practical experience in war was forming a school of thought which held that mounted infantry training must be given more prominence in peacetime. This particular question of reform must be set in the context of a quickening development towards a new 'professional spirit' in the Army from the late 1880's, exemplified by the displacement of the last of the 'bow-and-arrow' generals of the Crimean era by the reforming 'Wolseley Ring'.

It is ironical that the advent of these reformers coincided with a pronounced reaction towards the ideal of cavalry shock tactics in Western Europe. With the passing years the bloody and ineffectual cavalry charges of the Franco-Prussian and earlier wars were conveniently forgotten and the cavalry tradition revived, aided no doubt by the fact that the machine-gun—the horse's deadliest opponent—had been badly misused as an artillery weapon. A more tangible reason, however, was the accession of the uniform-loving cavalry devotee, Wilhelm II, to the throne of Imperial Germany in 1888, though a similar trend was admittedly occurring in France.[22] In 1890 the German Emperor ordered all his ninety-three cavalry regiments to be equipped with the lance, and massed charges were henceforth sedulously practised at German manœuvres. Britain followed suit by introducing the lance into the front rank of all cavalry regiments except the Hussars.[23]

The British Army's tendency at this time uncritically to follow German fashions was offset in the case of cavalry doctrine by a revival of interest in the American Civil War, which was initially inspired by the writings and teaching (at the Staff College) of one man, Colonel G. F. R. Henderson. As yet by no means an opponent of cavalry using lance and sabre—in suitable conditions—Henderson's studies through the 1890's persuaded him increasingly that it was firepower which provided the key to the 'unorthodox' cavalry tactics in the Civil War; and he therefore gave his considerable influence to the encouragement of the use of dismounted action and firepower by British cavalry.[24]

It was in this confused climate of opinion that the great controversy on mounted infantry took place: that is, the proposal that mounted infantry should be trained in Britain in peacetime and not improvised from regular infantry and miscellaneous irregulars at the seat of war. The chief propagandist for this idea, Major Hutton, received the support of Sir Garnet Wolseley, whose view was that although cavalry using shock tactics were still indispensable, owing to their small numbers and specialized training they would benefit from a supporting, though in no way rival, force. Wolseley also favoured the conversion of the Yeomanry into mounted infantry. Both men vehemently criticized the British habit of tamely following continental military fashions.[25]

Despite Wolseley's backing, the actual training of mounted infantry made slow progress in the decade before the South African war. In 1898 a *Mounted Infantry Training Manual* was issued which specified that a mounted infantry battalion should comprise four companies and a machine-gun section, and that on foreign service one mounted infantry company would exist in each infantry battalion, and two companies in each cavalry brigade. As often happened, paper organization anticipated the actual forces in being. Only one mounted infantry battalion took part in the 1898 manœuvres and only two were ready at the outbreak of war.[26] Fortunately, to this number could be added some 2,000 Volunteers whose unofficial mounted training was due to a few enthusiastic commanding officers such as Lord Wantage in Berkshire, Sir Thomas Acland in Devonshire and Colonel Bower in Hampshire. These Volunteer detachments, though only 'isolated fragments and disconnected atoms', were none the less a remarkable achievement in the face of hostile professional military opinion. The development of regular mounted infantry had been painfully slow considering that as long ago as 1886 Sir Redvers Buller had predicted that 'the value of mounted infantry will be the most noticeable feature in the next great war'.[27]

Superficially, the charge of the 21st Lancers at Omdurman in 1898, immortalized by Winston Churchill who was present as a subaltern in the Fourth Queen's Own Hussars, provided a fitting climax to a decade in which shock tactics took pride of place in British as well as continental drill books and training. Examined more closely, through the reactions of Churchill himself, Omdurman provides further evidence that *arme blanche* tactics were obsolescent.

In a flanking movement to prevent the retreating Dervishes from entering Omdurman the Lancers unexpectedly came across a large body of the enemy, previously concealed, in a shallow depression. There was no alternative but to charge through them. Churchill, after the excitement of the charge, recounts that he was 'very anxious for the regiment to charge back because it would have been a very fine performance and the men and officers could easily have done it while they were warm. But *the dismounted fire was more useful* though I would have liked the charge—"pour la gloire"—and to buck up British cavalry' (my italics).[28] In the two minutes taken up by the charge British casualties amounted to five officers, sixty-five men and 119 horses out of a total of less than 400.[29] And even after the rout of the enemy in the main battle, the fugitives, armed with rifles, were still able to hold off the pursuing cavalry.[30]

106

Broadly speaking the period 1870-99 was one of recuperation and consolidation on traditional lines by British cavalry. Except Omdurman, there had been no spectacular charges to offset the frightful massacres of the Franco-Prussian war, but the precise details of the latter were growing hazy and were in any case of only indirect concern to British cavalry, whose self-assurance was unshaken. The ominously rapid developments of firepower *since* 1870, including machine-guns, rifle magazines and smokeless powder, were either ignored or countered by the argument that each improvement in firepower would correspondingly increase the 'friction' of battle and so demoralize the infantry and gunners that opportunities for 'charging home' with cold steel would still occur.[31] On the eve of the Boer War, then, the cavalry was 'still concerned to far too great an extent with the charge of large bodies in close order, which the history of all recent wars . . . had shown to be *vieux jeu*, save under exceptionally favourable circumstances'.[32]

In South Africa the British encountered an enemy who were, paradoxically, nearly all mounted men and who yet had no cavalry at all in the European sense of men armed with lance and sabre and always looking for an opportunity to charge. The Boers were expert marksmen with Mauser rifles and, as hunters, were adept at making the best use of ground, whether to conceal themselves or to surprise the British. Their horses were employed almost purely for mobility. The Boers did make a few 'charges' in the later part of the war, but even then firing from the saddle took the place of physical shock, for which their lean, under-sized ponies were completely unsuitable. Against such an opponent shock tactics were practically impossible. Even Colonel Douglas Haig, a fervent advocate of the *arme blanche*, admitted later that 'in practice there was no real distinction between the use of "Mounted Infantry" and "Mounted Rifles" and, in the latter part of the war, the cavalry were armed and employed in much the same way. The lance and sword were discarded after the first year of the war.'[33]

The one indisputable 'lesson' apparent from the very beginning of the war was that the regular cavalry was too weak numerically for the duties confronting it on the veldt, and that the training of mounted infantry and mounted auxiliaries for war overseas had been seriously neglected. General Buller's famous telegram on the morrow of his reverse at Colenso underlines this weakness. He asked for '8,000 irregulars . . . able to shoot as well as possible and ride decently', to be amalgamated with the Colonial Volunteers.[34] The one military organization capable of meeting this urgent request was the Yeomanry, which in 1899 comprised thirty-eight regiments of about 10,000 effective men. Though both organization and training had been tightened up in the 1890's, serious defects remained. The force resembled medieval levies in its attachment to individual commanding officers and localities; it trained for only eight days a year; and it lacked the administrative structure essential for war. Worst of all, given Buller's particular requirement, the Yeomanry proudly adhered to the purest *arme blanche* doctrine; and though armed with Martini carbines, its principal weapon was the sword (or, in a few cases, the lance).[35]

The conversion of the Yeomanry into the kind of 'mounted riflemen' needed in South Africa was nominally the achievement of a committee of Yeomanry colonels, but in fact the credit belongs almost entirely to one man, the Earl of Dundonald, who disagreed with the majority that the force should retain either the world 'Cavalry' in its title or the characteristics of that arm. Dundonald, who perceived more acutely than anyone else at that time that theoretical training in both *arme blanche* and riflemanship would in practice mean the perpetuation of the former, won over the Secretary of State for War by his arguments and so the 'Imperial Yeomanry' was born.[36] The characteristics of mounted infantry were emphasized from the start by formation in companies and battalions, and by the issue of the long Lee-Enfield rifle as the principal weapon. The first contingent of 10,000 Imperial Yeomanry was despatched early in 1900, the majority of them civilian volunteers, and in the course of the war a total of 34,124 left Britain.[37]

Only by means of such brilliant improvisation as was exemplified in the case of the Imperial Yeomanry, by a great upsurge of patriotism, and by the invaluable assistance received from the Empire and South African Loyalists, were enough mounted men raised to contain the Boers and eventually cause them to surrender.

The regular cavalry was much criticized during the war, and the firepower versus *arme blanche* controversy was thoroughly aired in the exhaustive inquiries of the Royal Commission which speedily convened on the conclusion of peace. Its report provides a very apt example of how difficult it is to learn from history; how, confronted with the same facts and documents, each side interprets them differently in accordance with preconceived opinions or attitudes.

The most distinguished witness in favour of the *arme blanche* was Lieutenant-General Sir John French. Sir John was absolutely opposed to the rifle being made the principal cavalry arm because 'if the cavalryman is taught that he is to rely mainly upon his rifle, his morale is taken away from him, and if that is done his power is destroyed'.[38] Haig's complete confidence in the future of the *arme blanche* was more surprising, since in November 1899 in some 'Tactical Notes' he had stressed the importance of firepower and dismounted action by cavalry, including Lancers, and had even written: 'It is a question whether the Dragoon Lancer is not a mistake! His lance hampers him.'[39] In his evidence, however, he argued that it was not worth while to train any mounted infantry in peacetime since cavalry could perform all their duties, and more effectively. It had been a mistake to withdraw lances and swords from the cavalry in South Africa because although their actual use was small, their effect on Boer morale was considerable. He also went on record as believing that 'the necessity of training cavalry to charge is as great as it was in the days of Napoleon'. That Haig's reasoning was constricted by a stereotyped view of future European warfare is evident in his belief 'that horsemen armed with firearms only (even though highly trained as cavalry) cannot cope successfully with cavalry either in attack or defence'.[40] Yet the Boer horsemen had done reasonably well against cavalry, though they carried neither lance nor sabre. Indeed the most astonishing 'lesson' derived from the war by several champions of the *arme blanche* was that the Boers would have done even better had they possessed the *arme blanche*.[41]

On the other side Sir Ian Hamilton completely disagreed with Haig that the *arme blanche* had exerted a psychological influence on the Boers. 'Compared to a modern rifle', he remarked, 'the sword or lance can only be regarded as a medieval toy.' If the cavalry retained the sword it should be in the interest of their own morale, but it should not be issued to the mounted infantry or Yeomanry. Lord Roberts' great experience and reading also led him to the opposite conclusion from Haig: that shock tactics had achieved little since Napoleon's time and were even less likely to do so in the future.[42]

From such a medley of divergent opinions the Commission could only make compromise recommendations on the future of cavalry, though it did at least recognize the increased importance of firepower and the need for a much higher proportion of mounted men in the Army.[43] In short, training henceforth was to be shared between firepower and shock tactics, with the practical result that Dundonald had foreseen.

In the usual postwar confusion, the cavalry suffered excessively from lack of any clear directive on its future role. In 1904 the Inspector-General of the Forces, the Duke of Connaught, regretfully reported to the Army Council that 'though progress has been made the British Army at home is far from being ready and efficient for war'. Among the reasons for inefficiency listed by the Duke, several concerned the cavalry; for example 'doubts as to the efficiency of the cavalry armament; the cavalry except for Aldershot and Ireland not organized in Commands; inadequacy of training grounds; shortage of horses; and numbers of inferior soldiers enlisted during the war'. In 1905 the Inspector-General of Cavalry reported that the roles of regular cavalry and mounted infantry were still in confusion, both as regards their individual duties and in combination with other arms.[44]

The one man who was convinced that the South African war must not be ignored as a guide to the general character of future European warfare and who was also, briefly, in a position to implement his views, was Field-Marshal Lord Roberts, whose great career in India and apparent success in South Africa earned him the appointment of Commander-in-Chief of the British Army from 1900 to 1904. Roberts' ideas on the future of the *arme blanche* were probably influenced by Henderson, whom Roberts chose as his Director of Intelligence when he sailed for South Africa in 1900.[45] The cautious ambiguities in Henderson's earlier writing on the relative merits of firepower and shock tactics were resolved by his experience in South Africa. 'It is as clear as noonday', he wrote in April 1901, 'that a mounted force as mobile as the Boers . . . will be a most effective weapon, *even on a European theatre of war*, in the hands of the strategist who grasps its possibilities' (my italics). Few critics, he complained, had realized that the 'small-bore and smokeless powder have destroyed the last vestiges of the traditional role of cavalry'.[46]

Lord Roberts, like his predecessor as Commander-in-Chief, Lord Wolseley, did not allow high office to inhibit the public expression of his personal views. In an article on 'Cavalry Armament' in 1903 he developed the thesis of increasing fire-power as militating against steel weapons. In conflicts between cavalry and cavalry, he pointed out, enormous developments in quick-firing guns, etc., had taken place since 1870, whereas no comparable changes were possible in the horse, lance or sabre. He deduced that: cavalry is sure to use fire auxiliaries even against cavalry; and that the advance and deployment of cavalry masses would become increasingly difficult. On the prospects for cavalry against infantry and artillery he was even more pessimistic. Brittle lines of skirmishers would not be found in Europe as in South Africa and, in general, 'cavalry attempting shock tactics will meet a worse fate than the French at Worth, Vionville and Sedan'. It needs to be stressed that Roberts was not an extremist: though he insisted that the rifle must be the cavalry's principal weapon he favoured retention of the sword and was reluctant to abolish even the lance.[47]

By the time this article was published the first blow against the *arme blanche* had been struck. Army Order 39, of March 1903, directed that cavalry in future would be armed with a carbine (or rifle) and sword, the former being the principal weapon. Lancers, Dragoon Guards and Dragoons would retain the lance, 'but it will only be carried on escort duty, at reviews and other ceremonial parades; not on guard, in the field, at manœuvres, or on active service'.

Lord Roberts' last and most controversial action coincided almost exactly with his retirement from office early in 1904 in consequence of the Esher Committee's Report advocating the abolition of the post. Roberts took the unusual step of writing a short, signed Preface to the new edition of *Cavalry Training* dated 1st February 1904. Repeating the main points of his Memorandum in a moderate tone, Roberts said in effect that while he was no enemy of shock tactics, increased firepower necessitated that 'instead of the fire-arm being an adjunct of the sword, the sword must henceforth be an adjunct of the rifle'.

This was precisely the arrangement that the cavalry feared. To give the rifle priority entailed frequent dismounting, and a cavalryman who got off his horse was by definition no longer a cavalryman. The forces of reaction were now brought into the open and even Lord Roberts' great reputation did not protect him from a rather sordid controversy. In February 1904 the Army Council deferred publication of the new manual because of the controversial Preface. Roberts protested to Lord Lansdowne and told Sir Ian Hamilton that he would resign from the Defence Committee if it was not at once published. The insult stung particularly because Roberts had so recently submitted uncomplainingly to the verdict of the Esher Committee, by whom he had not been consulted. The manual was thereupon issued provisionally for six months and thereafter the Preface was omitted, despite Roberts' protest to the Secretary of State for War, Arnold-Forster. As Lord Roberts' most recent biographer remarks, 'The fact was that belief in the steel weapon was a religious mystique to the older school of cavalrymen.'[48]

The Russo-Japanese war of 1904-5 might almost have been regarded as a *deus ex machina* to settle the acrimonious debate on the role of British cavalry. Here was truly a major war involving the greatest European military power, at least numerically, and the most powerful Oriental nation whose Great Power status was now to be established. More to the point, the war promised to be a trial between the rival theories of shock and firepower since the Japanese Army, trained largely by German officers, had developed a cult of the *arme blanche* (i.e. the sword; the Japanese did not employ the lance), whereas Russia, since the 1870's, had been the only European nation consistently to follow the principles of firepower and dismounted action foreshadowed in the American Civil War.[49]

Unfortunately the one point of agreement was that neither cavalry played an important part in the war, and for this three reasons were paramount. First, Japanese inferiority in numbers of mounted men was so pronounced that some of the main duties of the arm, such as strategic reconnaissance and independent action on the enemy flanks, were quite beyond their scope.[50] Secondly, the Russian cavalry, though possessing overwhelming numerical superiority, put up an extremely poor performance in nearly all respects, and, as an example of mounted infantry, stood no comparison with the Americans or Boers. The very few regular regiments sent out performed creditably, but the Cossacks, taken as a whole, 'seemed of little value for war purposes'.[51] Lastly, in the Manchurian theatre there was little open country at all suitable for a fair test of cavalry tactics.

If the British observers' reports of what little cavalry action there was incline to the side of firepower and against the *arme blanche*, this was partly due to the colourful and decisive personality of Lieutenant-General Sir Ian Hamilton, who accompanied the headquarters of Kuroki's Third Army. Hamilton's impressions, later expanded into a fascinating book, reinforced Roberts' conclusion from the South African war: that the *arme blanche* simply could not be used against an unwilling opponent. 'If one side is so unfair as to dismount and shoot, the opposing side must follow suit or be shot.' Hamilton, like Dundonald, saw that the problem was one of emphasis; his arguments were not directed against the sword as such 'but only against those who would train cavalry so that they enter upon a field of battle thinking rather of where they may deliver a charge than of how they may employ their mobility to enable them to make use of their rifles with the best effect'.[52]

On the other side protagonists of the *arme blanche*, such as Colonel W. H. Birkbeck, who was later to edit the *Cavalry Journal*, could argue that the wretched performance of the Russian cavalry—in Mischenko's raid, in the battle of Mukden and in reconnaissance generally—was precisely due to their 'mounted infantry' training. If such training had indeed 'emasculated their Dragoons' then a strong case was made for greater emphasis on shock tactics.

Few who had observed or studied the war in Manchuria could deny that the destructive power of machine-guns and artillery had been demonstrated even more clearly than in South Africa. But the virtually inevitable effects of these weapons on the vulnerable target of the horse, assisted by the increasing use of entrenchments and barbed wire, were evident only to the minority with truly open minds. In postwar discussions the British cavalry concerned itself with comparatively minor issues, such as the poor horsemanship of both sides, the opportunities lost by the Japanese for lack of cavalry, and the uncritical assertion that training in mounted infantry tactics 'kills the cavalry spirit'.[53]

Lord Roberts, though cautious in his retention of the sword and in his views on the possibility of cavalry shock action in future wars, had turned the emphasis of British doctrine and training firmly towards the use of the rifle and dismounted fighting. The years immediately following his departure from the War Office saw a remarkable resurgence of the traditional cavalry outlook which succeeded in reversing Roberts' reforms and reinstating the *arme blanche* on at least equal terms with firepower.

The restoration of the lance was both a real objective and a splendid symbol. Lord Roberts realized this and as early as April 1904 wrote to Kitchener for his assistance in preventing its restoration. Kitchener agreed.[54] Pressure was applied on the Army Council through the annual reports of the Inspector-General of Cavalry, which called attention to the fact that the cavalry was lacking in effective steel weapons with which to oppose a continental opponent. When the 1st Cavalry Brigade at Aldershot (all Lancer regiments) flouted Army Regulations in 1907 by carrying lances at drill the Inspector-General of Cavalry,

Major-General H. Scobell, sympathized with them. Finally by Army Order 158, of June 1909, it was ruled that 'regiments of Lancers will in future carry the lance not only on escort duty [etc.] but also on guard, during training, at manœuvres, and when so ordered, on field service'.[55]

Another extremely effective step towards the defence and propagation of *arme blanche* doctrines was the foundation of the *Cavalry Journal* in 1906. Inspired from the start by enthusiastic advocates of lance and sabre such as Sir John French and C. S Goldman, its publication became the responsibility of the Cavalry School staff in 1908, and three years later the editorship was assigned automatically to the Commandant of the Cavalry School.[56] A study of the prewar issues shows the assiduity with which international military literature was combed for views favourable to the *arme blanche*, and also the disproportionate space given to cavalry performances in the pre-Crimean era.

In the following year a new edition of *Cavalry Training* was issued, without a Preface this time but known to embody the views of Sir John French, then commanding the Aldershot District. The previous emphasis on the rifle and dismounted action has been replaced by sword and lance; and in the section dealing with the attack of cavalry against cavalry confident instructions are given for 'The Charge', which is referred to as 'the culminating point of the mounted instruction of cavalry'.

By 1907 General Sir John French and Major-General Douglas Haig had consolidated the reputations which their dashing leadership had earned them in South Africa. Now recognized in the Army as the leading authorities on cavalry doctrine and training, the former underlined his support of continental cavalry doctrines by writing an introduction to Bernhardi's influential book *Cavalry in Future Wars*, while the latter expounded similar (though not identical) views in his own *Cavalry Studies* published in 1907. In his introduction Haig makes considerable concessions to the importance of firepower, even describing Civil War cavalry as 'the real article', but on the whole he is clearly a supporter of the *arme blanche*. Thus he believes that the quality of leadership affects cavalry performance

115

more than changes in weapons; that statistics showing the proportionate losses caused by bullet and sabre in battle are worthless because it is the latter's moral effect that counts; and that (allowing for increasing use of the rifle) 'all great successes can only be gained by a force of cavalry which is trained to harden its heart and charge home.'

The '*arme blanche* school', though now predominant in Britain, did not have things all their own way. Lord Roberts, despite his age and greater involvement in the campaign to introduce compulsory military training, re-entered the lists by adding his authority to a brilliant polemical book by Erskine Childers.[57] The latter, though not himself a soldier, had seen some of the fighting in South Africa and had written the last volume of the official history of that war. Childers was an extreme critic of the *arme blanche* in that he demanded the complete abolition of both lance and sword and reliance solely on firepower. Although perhaps a little harsh in his reckoning of recent cavalry achievements and appearing rather arrogant in his certainty that the *arme blanche* would achieve nothing in future wars, his books were unrivalled in the devastating logic with which he analysed such emotion-charged words as 'shock tactics' and 'the personal weapon'; and for the painstaking way in which he examined the evidence of recent wars where other controversialists were content to select convenient incidents. Childers' effect on official thought was limited by his civilian status (as well the acerbity of his pen), and also by the fact that Lord Roberts would not go the whole way and call for the abolition of the sword as well as the lance.[58] Though Childers and other accurate prophets had to wait until after 1914 for the melancholy proof of their contentions, it seems likely that their determined stand did at least influence the compilers of the new edition of *Cavalry Training* in 1912 to strike a more equitable balance than in the previous issue between the respective merits of sword and rifle, mounted and dismounted duties.[59]

Cavalry training in the field after the South African war was adversely affected, not only by the protracted controversy on its armament and duties, but also by a continuation of the two

factors that had provided a farcical element to pre-1899 manœuvres—lack of money and training grounds. As to the latter
the Inspector-General of Cavalry reported in 1904 that 'field
firing bears little resemblance to war conditions. Horses are
often not allowed on the range and owing to limitations of ground,
etc., the squadrons carry out the ordinary infantry attack on foot.'
Lack of money for field training was particularly pernicious in
delaying army manœuvres on a divisional level, brigade training
being the limit in both 1905 and 1906. In the following year, to
a request that a General Officer Commanding and Staff be
appointed for the Cavalry Division (then existing mainly on
paper), the Army Council returned the simple negative: 'The
net cost would be £2,300 per annum'.[60]

A new era of cavalry training may be dated from the appointment of General Sir John French as Inspector-General of the
Forces in December 1907. Allowing for the fact that inspectors
are expected to find faults, General French's report on the
Cavalry Division in 1908 was something of a bombshell. Among
scathing criticisms of the Divisional Commander, French wrote
that 'many of his moves could only have led to complete failure'.
The practice of dismounted action was extremely bad: men dismounted too far from the battlefield and were used like infantry;
the led horses were left exposed to fire, and machine-guns were
brought into action in almost impossible positions. Under
French's energetic supervision there was great improvement in
the next two training seasons. Divisional Training and Army
manœuvres took place at last. In 1911, French's last year of
office, the coronation of George V, followed by the Agadir crisis
and a series of strikes, interrupted brigade training and prevented
Divisional manœuvres.[61]

In the last two full training seasons before the war the criticisms
of French's successor, General C. W. Douglas, were directed
mainly towards the continuing inadequacy of the higher command
on manœuvres, due, not surprisingly, to lack of experience with
large bodies of men; and also to the cavalry commanders'
unimaginative application of shock tactics. In 1912, for example,
General Douglas reported 'Our cavalry commanders are inclined

to employ shock action whenever possible without reference to the circumstances of particular cases . . . many of the manœuvres showed a disregard of the effect of fire that could not be justified by our regulations, and the attempts to combine shock and fire action were seldom successful.' There were grounds for fear that 'the present training of cavalry shows tendencies that may lead to the useless sacrifice of our available cavalry force in war, and that it would be wise to impress on our Cavalry Commanders that while the mounted attack is the most effective method of obtaining decisive results . . . attacks of this nature which promise nothing but a useless sacrifice cannot be too strongly condemned'.[62]

Since the higher commanders were again criticized in 1913, and the Cavalry Division was not assembled during the year, it can safely be assumed that there was no radical improvement before the outbreak of war. On the evidence of these official reports it looks as if 'the cavalry spirit' had triumphed; that despite the judicious combination of fire and shock tactics inculcated in the drill books and by the inspecting generals, the brigade and squadron commanders remained wedded to the ideal of the charge.

A study of British cavalry doctrine and training in the era before 1914 illustrates just how difficult it is to learn from war, and from analyses of the likely effects of new inventions, 'lessons' which seem self-evident to a later generation. This is especially true in the case of personal weapons with a long and distinguished history. The cavalry, in this instance, could never be persuaded by statistics, since they were profoundly convinced of their ability to affect morale. A more practical and plausible defence was that no two wars were ever alike and no one could be sure where and under what conditions the next would be fought.[63] Thus Lord Roberts was reluctant to abolish the lance because he had witnessed its efficacy against savages. On a broader level, of course, lessons were learnt and peacetime cavalry organization and training improved considerably between 1870 and 1914.

A second point about the *arme blanche* controversy was the fact that the most progressive (and in this case prophetic) thinkers were—as is usually the case in military history—not high-ranking regular soldiers, and hence, in the case of men like Havelock, Denison and Childers, their opinions made little impression on official doctrine, at any rate in Britain.[64] On the other hand radical thinkers who did attain high rank and office were by then frequently too old or disillusioned to wrestle effectively with political apathy and the conservatism or actual hostility of the separate interests within the Army. The achievements of the 'Wolseley Ring' were certainly limited by these factors, and the powerful opposition encountered by Lord Roberts' comparatively modest reforms has already been discussed.

Even so it must be admitted that the *arme blanche* tradition of the British cavalry displayed a 'capacity for survival that bordered on the miraculous'.[65] Not merely did it resist the attacks of peacetime critics and reformers, but it actually effected a come-back in the period 1904-14 after two wars (in one of which British cavalry had failed to distinguish itself); and a Royal Commission had further questioned its effectiveness and a reforming Commander-in-Chief had attempted seriously to modify its doctrine and training. Much of this success was due to the fascination which the arm exerted, even over non-cavalrymen. Even the probing, academic mind of Colonel Henderson was evidently for some years under the spell of the *arme blanche*.

Less easy to understand, however, was the amazing extent to which the British cavalry continued to follow continental doctrines despite their knowledge of the latter's poor performances in recent wars and their own far more varied experience in colonial warfare. Yet the dogmas persisted that the next great European war would be virtually decided by a great opening cavalry clash, and that only cavalry armed with lance and sabre could defeat cavalry similarly armed, a vicious circle which the British cavalry were well placed to break; until the same blinkered approach, on a larger scale, committed the British Expeditionary Force to fight on the Continent several years before the outbreak of war in 1914.

In fairness to those who continued to put their faith in the *arme blanche* and were proved wrong by the first World War, it must be admitted that no British military thinker, not even

Erskine Childers, anticipated the full implications for the horse cavalry of the ingredients of twentieth-century warfare which were already making their appearance in the years between 1870 and 1914. The development of Maxims and other types of machine-gun, quick-firing artillery, entrenchments, mass-produced barbed wire, and aeroplanes, was bound to drive the horse from European battlefields except as a means of transportation.

Attempts after 1918 to pretend that the *arme blanche* was not finished and often at the same time to put most of the responsibility for the horror of modern war on to mechanical innovations, such as the tank, made for sad reading and bad history. Before 1914, however, in the cavalry's unavailing resistance to the inexorable development of modern mechanized warfare may be discerned a spirit of true pathos. Although the motives were perhaps subconscious, such phenomena as the cult of the horse and the *arme blanche* may now be seen as a last desperate effort to withstand the de-personalization of war; the same feeling of nostalgia for a more chivalrous era which in 1937 inspired Major-General J. F. C. Fuller—no supporter of the *arme blanche* —to entitle his recollections of the South African campaign *The Last of the Gentlemen's Wars.*

NOTES

1. Sir Henry M. Havelock, *Three Main Military Questions of the Day* (London 1867), pp. 33-65. Lieut.-Col. George T. Denison, *Modern Cavalry* (London 1868), pp. 7, 20, 29-31, 73.

2. Jay Luvaas, *The Military Legacy of the Civil War* (Chicago 1959), pp. 14-51, 100-118. This indispensable study is henceforth referred to as 'Luvaas'. R. A. Preston discerns a 'strong resemblance' to American tactics in British field exercises from 1870 but makes no specific reference to cavalry. 'Military Lessons of the American Civil War', *Army Quarterly*, LXV, No. 2, Jan. 1953, pp. 229-237.

3. Lieut.-Col. E. T. H. Hutton, *Five Lectures on Mounted Infantry* (London 1891), ii. 13-16.

4. Lieut.-Gen. W. H. Goodenough and Lieut.-Col. J. C. Dalton, *The Army Book for the British Empire* (London 1893), p. 194 (henceforth referred to as *Army Book*).

5. Field-Marshal Sir Evelyn Wood, 'British Cavalry 1853-1903' in *The Cavalry Journal*, i. (1906), 151-153: 'In the last quarter of the 19th century a subaltern's pay was about £120 per annum. Ten years or more might elapse before Captain's rank was attained, and then the pay was less than £200 per annum', Field-Marshal Sir W. Robertson, *From Private to Field-Marshal* (London 1921), p. 31.

6. Robertson, op. cit., pp. 15-18; Maj. E. W. Sheppard, *The Ninth Queen's Own Royal Lancers, 1715-1936* (Aldershot 1939), pp. 185-188. See also Maj.-Gen. M. F. Rimington, *Our Cavalry* (London 1912), pp. 156-157; and Lieut.-Col. Hon. E. G. French, *Goodbye to Boot and Saddle* (London 1951), p. 35.

7. *Army Book*, pp. 191-194, 207-211; C. R. B. Barrett, *The 7th (Queen's Own) Hussars* (London 1914), ii. 252-260; H. C. Wylly *XVth (The King's) Hussars, 1759 to 1913* (London 1914), pp. 362-364.

8. Col. H. C. B. Rogers, *The Mounted Troops of the British Army* (London 1959), p. 214.

9. Robertson, op. cit., p. 15; *Army Book*, pp. 202-203.

10. Col. H. Knollys, *Life of General Sir Hope Grant* (London 1894), ii. 273-282; and for the report in full Col. W. Verner, *Military Life of George Duke of Cambridge* (London 1905), ii. 435-436.

11. Knollys, op. cit., pp. 283-284.

12. Knollys, op. cit., pp. 286-288 and entry on Sir Hope Grant in *Dictionary of National Biography*; Verner, op. cit., ii. 55-58, 346, 387-389. See also *Details of the Force employed in 1871* (War Office Library).

13. The House of Commons was adjourned on the issue on 31st July. See *Lord Wantage: A memoir by his wife* (London 1907), pp. 211-213.

14. For the frustrations of energetic generals seeking manœuvring ground, see Sir E. Wood, *From Midshipman to Field-Marshal* (London 1906), ii. 217-221, and Robertson, op. cit., p. 162.

15. Sir F. Maurice and Sir G. Arthur, *The Life of Lord Wolseley* (London 1924), pp. 59-60.

16. M. J. Wise, 'The Cannock Chase Manœuvres', *Army Quarterly*, July 1954, pp. 248-256; Robertson, op. cit., p. 16.

17. *Army Book*, pp. 204-206. Entry on Sir John French in *D.N.B.* In the 'Report on Cavalry Manœuvres, 1894', it was stated that neither Brigade had executed the charge satisfactorily. 'No regiment of cavalry can be considered efficient until it can charge with cohesion and rally rapidly behind its leaders after the break-up.'

18. Memorandum on cavalry armament by Lord Roberts in *Royal*

United Service Institution Journal, XLVII, May 1903, p. 576 (note). Rogers, op. cit., p. 214.

19. Col. C. H. Melville, *Life of Rt. Hon. Sir Redvers Buller* (2 vols., London 1923), i. 83-127.

20. Rogers, op. cit., pp. 224-230; Hutton, op. cit., i. 1, ii. 17. Hutton realized that informal dress was essential if mounted infantry were not to degenerate into indifferent cavalry: 'you cannot get men who study appearance and foster a false idea of smartness to lie down in the mud and shoot steadily and effectively'.

21. Sir Frederick Roberts: Commander-in-Chief in India, 1885-93; Commanding in Ireland, 1895-1900. Sir Garnet Wolseley: Adjutant-General, 1882-90; Commanding in Ireland, 1891-95; Commander-in-Chief, 1895-1900. Sir Evelyn Wood: Eastern Command, 1886-89; Aldershot Command, 1889-93; Quartermaster-General, 1893-97; Adjutant-General, 1897-1901. Sir Redvers Buller: Quartermaster-General, 1887-90; Adjutant-General, 1890-97. Interesting appraisals of the comparative merits of these Generals may be found in Melville, op. cit., i. 261 ff. and Julian Symons, *Buller's Campaign* (London 1963), *passim*.

22. C. Ffoulkes, 'The Lance', *Army Quarterly*, XVII, No. 1, Oct. 1928, pp. 91-95.

23. Col. R. Home *A Précis of Modern Tactics*, revised Pratt (2nd ed. 1896), p. 62; *Army Book*, pp. 207-210; Maj. W. C. James, *The Development of Modern Cavalry Action in the Field* (Aldershot Military Society, 8th Jan. 1891) (Paper XXVIII), *passim*; T. McGuffie, 'The Lance in Battle', *History Today* (August 1958).

24. Luvaas, op. cit., pp. 170-202.

25. Hutton, op. cit., see especially iii. 5, 19, iv. 23-27. Wolseley remarked that in observing a large force of German cavalry for nearly a fortnight on manœuvres 'I saw but one squadron dismounted and I must say a more ridiculous sight I never saw'. On 17th Sept. 1880 he wrote to Lady Wolseley from Berlin: 'We can really learn very little here but I am delighted I came to assure myself of that fact.' (Wolseley Correspondence at Royal United Service Institution.)

26. Col. A. J. Godley, 'The Development of Mounted Infantry Training at Home', *Cavalry Journal*, i. 52-55.

27. Godley, op. cit.; Hutton, i. 29 and v. 2.

28. Churchill in a letter to Sir Ian Hamilton, quoted in the latter's *Listening for the Drums* (London 1944), pp. 246-247.

29. Ibid; and Rogers, op. cit., pp. 217-223.

30. Roberts's Memorandum, op. cit., p. 579.

31. See G. S. Hutchison, *Machine Guns: their History and Tactical Employment* (London 1938), pp. 1-118; and for the cavalryman's

'psychological argument', Capt. G. E. Benson, *Smokeless Powder* (Aldershot Military Society, XLV, March 1893), p. 16.
32. Sheppard, op. cit., pp. 185-186.
33. Royal Commission on the War in South Africa. Cmd. 1789, report para. 87, minutes of evidence para. 19472.
34. Quoted in Col. J. K. Dunlop, *The Development of the British Army, 1899-1914* (London 1938), p. 104.
35. Ibid., pp. 52-55.
36. Report of Committee on the Yeomanry Force. Cmd. 466, 1901, pp. 1-5. The Earl of Dundonald, *My Army Life* (London 1926), pp. 180-183.
37. Dunlop, op. cit., pp. 107-118.
38. Cmd. 1789, op. cit., minutes of evidence paras. 17218-41.
39. Duff Cooper, *Haig* (London 1935), i. 377-382.
40. Cmd. 1789. Report para. 88, minutes of evidence paras. 19468-80, 19502-32 and cf. Brig.-Gen. M. F. Rimington, paras. 12684-710.
41. e.g. C. S. Goldman: 'The Boers did all that could be expected of Mounted Infantry but were powerless to crown victory as only the dash of cavalry can do', Preface to von Bernhardi's *Cavalry in Future Wars* (London 1909). See also Rimington, *Our Cavalry*, pp. 74-75, 100; and F. N. Maude, *Cavalry: its past and future* (London 1903), p. 273.
42. Cmd. 1789, minutes of evidence paras. 13247-51, 13881-7, 17580-5.
43. Ibid., Recommendations, section II.
44. Inspector-General of the Forces, *Separate Reports, 1904-5*, pp. 34, 290-291, 317, 322, 343; *Annual Reports, 1904*, pp. 3-5, 33, 47-48, Appendix 2; *Annual Reports, 1905*, pp. 4-17, 52, 61.
45. For Henderson's influence on Roberts see Luvaas, op. cit., pp. 182 ff.
46. Henderson, *The Science of War* (London 1910), p. 379. For evidence that Roberts believed that the South African war embodied permanent lessons see *Report on Combined Manœuvres, 1903*, pp. 4, 30-31.
47. Memorandum, op. cit., *passim.*
48. David James, *Lord Roberts* (London 1954), pp. 439-442; *Annual Reports of Inspector-General of the Forces, 1904*, p. 3; Report by the Duke of Connaught dated 1st Nov. 1904.
49. See the Prefaces to George T. Denison's *A History of Cavalry* (2nd ed. London 1913). Only a few Cossack regiments carried the lance. *The Russo-Japanese War, Vol. III: Reports from British Officers with the Russian Forces*, pp. 130-133.
50. American observers estimated that the Japanese had about 6,500 cavalrymen in Manchuria, i.e. 1/70th of their total forces. *Reports of Military Observers attached to the armies in Manchuria* (Washington 1906), Part III, pp. 21-28.

51. *Reports from British Officers*, op. cit., especially pp. 261-265. The Siberian Cossacks were said to prefer the skyline when scouting, and all the Cossack regiments except those from Trans-Baikal considered dismounted action derogatory.

52. Sir I. Hamilton, *A Staff Officer's Scrap Book* (one-vol. edition, London 1912); for cavalry see especially pp. 86, 119-120, 167, 306, 340, 356 ff., 426. Hamilton's opinions are also prominent in *Russo-Japanese War Reports—Cavalry* (R.U.S.I. Library); see especially Report 35 'Fire action versus shock tactics', pp. 315-324 and cf. Reports 14 and 23 by Col. W. H. Birkbeck.

53. See for example, 'The Cavalry Spirit', *Cavalry Journal*, i. 12-23; 'The Use of the Horse Soldier in the 20th Century', *R.U.S.I. Journal*, LII, March 1908, pp. 307-330. 'Some Lessons of the Russo-Japanese War', *Aldershot Military Society*, LXXXIX, 3rd April 1906.

54. James, *Lord Roberts*, pp. 439-440. Spenser Wilkinson Papers 14/95, 107, Roberts to Wilkinson 30th Dec. 1903 and 24th March 1910.

55. *Annual Reports of Inspector-General of the Forces*, 1904, Appendix 2; 1906, pp. 7, 16; 1907, p. 16. *Cavalry Journal* i. 73. The lance was abolished as a weapon of war by Army Order 392 of December 1927.

56. Luvaas, op. cit., p. 198.

57. Erskine Childers, *War and the Arme Blanche* (London 1910); see also the same author's *German Influence on British Cavalry* (London 1911).

58. See for example the importance attached to this disagreement by the Military Correspondent of *The Times* (Col. Repington), in *Essays and Criticisms* (London 1911), pp. 81-88.

59. *Cavalry Training, 1912*, pp. 268-272; and Sheppard, op. cit., p. 225.

60. *Annual Reports of Inspector-General of the Forces*, 1904, p. 47; 1905, pp. 4, 11; 1906, pp. 21-22.

61. Ibid., 1908: 'Inspection of the Cavalry Division', pp. 1-6; Harold Nicolson, *King George the Fifth* (London 1952), pp. 147, 158, 188.

62. *Annual Reports of Inspector-General of the Forces*, 1912, pp. 4-21; 1913, pp. 4-20; Lord Roberts' Papers, R/3/55-56.

63. Lord Roberts's Papers R/52/133, 134. Correspondence with Sir William Nicholson, C.I.G.S., 1909. In 1911, for example, a staff officer was asked whether Belgium was suitable for cavalry charges. Very suitable, he replied: 'I have not been to Belgium myself, but everyone who has assures me the ground there is very like Salisbury Plain with a few farms here and there, no hedges and a few ditches': 'Mounted Troops in co-operation with other arms', *Aldershot Military Society*, CXI, 21st Feb. 1911.

64. Though Denison's books influenced or at any rate confirmed Russian mounted infantry doctrine. See his Preface to *A History of Cavalry* (1913 ed.) and Luvaas, op. cit., p. 113.
65. Edward L. Katzenbach, Jnr., 'The Horse Cavalry in the 20th Century' in *Yearbook of the Graduate School of Public Administration, Harvard University* (Cambridge, Mass. 1958).

Part II

§6§

Liddell Hart and the French Army, 1919-1939

GÉNÉRAL D'ARMÉE ANDRÉ BEAUFRE

L IDDELL HART'S name appeared in French military literature shortly after 1918. But to the best of my recollection he became a figure of major controversy only with his sacrilegious assessment of the major French generals of the first World War in his book *Reputations*. For the victorious French Army it was unthinkable that a young British captain should dare to pass unfavourable judgements on such men as Joffre and Foch, who were covered in a glory compounded of the inevitable semi-divinity conferred on them by war propaganda and of the gratitude due to men 'who deserved well of the Fatherland'. The scandal was all the greater for the fact that these heroes had unquestionably shown themselves to be the possessors of very real qualities.

However, it was in this way that, right from the start, Liddell Hart assumed the role—and it was an exceptional role at the time—of a champion of nonconformity, a nonconformity which provoked certain sympathetic reactions amongst those who had reason to question the way in which the war had been conducted.

Liddell Hart's reaction to the war—as far as I can judge—had been an instinctive one, provoked by the absurd spectacle of those massive manœuvres which had resulted in the gigantic slaughter of 1914-18, so foreign to British military traditions. His revolt led him not only to criticize, doubtless not always with absolute fairness, but also to sense that it must be possible to envisage the problem of war in a different way. It was this belief which fired him in his passionate search for new solutions, both in the tactical realm of mechanization and in the rediscovery of strategy as the only key to a proper understanding of war.

His preoccupations, totally removed from those of the official French military circles at the time, who were busy establishing a sterile conformity, echoed the concern of those French officers, particularly numerous amongst the younger men, who were not prepared to accept the view that the battles of Malmaison and Montdidier had fixed once and for all the future shape of war.

Their interest, alerted by *Reputations*, was henceforth to remain turned towards this young British writer.

The French Army was at that time entering an extremely critical phase, although this was still inadequately recognized. The crucial question was that of the conclusions to be drawn from the events of the Great War.

Now two major personalities had emerged from the war: Foch and Pétain. The first, a hot-blooded southerner from Joffre's team, stood for the great prewar tradition with his taste for manœuvre, his natural preference for the offensive and his faith in what was called 'strategy'—the careful distillation of a life's thought and brilliantly expounded at the École de Guerre, which he directed. Pétain, on the other hand, the cold northerner with his caustic turn of wit, was the leader of a new and very different school of thought. After a long and distinguished career as a regimental officer, he prided himself on his down-to-earth realism. Posted to the École de Guerre as lecturer on Infantry, he taught, in the teeth of official doctrine, that an extreme reliance on the bayonet was mistaken and that, above all, methodical operations and an organized combination of infantry and artillery were necessary. He placed little faith in brilliance and dash and even less faith in 'strategy', preferring to trust in thoughtful and carefully delimited tactics carried out by an army of stubborn peasants, and supported by superior technique and *matériel*. The correctness of his views, together with their practical success, brought him extremely rapid promotion, culminating in the negative victory of Verdun. Consequently, when in 1917 the failure of the Nivelle offensive brought about the final discredit of the old romantic approach to war, it was this great realist, the methodical adversary of all adventure, who was given supreme command of the French Army.

In his view, all our thinking previous to 1914 had been wrong. The cult of the offensive, 'strategy' and the traditional attitude to soldiering were all obsolete. The new style of war was one of *matériel* which made all the old formulae unacceptable and which should be based firmly on the empirical realities which he had perceived and which his experience had seemed to confirm. Even though Russia, torn by revolution, was on the point of negotiating for peace with Germany and as a result our superiority on the Western Front was soon to be lost with the return of German forces disengaged from the Eastern Front, he held to his formula (which must seem extremely modest to us today) of the offensive with strictly limited objectives. The battle of Malmaison, to which he gave his especial attention along with his Chief of Staff, General Debeney, stands as the model of this kind of battle. But when in 1918 the enemy, finally freed of their entanglements on the Eastern Front, launched major offensives which broke through all along the Allied lines, Pétain was momentarily disconcerted. However, thanks to Foch's tenacity, all the breaches were made good and the continuous front, if it had shown itself to be supple, proved none the less effective. Pétain was thus able to conclude that he was right and that any attempt at penetration from now on was useless and hence even dangerous. As for Foch's continual attacks launched during the battle of France, Pétain observed that they had failed to achieve a break-through and that all that had been realized, in fact, was a series of offensive engagements with limited objectives, and that thanks only to a superior potential in men and *matériel*. In consequence he believed his theory to have been definitively confirmed by practical experience and that it was his tactics which had won the war.

To anyone who is a student of the Great War, it is obvious that military victory was the product of the union of Foch's vigorous strategy and Pétain's cautious tactics. But after the war, Foch and Pétain were to work in very different fields and this divorce was to have the most serious consequences for France.

Foch, on the Interallied Committee, had a somewhat remote influence on the French Army. He was concerned with organizing the occupation of the Rhine, and the construction of the armies of Poland and of the Little Entente, which gave strategic formulation to the humiliation of Germany within the framework of Versailles. This strategy, written into the treaties, gave us for a long period a semblance of power—a power which, in our diplomacy, we accepted as basic and feasible until 1936. However, this strategy was inapplicable, simply because France did not have an army capable of implementing it, and this because it was not Foch who was in charge of organizing the French Army, but Pétain.

In fact Pétain stayed on as supreme commander of the French Army and it was he who was to give it its new peacetime form. The army which he organized was not that which Foch had foreseen, capable of conducting offensive operations in Germany, supported by our central and east European allies, an army such as was demanded by our place in the League of Nations. Rather was it the army of the battle of Malmaison, of massive mobilization, of defensive superiority with great prominence given to artillery, with its progress rigidly limited by successive bounds, and its units closely integrated on an unbroken defensive front. Ignoring its European commitments, the organization of the French Army was firmly based on concepts which were to render our military policy totally ineffectual and mummify it until the appalling awakening of 1940.

This disastrous evolution did not come about without a vehement opposition which was only tempered by a concern for discipline. There was a school of thought in France which had recognized the capital role which tanks might come to play in the future. The leader of these dissidents was General Estienne, known as the 'Father of the Tanks' because it was he who had perfected the first formulae of 1916 and who had organized what was then called the 'assault artillery'.

The rather restrictive character of this name should not be misunderstood. In fact the basic concept had much wider implications. In 1922 Estienne came to Saint Cyr to give a lecture, in which he foresaw a great battle relying on attacks in depth launched by tanks. It may be obvious nowadays that the idea of these attacks was simply to achieve a break-through of the fortified enemy positions and that further major penetration in depth was incompletely understood. But this was due above all to a failure to appreciate the problem of the strategic significance of such a battle. The main subject of consideration was still the problem of the break-through, the first essential in the resumption of mobile warfare. It should also be said that Pétain's belief in the necessity of massive war on a continuous front inevitably coloured the thinking of the innovators, who did not consider that they could ignore such a formula. Nevertheless their faith in tanks was such that the report to the Minister which laid down conditions for infantry manœuvre in 1921 conceived of the possibility of the infantry section developing into an armoured crew mounted in a cross-country vehicle.

Now, under the influence of Pétain and Debeney (the latter had been put in charge of the École de Guerre), these new ideas were gradually stifled. No advance was made beyond the use of the infantry tank. It was at this moment in 1927 that, under the influence of Liddell Hart and Fuller and in the teeth of official opposition, Great Britain resolved to experiment with a 'mechanized brigade', the first ancestor of the modern armoured formations.

This experiment at once aroused considerable interest amongst informed French opinion. Under English influence the concept of the use of tanks developed from that of simple infantry support to mobile manœuvre—in other words, to that of a cavalry role. From 1924 to 1932 the idea of a mechanized *corps de bataille* gained such ground that we, in turn, began gradually to mechanize our cavalry. In 1930, during the Lorraine manœuvres, we experimented with a mixed detachment with such success that three years later the first light mechanized division was created, a medley of armoured cars, tanks, motor-cycle troops and mounted cavalry. It seemed that we were on our way towards an important revision of our military thinking. Finally, at the École de Guerre, serious attention was given to the possibilities of these new units and above all to the considerable dangers that armoured vehicles presented to traditional troop formations. In the 1934 manœuvres, despite a rather biased umpire's decision, a raid by armoured cars completely disorganized the movements of the opposing side.

It was at this time that Commandant de Gaulle published his *Vers l'Armée de Métier*, in which he expounded the view that, for geographical, political, strategic and tactical reasons, France could not fulfil her role unless she possessed an army of a new kind, equipped with armour and long-service specialists. This thesis was to become the basis of legislation proposed by Paul Reynaud in 1935. Also, in Germany, Colonel Guderian published his book, *Achtung Panzer*, a less theoretical paraphrase of Liddell Hart's proposed solutions, and the progressive elements of the young Reichswehr adopted this line of thought which had begun in England and announced the creation of several *Panzerdivisionen*. It really seemed that the modern school of thought was about to triumph and that at last the French Army would rejuvenate itself.

But this was not to be. The movement of ideas and the evolution of our opponents' armaments did force a partial modernization on the army (in 1939 we entered the war with two small mechanized divisions, 3,000 small-bore anti-tank guns and 2,000 tanks new in model, but generally too slow and too limited in range of action). But our strategic and tactical thinking was still based almost entirely upon the experience of 1918. Everything continued as if the intellectual ferment caused in our Army between 1928 and 1930 by the British example, inspired by Liddell Hart, had never been.

The fact was, as Liddell Hart had foreseen from the beginning, that the solution to modern warfare was not to be found in tactics but in strategy. Our strategy being basically unchanged we could not see any need to change our tactics. Now it was in the realm of strategy that Liddell Hart was to make his most original contribution and open the way to a total revision of military thought which might, had it been followed up in France, have prevented the disaster of 1940 and its consequences, consequences from which the West has still not recovered. His brilliant book, *The Decisive Wars of History*, appeared in 1929. Almost at once a translation was published in France. The ideas it contained seemed like a breath of fresh air.

In fact the issue at stake was nothing less than the rediscovery of strategy, in the sense of the art of achieving victory in the surest and least costly way. Nowadays such an objective might seem obvious, but it was not so in France in 1930, for strategy at that time was very seriously underestimated. This eclipse was due to the combined effects of two successive mistakes.

The first mistake was a distant consequence of our defeat in 1870, which had brought the French Army to adopt the theories of the Prussian High Command, born of Clausewitz's monumental work which had become the strategists' bible at the end of the nineteenth century. This posthumous work, incomplete on publication, contains a number of internal contradictions, with the result that it was possible, according to a choice of passages, to find in it a justification of limited operations as well as an extreme theory of total war. Now far from noting and pointing out these discrepancies, the Prussian school had come to present as 'Clausewitzian' a systematically extreme strategy, insisting upon the necessity of 'a decisive battle' achieved through 'bloody sacrifice'. The sinister Wagnerian beauty of such a concept was without doubt more appropriate to the psychology of his commentators than to the more complex experience of Clausewitz himself. But as *Vom Kriege* is no easy book to read, opinion tended to crystallize most often around commentary rather than the text itself. From one distortion came another and it came to be agreed that the major modern strategy based on Napoleon's example could only be that of a single-minded seeking after the 'decisive battle' by the confrontation of massed armed forces in the principal theatre of war.

This thesis, which had been adopted by the German High Command, was adopted in turn by our École de Guerre. Foch's exposition of the theory was remarkable for its Cartesian clarity, which gave an admirable precision to certain aspects hitherto left ambiguous by the Germans. If it was necessary to force a decision, then this decisive battle must be fought as soon as possible with the maximum combined strength on the line of advance which offered the greatest threat to the enemy, with the object of breaking through his defences. This was the outline of the famous Plan XVII which was to fail completely in the first weeks of the 1914-18 war. The Schlieffen Plan, symmetrical to Plan XVII and as 'Clausewitzian' as Foch's, sought for the decisive battle by a vast enveloping movement, achieved also by concentrated forces.

Here we may note that these two plans completely miscalculated the operational potential of the means at their disposal at the time. The first made a fatal mistake in its assessment of the offensive capacity of troops under modern fire. The second did not allow for the fact that enveloping movement on such a scale could only have succeeded if the speed of advance of the moving wing had been two or three times greater. Instead of the decisive battle, these two combined mistakes resulted in the deadlock of trench warfare which surprised and scandalized contemporary opinion. An attempt was then made to resume the decisive strategy by major offensives which became more and more costly in lives and material; but in vain. At this point, faced by this astounding reversal, Pétain's school of thought made triumphant headway with the theory that strategy was irrelevant to modern warfare and that from now on our thinking had to be based on an assessment of tactics and *matériel*.

However, even if one doubts the validity of strategy, one still cannot avoid having some kind of strategy. The strategy more or less implicit in Pétain's position, and which was to dominate the thinking of the French Army in the 'thirties, was not, as one might have thought, the denial of those theories which had been drawn from Clausewitz's book. On the contrary, it was simply a translation which monstrously aggravated its basic errors. It was still the battle which would bring about a decision, and this by the mobilization of always vaster and more powerful forces. The art of war was reduced to the full mobilization of these resources and then their rational engagement in massive operations conceived and conducted according to engineers' calculations.

It was in this oppressive atmosphere which, it must be said, did not enjoy the unanimous approval of the French Regular Army, that a new book by Liddell Hart appeared. In it we could read in clear and straightforward language a series of truths backed up by innumerable historical precedents which seemed quite extraordinary at the time.

1. The end of war is not battle but the defeat of the adversary.
2. Battle is only a means, *among others*, to this defeat.

138

3. Success must be sought as far as possible by combinations which set out to deceive the enemy.

4. In order to deceive the adversary it is always essential to confront him with a dilemma.

5. Victory is not achieved by the physical destruction of the enemy but by his demoralization—and this may be achieved by manœuvre.

6. The most economical means must always be sought and extreme of total military effort avoided . . ., etc.

I do not wish to analyse Liddell Hart's doctrine in detail here, simply to show what a contrast his views made with official doctrine in France. It was as dazzling a discovery as the rediscovery of antiquity must have seemed to the men of the Renaissance after the conformist sterilities of medieval scholasticism. My personal experience on reading his book (I was then at the École de Guerre) was like that of a revelation that I had been waiting for —the ordered and complete formulation of everything that I had been groping towards. At last the art of war could emancipate itself from the sterilities which had sprung from the misinterpretation of Clausewitz's ideas and the lessons of 1914-18.

The book made a profound impression on my generation in the Army and on our immediate predecessors. De Lattre and Juin, for instance, were much influenced by it and were later to put its lessons into practice. But these generations were then still part of the lower strata of the military hierarchy and lacked any real influence.

At a higher level, on the contrary, the prejudices against Liddell Hart as the author of *Reputations* were an initial handicap. Furthermore, Liddell Hart had called his new book *The British Way in Warfare*. It was thus construed to advance a strategy which might be appropriate to an island power but which was inapplicable on the Continent with its fundamentally different problems. If Liddell Hart's thesis was interesting, it did not concern us directly, since we had the Maginot Line and a mobilized army of 100 divisions. However, as the movement of opinion mentioned above with reference to the use of tanks grew in strength, General Gamelin signed in 1935 a circular reminding us that the High Command alone was qualified to define military doctrine and that officers should refrain on all occasions from advancing any personal views on the question. This unbelievable decision unfortunately met with total success, so strong was discipline at the time. Military reviews, lectures and books became nothing more than paraphrases of the official doctrine. The Army's interest, which had been stirred for a brief time, was lulled again into conformism. The course of the second World War was mapped out from that moment on. The Gods had ordained it. . . .

It was in 1935 that I met Liddell Hart when I was given the job of welcoming him to the Army High Command and to answer any questions he might like to ask.

I had read just about all his books and was overjoyed at being given this task. In the little office which had been put at our disposal I met a pleasant, easy-mannered man, tall and thin, who proceeded to launch a whole broadside of questions, and who, despite the rapidity of his speech, seemed to find words too slow to match the speed of his thought. He sucked at a pipe which was nearly always out or going out and which he would constantly relight for a couple of puffs, slowly building up a little pile of burnt-out matchsticks in front of him. Our discussion began at about ten o'clock in the morning. At one o'clock I hesitantly mentioned lunch—which we had together. Back in the office in the afternoon we went on talking until seven o'clock but, as we still had not finished, we remained together until late into the night. I cannot remember whether our discussions went on the next day . . . in any event after the warmth of that first meeting, we were to keep constantly in touch with one another.

What struck me most about that interview was the quickness of mind and the very un-British vivacity of this great nonconformist. I was also impressed by his immensely lively curiosity, his objectivity in attacking a problem and his total lack of prejudice. But at the same time I noticed something which was already evident in his books and which I had not until then appreciated at its true value, no doubt because of my lack of sympathy for the official French doctrine. From his criticism of the first World War and also perhaps of certain British traditions (Torres Vedras, Waterloo), Liddell Hart has shown a certain preference for the defensive, in which (like Clausewitz!) he sees a way of exploiting to the maximum the advantages of modern firepower. My exposition of the French point of view—no doubt slightly embellished—provoked in him certain favourable reactions just where I had expected him to offer particular objections. Something of this attitude of mind is apparent in his book published three years later, *The Defence of Britain*.

If I mention such a nuance now it is because it seems worth while pointing out every aspect of the exceptional genius who was the initiator of the renaissance in strategic theory in our times. A nonconformist, he pointed the way towards the war of manœuvre based on armour and rediscovered, in his expression 'the indirect approach', the basis of the decisive strategy of history's great generals. It was unfortunate that what he had to say was better understood by the vanquished than by the victors of 1918, but it was natural that this should have been so. A pragmatist as well as a nonconformist, he had also recognized the enduring importance of the defensive, the essential mode of action for achieving the decisive manœuvre, either by means of the economy of force which it makes possible in preparation for an offensive, or by an active counter-offensive manœuvre. No man is less ready to systematize than Liddell Hart. But there again it was unfortunate that the French concept of the defensive amounted to nothing more than complete passivity, rendered even more inadequate by ill-considered tactics.

It is beyond doubt that Liddell Hart's influence has been immense. For my part I have simply tried to show here how that influence, which might have saved us from the catastrophe of 1939-40, was insufficient to change the course of history, at least insofar as the French Army was concerned.

Quos vult perdere Jupiter dementat

§7§

Doctrine and Training in the German Army 1919-1939

CAPTAIN ROBERT J. O'NEILL

WHAT makes this story worth telling is the development of one idea: the Blitzkrieg. Between the two World Wars, most armies were carrying out experiments to improve their fighting methods. Apart from Germany, their efforts tended to be hesitant and spasmodic. High Commands and political leaders had to be urged by small groups of individuals, sometimes from outside the military establishment, to try new ideas; and when they had been tried, the wrong conclusions were often drawn. The German Army, on the other hand, had a greater grasp of the effects of technology on the battlefield, and went on to develop a new form of warfare by which its rivals, when it came to the test, were hopelessly outclassed. The German Army was by no means alone in perceiving the power of mechanized units to break the current stalemate caused by the dominance of the defence—indeed its best ideas came from abroad—nor did it lack a heavy group of conservatives who clung to the cavalry notions of the Great War. The German advantage consisted in sufficient, even barely sufficient, combination of factors, part random, part deliberate, to bring the idea to fruition.

The Preparation of the Soil, 1919-22

Defeat is the best killer of complacency. The questing minds of Germany's military thinkers did not lack a perceptive guide to channel their new-born energies towards productivity. General Hans von Seeckt had a horror of trench-warfare and was determined that its power should be overcome. He had fought for most of the Great War on the Eastern Front and, as Chief of Staff to von Mackensen's Army of German and Austro-Hungarian divisions, had played a leading part in the great break-through that Mackensen made in May 1915, at Gorlice-Tarnov, just north of the Carpathians, which cleared the Russians out of Galicia.

The strategic situation of Germany gave little cause to hope that she could survive another major war in the near future, and so an air of detachment could be permitted. The internal troubles of the early 1920's left little time for tactical training, while the Army, being composed of a selection of veterans, was already quite proficient in the basic elements of soldiering. What doctrine there was in the early years after the war seems to have consisted largely of keeping an open mind, of searching until the right riposte to the *Stellungskrieg* be discovered. Seeckt set in motion a thorough examination of all the major phases and problems of the Great War. He was not convinced that Germany's defeat had been brought about by any one obvious factor, but if there was a hidden truth lurking in the bewildering complexity of experience that was Germany's harvest of the war years, he was out to find it.

It is easy enough now, after another war and forty-five years, to see the bright needle that was eluding Seeckt's team in the haystack of the *Reichsarchiv*, but Seeckt never really had it in his grasp. He certainly played with it, turned it over in his hands once or twice and looked at it closely; but he laid it down, although still with an open mind. His desires for mobility seemed, at this time, to base themselves on cavalry concepts, but this was not a dogma. His writings of the period show that he wanted to establish, when the time was ripe, large units of motorized troops. Never again, he wrote, could cavalry be used in great masses for a dashing frontal attack.[1] His doubts concerning the use of mechanized armour were centred on practice rather than principle. He simply did not believe that a mechanical contraption could equal the cross-country performance, the speed, flexibility, invulnerability and firepower of cavalry, working with the close tactical support of aircraft. That he ever considered the combination of tanks and aircraft is doubtful; his papers certainly do not show this. But it is certain that he stimulated discussion of these ideas, making young officers receptive to what was being thought elsewhere and keen to get closer to a solution. Perhaps his greatest legacy to the field of doctrine was his refusal to be doctrinaire.

The training of higher commanders was led by Seeckt personally. He ridiculed the view that 'a Commanding-General has nothing more to learn'.[2] In early October 1921, the first *Führerreise* took place, at Bad Kissingen. This tradition became so well established that it was continued, and further developed by

Seeckt's successors. Seeckt was particularly disturbed by the contrasts that the past had shown between the uniformly trained General Staff and the totally uncoordinated outlook of the various higher commanders, and, through this concern, he was able to defeat yet another concomitant of the Versailles system: he kept his generals alert and conscious of the time to come when Germany would again have an adequate army. These exercises also led for the first time to the development of a unified doctrine for the handling of larger formations. The customary *Generalstabsreisen* were also recommenced, and ran unbroken throughout the whole period. One particularly valuable form of training was the introduction of the telephone battle for commanders and staffs. It must not be forgotten that the Army was also responsible for all air training and tactics until the Luftwaffe was formed and placed under Goering.

The Sowing of the Seed, 1922-28

On 1st April 1922, Hauptmann Heinz Guderian received the somewhat puzzling appointment of a General Staff Officer on the staff of the Inspector of Transport, employed in the Motorized Transport Department. Guderian was a signals specialist and knew nothing about mechanical vehicles. However, as in most armies, he had to get down to the job and start learning. The Inspector of Transport, General von Tschischwitz, was himself an original thinker and was making a lengthy study of the question of moving troops about in motorized vehicles. Guderian was pressed into service and some small test exercises were conducted in the attractive but difficult country of the Harz. Once Guderian had been made to think seriously about the problem, his own views began to crystallize and Tschischwitz devoted a good deal of time to criticism and encouragement of his young assistant. Guderian thought that Germany's weakness effectively precluded the recurrence of static warfare in any conflicts that might arise in the foreseeable future.

If Germany did find herself at war, the relative smallness of her forces would require high mobility and exploitation of the principles of surprise and local concentration to offset the overall numerical superiority that an opponent would possess. As is so often the case with junior officers, Guderian felt acutely aware of the need for developing some form of defensive technique which would foil any aggressive intentions of neighbouring countries. He was not able to take the more relaxed view of Seeckt. He knew that the best way that Germany could defend herself at the time was by moving units about at high speed to crush the enemy's blows and keep him from making deep penetration. This soon raised the problem of protecting the troops during movement and hence the use of armoured vehicles suggested itself.

While casting about for any available information on experiments that had been made with their use, he got to know a Leutnant Volckheim, who was engaged on a study of the use of armour in the Great War for another department of the General Staff. Volckheim was a mine of information, particularly on what had been done by the English and French. As part of the great renaissance of thought that was going on within the German High Command, a special periodical review, *Wehrgedanken des Auslands*, had been set up to give full coverage of the military field abroad. It is significant that the distribution of this confidential paper was not confined to the Reichswehr; certain civilian brains were also being stimulated by it.

Through studying these sources the English school of Fuller, Liddell Hart and Martel soon impinged upon Guderian. It provided the necessary impetus for him to get beyond the use of armour as a mobile defence and to its use in the attack. He recognized the fallacy of using armour merely as an infantry support weapon or for light, 'cavalry' function. His resultant ideas were published to the whole Army in the *Militär-Wochenblatt*. These articles aroused interest and he was encouraged by his superiors to write more. Guderian attributes his success to the old proverb: 'In the country of the blind, the one-eyed man is king'.[3]

During the winter of 1923-24, Guderian assisted the then Oberst-Leutnant von Brauchitsch in the conduct of exercises in co-operation between motorized troops and aircraft. His efficiency earned him a posting to *Wehrkreis II*, Stettin, as a General Staff instructor in tactics and military history. Here, Guderian further developed his ideas in the course of his lecturing. It says a good deal for the degree of enlightenment within the German Army that he was allowed to do this, instead of being handed a detailed syllabus and told to teach that and nothing else. Furthermore, the standard of officers taking the course was such that Guderian was constantly stimulated to higher levels of thought—he dared not put across anything that was poorly conceived. His historical instruction led him farther on in the study of mobility through the use of the cavalry tactics of the opening phases of the Great War.

While Guderian was thus accelerating himself along the line leading towards Blitzkrieg, the Heeresleitung was busy with building the Seecktian 'Army of Leaders'. One of its most significant pieces of work was the production of the training manual, *Führung und Gefecht*, under the direction of Oberst Herrgott of the Training Branch, General Staff.[4] Prior to 1914, each arm had had its own publications governing command and tactics and much disunity had arisen. *Führung und Gefecht* united all these into a single set of principles for the Army and remained in use without modifications until the early 1930's. A welter of various training courses led to protests that the regimental training of the Army was being neglected, because officers were too often away from their units. The troubled internal circumstances of the time effectively prevented any large-scale manœuvres and the Army was totally dependent on company and battalion exercises; these were scarcely novel, but the official slogan was 'Defeat boredom by activity'. There were not many physically unfit soldiers in the German Army of those years.

In 1925, the first large manœuvres were held. The shortage of man-power for the exercises was overcome by the use of *Zeit-freiwilligen* (short-term volunteers) who served for periods of a few weeks at a time. Training was stimulated by competitions of many varieties between the *Wehrkreise*. By this time, the significance of the tank was having a greater impact on Seeckt.[5] He began to see it as a special weapon with its own distinct role, quite apart from infantry, cavalry or artillery, but as yet attached no vital importance to it.[6] As a result of the secret negotiations with the Russians, training centres for military aviation and for tank warfare were to be set up, as well as factories for the production of aircraft, ammunition and poison gas. The tank centre was located near Kazan on the River Kama. The Russians were slow, however, and despite German exhortations, it was not in action until 1929.[7]

The manœuvres of 1927 were the first to see the use of dummy tanks on a large scale, although no effort was made to relate the tactics of the tanks to the other arms. By this stage, Guderian had been at his instructional post for three years and had met with the approval of his superiors, and received good reports. His propensity for tactics and war games caused him to be posted to the Operations Branch of the General Staff, in the Transport Section. His post was newly created and its purpose was to produce tactics for moving troops by lorry. His plans were ambitious and soon struck resistance among, for instance, those who complained about the difficulties of putting the gun horses on to lorries.

His next opportunity to work with tanks came in 1928, when he was asked to give a course of lectures on tank tactics for the Instructional Staff of the Motor Transport Section. Here he was an originator—no one had ever done anything like this in the German Army before. Fortunately he had one tool ready to hand: having built up his own translation service, he did not have to wait for the official distribution in order to read the new English books and articles and to circulate them amongst his associates; he had also had the rudimentary British manuals translated. These he used as the basis of German mechanized training for many years, until German books were written in the late 'thirties. But so far as practical experience of tanks went, Guderian had only that gleaned from the exercises with dummies, made of wood and canvas and pushed about by soldiers on foot. He was not to see his first 'live' tank until he went to Sweden for four weeks in 1929.

Germination, 1929-35

Although Guderian was the leading exponent of armoured warfare in the German Army, he was by no means alone in this field. During the interval in which he was at Stettin, the Motor

Transport Section had been working in conjunction with the Army Ordnance Office and ten trial tanks were produced—two of each of five models. These were very rudimentary, with speeds of up to twelve miles per hour, lightly protected with mild steel and armed with thirty-seven-millimetre and seventy-five-millimetre guns for light and medium models respectively. They were gas-proof with an all-round arc of fire, but without wireless of any sort and with the commander seated next to the drive in the body of the tank. In 1929 some of these tanks were shipped in pieces to Kazan, where they were reassembled and put through trials. With them went one instructor and ten trainees. However it was the Soviet tanks that were used for instruction.

The tank centre had three main purposes: to train officers in the handling of tanks and tank units; to test German models; and to run comparison tests with foreign models on the proving ground. The training syllabus for both Soviet and German students was compiled by the Inspectorate of Motorized Units in Berlin. The instructional staff soon became all German in composition and taught theory, general mechanical and technical work, gunnery and communications. The school was visited each year by the German Chief of the General Staff (*Chef des Truppenamts*) from 1928 onwards. On 15th September 1929, Guderian's chief, Oberst Halm, was sent to Russia as Senior Officer attached to the Red Army Staff with the rank of Generalmajor. Other visitors to Kazan were Oberst Lutz (the first Commander of Motorized Units, 1934) and Major Pirner, who was responsible for the construction of the test model tanks. Early in 1930, the Soviet Government purchased sixty tanks from Britain—the Vickers Medium, six-ton and Carden-Loyd types—which formed part of an equipment exchange programme between the Red Army and the German Army.

During the early years of the 'thirties, Guderian filled various posts in Berlin and began to work with intensity on theoretical aspects of tank use. During 1929 and 1930, as a consequence of the preparation for his great work on Sherman, Liddell Hart evolved the concept of the deep penetration role of armour, which was the first definition of what is now known as 'Blitzkrieg'. The content of this notion was divided into two categories, tactical and strategic. The tactical aspects were bound up with the selection of the point for penetration of the enemy front. The variability of the thrust point could be used to keep the opponent on the defensive and to defeat him by surprise. Airpower would also be exploited and used in close co-ordination with tanks to achieve tactical domination. The strategic aspects were associated with the thrust itself. The most vital consideration was the maintenance of momentum. After tactical surprise had been exploited to the utmost, strategic surprise could be obtained as the enemy would face a multiplicity of unknown thrusts severing his communications and breaking up counter-attacks before they were formed. Every time he moved his reserves they would arrive too late to prevent resistance from collapsing. But the essential condition for achieving this paralysing effect was the maintenance of pace. A torrent of tanks must pour through the gap at high speed to prevent the spearhead of the thrust from becoming too weak as it raced through to the other side and expanded. Sufficient tanks must be concentrated initially to provide the reservoir. For strategic penetration of hundreds of miles a concentration of a few divisions would be useless except against the weakest of foes. Whole armies of tanks were required. Commanders should not have to wait for orders. They should be told the general aim and left to achieve it in as independent and flexible a way as possible. The thrust should never be halted. It must swerve round opposition or punch straight through a weak point. In negotiating defiles, speed must be increased as the front of the thrust becomes narrowed. The stream must keep on pouring from start to finish at an even, fast pace. The thrust should move by night as well as by day. Supplies for several days of operations should be carried with the stream as an integral part. Commanders must have that feeling in their fingertips for detecting when resistance is stiffening, so that indirect approaches would always be used and put into effect before any appreciable slowing down had been forced.

In 1931-32, Guderian was in the right stage of development to absorb these ideas and to start turning them to practical effect.

These were revolutionary theories, and would never be put into practice, Guderian realized, unless the tanks could be kept separate from infantry on foot. The maximum effects could be achieved only if the tanks were accompanied by supporting troops which could equal them in cross-country performance and speed. Special tank divisions containing infantry, artillery, engineers and signals units that were fully mobile must be formed. This was the stage at which Guderian resolved that his work must be the creation of Panzer Divisions, the future teeth of the German Army.

All of these great developments to restore the power of the offensive were accompanied by attempts to improve the defensive. The doctrine of delaying defence had been formulated by General Beck in the early 1920's and had become firmly established. While in theory it enabled the defenders to withstand a higher attack-to-defence ratio, the doctrine was clumsy and dangerous in the hands of a non-expert. It faded out of use during 1934. The early 'thirties were busy years for General Beck. From 1930-32, he was working on his *magnum opus*—the manual *Truppenführung*. This became the successor to Herrgott's *Führung und Gefecht* and is one of the great classics of Germany military literature.

There were altercations over the nature of defended lines and fortified positions. One school propounded massive 'Maginot Line'-type constructions which were cheap in terms of man-power, but enormously costly and difficult to erect and lacking in any form of defence in depth. The counter-proposal was for a 'Milky Way' system of pill boxes, mutually supporting, and in great depth. The former won the day, but when the time came to build the Siegfried Line, opinion had swung back, and the Chief of Staff of the Fortifications Department was dismissed.[8] It was by then patently obvious that the 'hard thin skin' approach was very inferior to the depth afforded by the 'Milky Way' system.

One of the chief centres of activity was *Wehrkreis I*, in East Prussia. East Prussia was in an exposed position through the establishment of the Polish Corridor and Pilsudski's plans for a preventive war before Germany regained her strength. Consequently there tended to be a concentration of top men in

Wehrkreis I. From 1929-32, General von Blomberg (later to be War Minister) was the Commanding General, with Oberst von Reichenau as his Chief of Staff. These two men were both of an adventurous frame of mind, always looking for new ideas and making their own experiments. Both of them were very conscious of the foreign environment. The spoke fluent English and read widely in the works of the British school. They also ran a translation and distribution service which was put into top gear when they both went to the Reichswehr Ministry after Hitler came to power. Training of short-term volunteers reached such a pitch that recruits could produce accurate fire with field artillery in three weeks. Heavy artillery was one of the weapons forbidden to Germany; so where should the secret heavy artillery school be but Königsberg? Also present in East Prussia at this time was Oberst-Leutnant Heinrici (later General-Oberst and Commander of the Fourth Army in Russia), who had begun to elaborate the theory of space-to-force relationship which he was to use at Orsha, in 1943, where he held attacks by thirty Russian divisions on a front of three and a half German divisions during five successive battles. When fully developed in the early 'forties, Heinrici's methods called for an attack ratio of six or seven to one, while he usually held his own against twelve to one.

In 1931 Guderian had been given command of his first motorized unit—a battalion that was composed of reconnaissance troops, a company of dummy tanks and a company of dummy anti-tank guns. This was a humble beginning, but to Guderian it was all that a set of building-blocks are to an intelligent child. In the spring, the Inspector of Motorized Units, General-Major Otto von Stülpnagel, was replaced by the keen, progressive General-Major Lutz.

Guderian's consistent drive and brilliance throughout this period are striking, as is also the fact that his merit was appreciated. He had no personal influence with the High Command, but it seemed to approve of him. He constantly got good opportunities and was making fairly rapid progress in his career, despite the numerous sharp clashes that this angular personality had with his superiors. He was not made to sacrifice his prospects for his ideas or vice versa. Responsible people were taking such far-reaching decisions as the experiments with tanks in Russia, the tank field exercises and the organizational changes in the motorized units. Certainly there was plenty of room for improvement, as 1939-40 was to show, but considering that the German General Staff was not planning to be at full strength until 1944, and the slow progress that other armies were making, credit must be given where it is due.

Lutz soon took Guderian on as his right-hand man in the Inspectorate as Chief of Staff. Together they worked at making the Panzer arm into a decisive force. Their prime task was the creation of Panzer Divisions, and then Panzer Corps. They had to overcome strong resistance from the Inspectorate of Cavalry, while the infantry refused to regard the odd little wood-and-canvas dummies as anything other than faintly ridiculous forbears of an infantry support weapon. Some cunning persuaded the Inspectorate of Cavalry to abdicate its reconnaissance functions in favour of the Panzers. A new Inspector tried to regain this lost ground by flooding the embryonic Panzer reconnaissance battalions with young cavalry officers, but Guderian and Lutz captured the imaginations of these infiltrators and the tables were turned.

The results of the field tests at Kazan were used to plan the tank that would be capable of making the decisive blow—the break-through and strategic penetration. Guderian did not bother about the time problem but designed what he knew he needed. He was fortunate in being free of the large stock of obsolete equipment which impeded other armies. His requirements were for two types of tank: a light and a medium. Both were to have an armour-piercing gun, machine-guns, radio-communications and a speed of the order of twenty-five miles per hour. There was a lot of trouble with the Army Ordnance Office to get big enough guns on the tanks, and compromises had to be made. These tanks were actually the Panzers III and IV, which were not produced until 1938 and 1939 respectively. For the Polish campaign the Army had only one battalion of them. They were to form the great bulk of the German armour throughout most of the war, as the newer models, the Panther and the Tiger, did not appear in battle in appreciable quantities until 1943.

Obviously a stop-gap was needed for training purposes as no one knew when the proper tanks would appear. Accordingly a small five-ton run-about was designed that could be built around the British Carden-Loyd chassis. This mini-tank was armed with two machine-guns and moved at twelve miles per hour. It was to be made by Krupp, but production difficulties threatened to delay its appearance beyond the desired 1934. A second stop-gap model was designed with a twenty-millimetre gun and a machine-gun. It weighed 8·9 tons and was built by the Maschinenfabrik Augsburg-Nürnberg AG. Thus were Panzers I and II born. Little did their creators realize that they would be going to war in them, behind a maximum protection of fifteen millimetres of steel plate!

Like everything else in Germany, the Panzer idea was greatly affected by Hitler's accession to power. Besides having such men of foresight as General von Blomberg and General von Reichenau in the key positions in the Reichswehr Ministry, the new Chancellor himself was interested in mechanized warfare. He saw Guderian's demonstrations of Panzer I's scout cars, motor-cycle troops and anti-tank guns and became enthusiastic. This gave Guderian the reassuring knowledge that at the head of the Government was a sympathetic ear. All he had to do was to be able to beat his way through the thickets that surrounded the Führer. However, Hitler was, even from the outset, a very mixed blessing for the Panzers. His attitude towards Russia caused the closure of all the German military establishments there, thus threatening the secrecy of the German armoured training.

In the autumn of 1933 came the first experiment in the system of trebling the size of the army that had been planned under Seeckt's direction in the early 'twenties. Battalion III of Infantry Regiment Nine (Prussian) was expanded to the size of a regiment and exercised against the other two battalions of Infantry Regiment Nine, under Generalmajor Freiherr von Weichs at Spandau. The results were surprisingly good. The Army manœuvres of 1933 further convinced Guderian that tanks must be used as the Army's principal weapon and must be provided with fully motorized support. On 1st February 1934, General der Artillerie Freiherr von Fritsch replaced General der Infanterie von Hammerstein as Army Commander-in-Chief. Fritsch was not a technically minded man but he was not opposed to Guderian's ideas. Guderian found him rather conservative but, to do Fritsch justice, it must be remembered that he had to balance the requirements of the whole Army against Guderian's urgent and revolutionary requests. These problems were often complicated by the slavish devotion of Blomberg, the Reichswehr Minister, to Hitler.

The new Chief of the General Staff, Beck, was a much more difficult man to handle. He was much more conservative and, because of his position, Guderian's plans often came directly before him. Manstein relates that Beck would sometimes 'pour a little water in Guderian's wine'[9] to calm him down. Guderian certainly did not see things in this light and regarded Beck as 'a centre of reaction at the very centre of the Army'.[10] In all his writings Beck gives no indication that he really caught the essence of armoured warfare, but the conduct of his exercises suggests that he was sympathetic to the creation of the Panzers. The General Staff Exercise of May 1935 at Bad Elster, five months before the formation of the first Panzer Divisions, studied the use of a whole Panzer Corps. In the next exercises, in 1936 at Bad Nauheim, operations involving the use of Panzer armies were studied.

In October 1934, the long-awaited trebling of the Army began. Twenty-one infantry divisions were formed as the backbone, with the three cavalry divisions of the old Army remaining as they were. The first tentative step towards the development of a mass of armour was taken with the raising of the First Panzer Brigade. This consisted of three regiments of two battalions each, stationed at Zossen (Regiment One), Ohrdruf (Regiment Two), Dresden and Kamenz (Regiment Three).[11] These units were gradually equipped with Panzer I's as they became available.

In 1934 and 1935, the First British Tank Brigade, under Hobart, was busy conducting experiments with the techniques of deep strategic penetration. By reading Liddell Hart's articles, Guderian discovered the details of these exercises and they were worked into his own field training for 1935 when, in July, at Munster Lager, the first manoeuvres for an entire Panzer division were held by

General Lutz. This division had been built up out of various elements, chiefly the Third Cavalry Division and First Panzer Brigade, and was commanded by General von Weichs. The purpose of the exercises was not so much to instruct the members of the division as to demonstrate that the movement and control of large masses of tanks in battle was feasible. The exercises were a great success—so much so that someone remarked to Weichs that the tanks should be placed under the command of the Minister for Propaganda. Blomberg and Fritsch, particularly the former, were convinced that the time had arrived for the birth of the new arm in a suitably decisive manner.

Growth, 1935-39

On 15th October 1935, the first three complete Panzer divisions were formed, along with three extra infantry divisions. The Panzer divisions were organized on the lines of the strategic-thrust principle. Each had a Panzer brigade and a motorized rifle (or Panzer grenadier) brigade as the main striking force. For reconnaissance, there was a special armoured car and motor-cycle battalion. The artillery, engineers, signals and anti-tank units were all motorized, but only partly capable of following the tanks across country. Both the General Staff and the Panzer officers wanted complete mobility for these units, but the bowstring of the German armaments industry was far too taut. Only one infantry battalion and one engineer company could be mounted on 'half-track' vehicles. This unsatisfactory situation was to persist, in some cases, throughout the war. Even the best-equipped divisions only reached a stage where a whole Panzer grenadier regiment (i.e. half of the brigade), some anti-aircraft artillery and some field artillery and parts of the signals and engineer support units were on half-tracks. The tanks were chiefly the tiny, air-cooled, Panzer I, although the larger, water-cooled Panzer II was slowly coming into service. Initially, each Brigade had 561 tanks, all of the Panzer I variety.[12]

The Second Panzer Division was commanded by Guderian, who was at the time only of the rank of Regimental Commander (Oberst). He had gone a stage farther in considering how to deal with pockets of strong defence without robbing the attack of its momentum. Here he was utilizing Liddell Hart's concept of 'tank marines', i.e. assault infantry, carried in armoured vehicles, who could accompany the main tank thrust to deal with particularly troublesome defended points. Detailed exercises were held, covering infantry–tank co-operation, in order to develop thoroughly the necessary tactics.

The night attack and the synchronization of air and tank attacks were also studied. All this was building up a force that could gain the advantage of surprise under almost any conditions and maintain it by a sustained speed of movement which would constantly outstrip the expectations of the enemy. The strategic use of huge masses of armour was studied by means of map exercises, designed to find out the limits of what could be used in the field for large-scale break-throughs and how those limits could be widened.

In trying to develop the principle of freedom for the tanks from the clogging influence of the infantry, difficulties arose with some of the senior infantry officers, who felt that they were being deprived of their necessary supporting weapon. Supply and ordnance staffs tended to dismiss the whole notion as impracticable fantasy and wanted to concentrate on other new ideas, such as the Infantry Assault Gun described in a pamphlet by the then Generalmajor von Manstein, Deputy Chief of the General Staff and head of the Operations Branch. Guderian himself opposed this project as he felt that it would interfere with the development of the tanks, but his opposition was of no avail. Manstein's ideas were fully adopted and proved to be highly successful during the war.

On 21st September 1936, on the Vogelsberg, the biggest manœuvres since 1913 began. This was the test of the first year of the conscript army, and the troops had been carefully built up to it. Each of the individual *Wehrkreise* had conducted its own exercises up to divisional level. Eighty thousand troops took part. A Corps of three divisions fought another of two. This was primarily an infantry exercise and as such showed how little the German infantry had changed since 1918. The proportions of artillery to infantry were the same and the transport and guns were still horse-drawn. A battalion of tanks (112 Pz. I) was used, but only in support of an infantry attack. It was fairly obvious that the tanks, if used in this role, would have suffered heavy casualties at the hands of the new, improved anti-tank weapons. From this the cavalry school concluded that the tank was totally useless. The most striking feature of the manœuvres was the use of armoured car and motor-cycle reconnaissance companies. Aerial fire control and command reconnaissance was also in vogue. The physical standard of the troops is evidenced by one battalion that marched fifty-one miles in thirty-four hours without a single man falling out.

However, the tank was not being neglected by the Planning Staff. After Hitler's order on 24th June 1937 to prepare a surprise attack on Czechoslovakia (*Fall Grün*) the plans made involved the use of a complete Panzer Army, although this was a thing that Germany did not then possess. De Gaulle's well-known book *Vers l'Armée de Métier* came to the notice of a few members of the German Army in 1937. This was a little too late to make much impact on them and they tended to regard it as too theoretical. However, it was eagerly read to discover what the French might do if they accepted de Gaulle's ideas: unfortunately the Germans need not have bothered.

Yet enlightenment within the High Command was still far from ideal. In October 1937, the Fourth Panzer Brigade was formed to provide close support for the infantry. This brigade was composed of two regiments, the Seventh and Eighth Panzer, which had been formed twelve months previously and placed under the care of First and Third Panzer Divisions respectively, to receive their initial training;[13] so the move was a result of long-thought-out policy by the General Staff.

The 1937 exercises took place in brilliant late September weather on the broad, lake-dotted plains of Mecklenburg. These exercises involved land, sea and air forces in co-ordination. 300,000 men took part as two armies, of five and four divisions respectively, battled for possession of the country between Strelitz and Schwerin. Rundstedt's Blue Army had the advantage of having the Third Panzer Division under command. On the final day, it made a massed attack on the Red Army, turning the southern flank in a style that made a huge impression on the watching Hitler and Mussolini. The vastness of the scope of these exercises had aroused troubled thoughts in the minds of many regimental officers. They thought it was expecting too much so soon from conscript troops. Yet, despite a lot of hard marching, discipline was maintained and much was learned by the participants. From the armoured side, many shortcomings in the supply and repair systems were evident. Despite earnest recommendations from the Panzer Corps Commander, these failings were not remedied until they had been exposed to the full glare of world publicity, six months later.

During this time, the early German tanks had been getting a thorough trial in the Spanish Civil War. One and a half Panzer regiments were sent, although with only 180 tanks, under Oberst von Thoma.[14] Apart from small sub-unit tactics, not a great deal was learned from the Spanish experiences, as there was no use of tanks in significant numbers. Thoma continually had to resist Franco's tendency to scatter the tanks about too much. The Republican forces were equipped with Russian tanks, some thirty of which were captured, examined with great precision and used by the German crews against their former owners.

The operations of the German Panzer forces during the Austrian Anschluss gave rise to a great deal of criticism. Some of this was justified, but it should be borne in mind that in forty-eight hours, the Second Panzer Division covered 420 miles, while the Waffen S.S. Leibstandarte 'Adolf Hitler' covered 598 miles, without any preparation of fuel, supply, or repair facilities beforehand.[15] Many of the troops had just been called up in the previous October.

The Anschluss focused enough attention on the Panzer question to assist the formation of two further Panzer Divisions, the Fourth and Fifth, during the following months. But still the High Command felt unable to take the big gamble of confining all tanks to a deep-striking, spectacular role. Another independent Panzer brigade, the Sixth, was raised as an infantry support formation, while in November, three new Light Divisions were added to the one that had been incorporated from the Austrian Army. The Light Divisions were basically motorized infantry with a tank battalion and a reconnaissance regiment in each. This was a further reversion to the cavalry ethic of reconnoitring and skirmishing. It involved another defeat for the principle of concentration and further delayed the addition of more Panzer Divisions. The Light Divisions were shown in the Polish campaign to be of little value and were scrapped in 1940.

During 1938, the first Panzers III and IV appeared. The year was officially a 'Small Exercise Year', with only individual divisional exercises, as the experience of the previous year indicated that a much greater consolidation of the basic essentials was necessary. Exercises went on in the late summer and early autumn, when the order came to prepare for entry into the Sudetenland. This time the operation went forward very smoothly, although not a huge amount was required of the infantry and Panzer divisions that took part. The operation was a classic example of thorough preparation. The troops were even issued with a 'Guide Book' for the operation containing, *inter alia*, detailed reproductions of each bridge in the area, and instructions for its demolition, topographical hints, and, for horsed units, an appendix with all the addresses and telephone numbers of the local German and Czech horse-butchers and knackers' yards, just in case. Every unit participating had been preparing studies entitled 'Prospects of Success', which were basically very detailed appreciations of the situation. A regiment's study contained some 50,000 words. The maps issued showed the entire Czech dispositions with every single weapon down to light machine-guns. Nevertheless it could have been a very bloody battle for the Germans had they had to fight their way in. The Czech defences were well sited, protected by forests, strongly fortified and heavily manned.

On 20th November 1938, the post of Commander of Mobile Troops was formed. Naturally, the first incumbent was Guderian. The creation of this post was Hitler's own idea and it was by his order that Guderian occupied it. Hitler saw the difficulties that the new commander might have in dealing at close quarters with the Army High Command and gave Guderian the right of direct access whenever he felt himself blocked on a vital issue. Guderian was now in personal charge of the development and training of all the remaining cavalry and of the motorized units. He went to work with customary vigour. The first problem was that there were no specifically German training manuals for the Panzers. This was put right by dint of overworking his small staff. He also wanted to reorganize and re-equip the cavalry completely, forming divisions that would be easier to handle and administer. He made no progress on this point. Despite the large amount of currency gained by the Blitzkrieg idea, there were still appreciable segments of reaction and indifference within the German Army, as is shown by the writings of many middle-ranking officers in this period. Their doubts were not to exist for much longer.

Troubles were being experienced with the supply of tanks and it became necessary to reduce the number of tanks in a company from thirty-two to twenty-two. This reduced the number of tanks available for combat in a division from 433 to 299. Even when France was attacked, the total number of tanks and armoured cars on issue to the Panzer divisions was only 2,574.[16] Such was the effectiveness of the Blitzkrieg doctrine that this was enough to achieve in six weeks what the entire German Army had failed to do in four years when it relied on the muscles of horse and man.

Conclusion

Thus it was that the technique of Blitzkreig was developed. The early post-first World War years provided a good environment for the discovery of new ideas and once this potential value had been recognized they were developed and applied. Each idea had to vie with rivals, while its sponsors hoped that it would attract the favourable attention of the High Command. Blitzkreig had dedicated sponsors who ensured that the technique was not choked by its competitors. The High Command eventually perceived its power and its development was turned into a rapid process of escalation.

The basic elements of this story are threefold: an idea, a man and an environment. The environment is that of hard work and intelligent application which has been, over the centuries, the most outstanding characteristic of the German Army. However, while it contributed to the German Army's success, it was not sufficiently strong to withstand the ruinous effects of Hitler.

Of the man, Field-Marshal von Manstein has written:

> In the overall reconstruction of the Army and the introduction of the weapons that were forbidden up till then, the question of the creation of a Panzer arm stood out foremost. . . . No one who is familiar with the development of this question will deny that the German Army would not have had the Panzer arm without the perseverance and the striving temperament of Guderian.[17]

Of the idea, Guderian's own words are eloquent enough:

> It was principally the books and articles of the Englishmen, Fuller, Liddell Hart and Martel, that excited my interest and gave me food for thought. These far-sighted soldiers were even then trying to make of the tank something more than just an infantry support weapon. They envisaged it in relationship to the growing motorization of our age, and thus they became the pioneers of a new type of warfare on the largest scale.
>
> I learned from them the concentration of armour, as employed in the battle of Cambrai. Further, it was Liddell Hart who emphasized the use of armoured forces for long-range strokes, operations against the opposing army's communications, and also proposed a type of armoured division combining panzer and panzer-infantry units. Deeply impressed by these ideas, I tried to develop them in a sense practicable for our own army. So I owe many suggestions for our further development to Captain Liddell Hart.[18]

He sums this up, with characteristic generosity, in his acknowledment in *Der Grosse Brockhaus*:

'*Liddell Hart*—The creator of the theory of the conduct of mechanized war'.

NOTES

1. Hans von Seeckt, *Gedanken eines Soldaten* (Leipzig 1929), pp. 120-121.

2. Friedrich von Rabenau, *Seeckt—Aus Seinem Leben, 1918-1936* (Leipzig 1940), p. 520.
3. Heinz Guderian, *Panzer Leader* (London 1952), p. 20.
4. Waldemar Erfurth, *Die Geschichte des Deutschen Generalstabs, 1918-1945* (Göttingen 1957), p. 129.
5. Von Seeckt, op. cit., p. 123: 'Die Motorisierung der Armeen ist eine der wichtigsten militärischen Entwicklungsfragen'. (Motorization of armies is one of the most important questions of military development.)
6. Ibid., p. 124.
7. The details of the operation of Kazan are well set out in John Erickson's *The Soviet High Command, 1918-1941* (London 1962), pp. 251–271.
8. Letter of General Dittmar to Captain Liddell Hart (undated).
9. Erich von Manstein, *Aus einem Soldatenleben* (Bonn 1958), p. 241.
10. Guderian, op. cit., p. 32.
11. Georg Tessin, *Formationsgeschichte der Wehrmacht, 1933-1939* (Boppard am Rhein 1959), p. 186.
12. Letter of General Guderian to Captain Liddell Hart, 16th May 1949.
13. Tessin, op. cit., p. 189.
14. Letter of General von Thoma to Captain Liddell Hart, 1st November 1945.
15. Guderian, op. cit., pp. 50-54.
16. Letter of General Guderian to Captain Liddell Hart, 30th July 1949; Guderian, *Panzer Leader* (London), p. 472.
17. Manstein, op. cit., p. 240.
18. Guderian, op. cit., p. 20.

Note on Sources

Apart from the references given, most of the details of Guderian's career are found in his memoirs, *Panzer Leader*. The details of the exercises of the period come from British press reports and from German Army documents. The development of tactical ideas is taken from the German Army Documents, from the papers of Captain Liddell Hart and from conversations with retired German generals.

§8§

Liddell Hart and the British Army, 1919-1939

GENERAL SIR FREDERICK PILE

M^Y first meeting with Captain B. H. Liddell Hart was on manœuvres on Salisbury Plain in 1927. I had seen him on many other occasions but this was the first occasion on which we had talked plainly and frankly. I was then in command of what was known as 'the Light Group'. It was really a rather polyglot force consisting of armoured cars and Carden Loyd light tanks. My orders were to advance to a certain line and there to consolidate. I had never believed that with armoured vehicles consolidation was practical and on this occasion, when I got to the line on which I was supposed to consolidate, I found no enemy anywhere in sight. I sent on my armoured cars to see if there was any sign of them and when they reported back I came to the conclusion that the sooner I got going again the better.

So I advanced in the direction from which I knew the enemy was coming. In the event the enemy force was met a long way away from Salisbury Plain and this completely put a stop to the manœuvres, the umpire deciding it was not possible to go on. I then came back to my rendezvous on the Plain and there Captain Liddell Hart drove up in his car. He asked me what had happened and what I was going to do. We discussed armoured war and he held as strongly as I did that it was folly to try to consolidate with armoured vehicles; one should keep on going on until meeting the enemy and then there should be some form of motorized infantry coming up behind to take over the position.

This was the first of many talks I had with Captain Liddell Hart on armoured war, and I would like to say now, at the beginning of this essay, that he influenced me very greatly. His ideas seemed not only practical but very sound; he was always putting before me new ideas which at times I felt were difficult to swallow, but when I sat down and thought about them, there was every possibility that they would be a success, and as history has proved time and again, these ideas were sound.

There was a sequel to the attack on the enemy from Salisbury Plain. At the pow-wow which took place the next day General

Sir John Burnett-Stuart, who was in charge of the manœuvres, said, 'I know a lot of you will not like the tactics which you saw employed by the Light Group in these manœuvres. You will think them risky. But I assure you in armoured war these things will be tried, they will probably come off, there will always be people who chance their arm in this way and you've got to be prepared to meet them when they do.' It was a fortunate thing for England that Sir John Burnett-Stuart was in charge of these particular manœuvres. A few years later, as we shall see, he was commanding in Egypt when Lieutenant-Colonel B. L. Montgomery (later Field-Marshal Viscount Montgomery of Alamein) was commanding the First Battalion of the Warwickshire Regiment. Montgomery was a typical infantryman and the influence that such a forward-thinking Commander had on him was very great.

The years between the wars gave time for radical thinking. The General Staff had never accepted tanks as the major force on the battlefield, and in spite of the cavalry disaster at Arras, there was a strong body of opinion which held that cavalry was still the ideal weapon for a break-through and that infantry was the queen of the battlefield. Every resource should be employed for the support of these two arms. Further, to many of these people tanks were anathema. The Director of Mechanization at this time, Major-General S. C. Peck, had become imbued with the idea of fast mechanical vehicles. He ordered three sixteen-ton tanks from Vickers and these tanks had an astonishing speed—about twenty-five miles per hour on good terrain. They were lightly armoured and only mounted a three-pounder gun. This weapon, although a great step forward, was only adequate to deal with a similar tank. It was unable to penetrate the thickness of armour which future tanks were sure to have.

In addition, a Mr John Carden greatly impressed the Director of Mechanization with his ideas of a light, speedy tank carrying a machine-gun and a crew of two. This machine was produced in a small workshop at Chertsey and in due course it developed into the light tank which was used in the war. Unfortunately, Carden was killed in an aeroplane accident, or he might well have produced something startling in the way of medium tanks. At the time of his death he was exploring a heavily armoured fast tank. Carden became a great friend of mine and on many occasions he told me what an inspiration Liddell Hart had been to him. He used to say: 'Whatever the General Staff may think, speed and armour as visualized by Liddell Hart must be the outstanding land weapon of the next war.'

But we were still in the 1920's. There was not going to be a war in our lifetime. Money was scarce, the research into armoured fighting vehicles cost money, the Royal Air Force was clamouring for its place in the sphere of things; so it was left to Liddell Hart, almost alone among war historians and military commentators, to preach a new kind of war: armoured war. He did not become popular with the General Staff by advocating these ideas, but history and the German General, Guderian, who read and imbibed every word which Liddell Hart wrote, proved in 1940 how abundantly right he was. There is no need to dwell on the brilliant Blitzkrieg of 1940, which resulted in the forced re-embarkation of the British Army at Dunkirk and the surrender of France, to prove that Guderian had learnt the lesson which Liddell Hart preached.

After 1932 the General Staff moved even farther away from any idea of tanks acting independently. They favoured a heavily armoured tank equipped only with a machine-gun. One infantry expert actually gave it as his opinion that the tank must not be able to go faster than infantry, the idea being that the two arms should advance hand in hand against the enemy. In effect this tank, when produced, moved at eight to ten miles an hour but had only a two-pounder gun. It was reasonably heavily armoured but of course was completely inadequate. It was not sufficiently armoured to resist the 88-millimetre gun which the Germans were to bring to bear against it; it had no gun capable of piercing the German armour; and it was too slow to fulfil the break-through role at which the cavalry, in its heyday, was supreme. However, from the General Staff point of view at that time, it had advantages. Liddell Hart's theories on tank warfare envisaged the tank break-through and here was a tank that just could not support that role. So the break-through was still a matter for the horse soldier, and the infantry would still remain the queen of the battlefield while being reinforced by the added offensive power of a slow-moving tank.

It is advisable at this point to give a more detailed description of Liddell Hart's vision of lightning war and decisively deep penetration. In his exposition of the 'expanding torrent' method of attack with mechanized forces he said:

The secret lies partly in the tactical combination of tanks and aircraft, partly in the unexpectedness of the stroke in direction and time, but *above all* in the *follow-through*—the exploitation of a break-through (the tactical penetration of a front) into a *deep strategic penetration*, carried out by armoured forces racing on ahead of the main army and operating *independently*.

The pace of such forces promises a decisively deep penetration *so long as* it can be kept up. It is kept up by a torrent-like process of advance, either swerving round resistance or piercing it at a weakened spot—in which case the tank-torrent contracts in pouring through a narrow breach, and then expands again to its original breadth.

It is the *persistent pace*, coupled with the *variability* of the thrust-point that paralyses the opponent. For at every stage, after the original break-through, the flexible drive of the armoured forces carries simultaneously several *alternative* threats, while the threat which actually develops into a thrust takes place too quickly for the enemy's reserve to reach the spot in time to stiffen the resistance there before it collapses. In effect, *both tactical and strategical surprise* are maintained from start to finish. It is a high-speed 'indirect approach' to the enemy's rear areas—where his vital and vulnerable organs of control and supply are located.[1]

This is Liddell Hart's original definition of the method which the Germans called 'Blitzkrieg'—a definition with which General Guderian wrote that he entirely agreed. He epitomized it as a combination of mobility, velocity, and indirect approach.

Liddell Hart deduced the potentialities and practicability of this deep-penetration method with mechanized forces mainly from the Mongol drives of the thirteenth century together with a comparative analysis of Sherman's marches and Forrest's hamstringing raids in the 1864-65 campaigns of the American Civil War. He developed its theory by strategic adaptation of the tactical expanding torrent method of attack which he had worked out in 1920.

In addition to his theories regarding a new tempo of action in a tank sense and a new technique for exploitation, Liddell Hart also developed the use of obscurity, particularly by the use of night action, a development which was later to play its part in the great battles in the Western Desert. He also developed the use of armoured infantry working in company with tanks and, finally, he was responsible more than any other man for the development of operational research.

Guderian in his memoirs refers to Liddell Hart's influence on his thinking and says how deeply impressed he was by his ideas. The thing that he remarks on mostly is that Liddell Hart emphasized the use of armoured forces for long-range strokes, operations against the opposing enemy's communication and also his proposal for a type of armoured division containing panzers and panzer infantry units.[2]

It would be worth pausing for a moment to see what in fact Liddell Hart at that time (1922-24) was thinking. He had first of all considered the new model division composed of three composite brigades each of two battalions of fast tanks, three small battalions of mechanized infantry mounted in armoured carriers, a mechanized signal company, a mechanical workshop section and three mechanized field batteries and one medium battery, self-propelled. One of the two tank battalions was to be equipped with heavy tanks mounting an eighteen-pounder or equivalent weapon so that the brigade should have assaulting power. The other was to be a medium tank battalion. Both types of tank were to be of high if not similar speed. This composite brigade was intended to be capable of operating independently as self-contained combat teams.

Major-General J. F. C. Fuller, a great exponent of the new ideas in warfare, at the same time as Liddell Hart produced his idea of a new model division, produced a 'Fuller Model Division'. In his book, *The Reformation of War*, which was published in 1923, he sketched a striking picture of mechanized warfare. He said: 'There will be two types of tank, a light cavalry tank possessing a speed of 25 m.p.h. and a heavily armoured tank with a speed of 15 m.p.h.' And he added that in the near future infantry if they exist will only continue to do so as police in the defence of a position, railheads, bridgeheads, etc. Artillery will become doubly important and as speed is added to this arm the old naval struggle between gun and armour will find its counterpart on land. He added: 'Then the infantry tank as we know it today will disappear and be replaced by the heavy gunned and strongly armoured land battleship—the artillery of the future. Then will the cavalry tank, relying on less armour and greater speed, become the battle cruiser.'[3] He believed that on these two types the land fight of the future would be founded. And in another book which he produced in 1926, Fuller set forth in his final chapter his developed view of the ideal army of what he called 'the artillery cycle'. The heavy division would comprise two tank brigades, two self-propelled artillery brigades and a horsed cavalry regiment. There would be no infantry units in it but the tanks should have three spare crews apiece and these should be trained to fight as infantry. Each of the two tank battalions should consist of a battalion of scout tanks, a battalion of assault tanks and two battalions of destroyer tanks, a total of 320 tanks to a division. The Light Division would have a cavalry role and would consist of two tank brigades each and one battalion of scout tanks and three battalions of the destroyer tanks. The pursuit division would consist of two brigades each of three battalions of pursuit tanks and one divisional battalion of destroyer tanks, a total of 280 tanks in all. He added that the future gun is likely to be of comparatively small calibre with high velocity and accuracy of fire. 'In my opinion', he said, 'two main types are likely to be evolved. A cannon superior to but of the nature of existing three- and six-pounders and a heavy machine-gun firing $\frac{1}{2}''$ to $1''$ bullet.'[4]

It will at once be apparent that Fuller's and Liddell Hart's ideas were fundamentally opposed in one essential. Whereas Liddell Hart considered the use of infantry a necessity, though he made arrangements for them to be taken to the battlefield in a protected manner, Fuller considered they were only useful for holding certain specific places.

In 1929 the War Office issued the first official manual on

armoured war. It was commonly called the 'Purple Primer'. It was written by Colonel (later Lieutenant-General Sir) Charles Broad. This manual laid down the higher organization of the Army: mobile troops, cavalry divisions or brigades and light armoured divisions or brigades; combat troops, divisions with non-divisional troops and medium brigades. The light armoured division brigades would comprise two or three battalions of light tanks, one close-support battery, and one anti-aircraft armoured battery. The medium armoured brigades would comprise one medium tank battalion and two light tank battalions, two close support tank batteries and one anti-aircraft armoured battery. Such brigades would be used to co-operate with the infantry divisions. The manual laid down a detailed specification of what was required in the design of tanks but only specified a small gun for the medium tank and did not suggest that a machine appreciably heavier than the existing thirteen-ton Vickers tank would be required.

In 1931 a revised Manual was issued under the title of *Modern Formations*. This said that the Army would be organized in mobile divisions and infantry divisions. The former might be of three types: entirely of horsed cavalry brigades; two tank brigades and an embussed infantry brigade; entirely of tank brigades. Tank brigades were to be of two types, light tank brigade and the mixed tank brigade. The latter was to have three mixed tank battalions, one light tank battalion and one light anti-aircraft section.

It will be seen from this modified 1931 edition that the General Staff were still convinced of the place and use of horses in war. Liddell Hart, however, had moved a long way from both Fuller's and the General Staff's ideas. He could not visualize a war in which horse-cavalry was still a practical proposition. Nor did he accompany Fuller in his idea that infantry would not still be useful on the battlefield.

This light-cavalry trend became still more marked when in 1935 the War Office decided to embark on the mechanization of the cavalry in preference to expanding the Royal Tank Corps. The mobile division was now replanned to comprise a reconnaissance echelon of two armoured car regiments, a fighting echelon of two mechanized cavalry brigades and one tank brigade and two tractor-drawn artillery brigades. A mechanized cavalry brigade was to have two regiments in light trucks and one in light tanks. However, in 1937, after Mr Leslie Hore-Belisha had become Secretary of State for War, a mechanized division was at last formed. It was an improvement in its composition because all the cavalry were converted into light tank regiments, and it included two motor rifle battalions. In this reorganization Liddell Hart played a major part. He had become Hore-Belisha's adviser and as he himself described it, 'We succeeded in defeating a cavalry-minded proposal to take the tank brigade out of the division which would have left us with nothing beyond light tanks.' Even as it was, seven-eighths of its machines were fit only for reconnaissance. The following year, the General Staff was induced to agree that the division should be re-cast on a smaller but stronger pattern and that one of the two cavalry light tank brigades should be dropped. It was, however, unfortunate that one of the two motor rifle battalions was dropped in the reduction. This was contrary to Liddell Hart's proposal.

These 1937-39 changes represented a breakaway from the light-cavalry idea that such mechanized divisions should merely take over the role of the former cavalry divisions.

When the mobile division was renamed the Armoured Division to emphasize its fighting role, the cavalry trend had gone so far and the turn came so late that it was impossible to make up the leeway before the war—especially as the production of medium tanks had also been deferred for so long.

Here we can leave for the moment the influence Liddell Hart had on the formation of an armoured division and revert to the other things which he recommended. Perhaps the most important, though it did not come into effect till well on in the war, was an effort to create an operational research organ. As long ago as 1921, in a paper on a 'New Model Army', one of the conclusions he came to was: 'It would seem essential therefore that a tactical research department should be created to work in close co-operation with a technical branch. At the same time we need to maintain an experimental formation to test out practically the application to the troops of new tactics and technical ideas.' This paper was later published in the *Army Quarterly* for 1924. It attracted much attention abroad, especially in the German Army.

When Field-Marshal Sir George Milne became C.I.G.S. in 1925, he expressed general agreement with the principle of creating an operational research organ, but he claimed that there was no money available for it. So nothing really happened between 1925 and 1937, when Mr Hore-Belisha became Secretary of State for War and called on Liddell Hart to act as personal adviser in drawing up a programme for modernizing the Army. At this same time Liddell Hart suggested a Director of Military Research working under the General Staff. Mr Hore-Belisha welcomed the project and General the Viscount Gort, who was then Chief of the Imperial General Staff, assented to it. But it was never fully implemented. Indeed, I rather doubt if Lord Gort was very much in favour of it. All that was eventually produced was a small section to study the practice and lessons of actual warfare. At the same time the scientists working for the War Office would be co-ordinated by a Director of Scientific Research.

This decision constitutes the first official acceptance of the need for operational research and the birth date of the first organ for that purpose. Its effect was much curtailed by its diminished scale and by separating the scientists from it.

At the end of April 1938 the Chief of General Staff in India and the Financial Adviser for the Defence Department, Sir Archibald Rowlands, arrived in England for discussions about modernizing the imperial forces. Sir P. J. Grigg, then Finance Member of the Government of India, wrote in advance of their coming to ask that Liddell Hart should see Rowlands, who had been Principal Private Secretary to three successive War Ministers preceding Hore-Belisha and who had also passed the Imperial Defence College. After several meetings Rowlands became entirely convinced of the necessity for an operational research organization. At the same time Professor P. M. S. Blackett became interested in the subject and Professor J. D. Bernal sent to Liddell Hart a memorandum which he had drawn up in consultation with

Professor Julian Huxley and Professor Solly Zuckerman on the possible uses of scientific research in relation to war preparation. It is of interest that all these men—Rowlands, Blackett, Bernal, Huxley and Zuckerman—became of supreme importance in the war effort of 1939-45.

It was about February 1940 that Sir Henry Tizard came to me at Stanmore, where I was G.O.C. in C., Anti-Aircraft Command, and asked me whether I would wish for a scientific adviser. I was then in great difficulties over radar and training the troops how best to use it. I was given Professor Blackett as my first scientific adviser and from the team of scientists which he formed there were developed the operational research sections for all the other spheres of the Army. He produced in Anti-Aircraft Command quite a first-class research department. In the spring of 1941 Blackett left me to go to Coastal Command where he initiated similar developments, and at the end of the year he went to the Admiralty as Director of Naval Operational Research.

The Royal Air Force was always more scientifically minded than the Army. Long before the war the Air Ministry had a scientist with an adequate staff. This department carried out very much the role and duties advocated by Liddell Hart for the Army. Scientists were maintained at all Command Headquarters and, what is more, their advice was sought and taken. Except in A.A. Command, where scientists were used abundantly, the Army in the field paid scant regard to them. It is true that the Eighth Army eventually had its scientist, but he was never used in the way, for example, Fighter Command used theirs to analyse success. At the same time, thanks to Liddell Hart's advice and work, the War Office did before the end of the war have a very good operational research department, though it is probable it would have been even more effective if it had been in existence in 1939. There was no doubt that, thanks to the very distinguished scientists who were appointed, it did bring about a large number of reforms which were badly needed.

It is of interest to have a look at the pre-war pieces of operational research advocated by Liddell Hart. First there was the question of the age of commanders of various grades in various types of command. This research he advocated in 1923 and more fully in 1937. It began to bear fruit with revised age limits which were adopted in 1938; and during the war it reached its climax, when the age of commanders was very much in keeping with the job that they had to do. Secondly, he considered the scale of artillery concentration required to subdue hostile machine-gun fire and make an infantry advance possible on given frontages. Thirdly, he considered the effect of different modes of mechanized movement in relation to factors of time and space. At this time the General Staff and most commanders persisted in moving mechanized columns closed-up, like marching columns, until the advantages of a more flexible type of movement were made clear by statistical analysis. Fourthly, he considered the relative effect of operating on a line which threatened alternative objectives compared with one that was visibly directed to one single objective. This analysis led to an important development in the theory of strategy. Fifthly, the relative effect of attacking in conditions of obscurity was compared with that where such a cloak was lacking. This was considered in 1930 and came to its full effect in the desert war.

There were many more subjects for consideration: the strategic and technical effect of a superiority in mobility; the most suitable ratio between mobile forces and infantry in a field army; the relative effect of cutting an opponent's communications near to his forces or to his base; and the ratio of forces to space and its effect on the chances of successful attack and defence.

Liddell Hart would be the first to admit that the analysis is still incomplete, but its significance has been strongly emphasized since the war by a number of the leading German generals.

In 1932 when controversy regarding the kind of tank most suited to our own Army and, even more acutely, as to whether the tanks should be completely subordinated to the old arms was at its very height, I had been appointed to the command of the Canal Brigade in Egypt. Liddell Hart's influence reached me there very promptly. For some time he had been writing of the importance of invisibility in the attack—by night or under a smoke cover. In Egypt at that time was a brilliant Commander-in-Chief, who has already been mentioned: Sir John Burnett-Stuart. Of all the men I have served under he was the most forward-looking. He told us in his first training instruction that we were to make the desert our friend, that we should try out every possible plan. Tanks were in short supply but new and more modern methods for using infantry and cavalry were required.

Having become thoroughly imbued with Liddell Hart's ideas I set about training my brigade in accordance with them. My brigade major was Captain (afterwards Lieutenant-General Sir) Alexander Galloway. He was seized with the idea of surprise through invisibility which Liddell Hart was preaching. Galloway soon discovered that with the best will in the world our units were incapable of finding their way about the desert at night. It was by no means easy to do so even by day. So he started a series of night exercises for platoon leaders. This developed into exercises for small bodies of troops and finally battalions were expected to carry out by night every military exercise that is possible by day. It was not easy to persuade commanding officers who had fought in the 1914-18 war and who had seen how easily even in daylight things became disorganized, but gradually most of them appreciated that movement at night was feasible. They still considered, however, that it should take the form of an approach-march followed by a daylight reconnaissance and attack in broad daylight. A night attack itself was felt to be hazardous. During the manœuvres north of Cairo in 1934 the Canal Brigade was set to capture the city, which was held by the Cairo brigade. The two forces were seven miles apart. Orders were given to one commanding officer to advance at full speed and attack the enemy in the dark without previous reconnaissance. The general line of defence of the enemy had been fairly well established by aerial reconnaissance. The commanding officer, afterwards the most successful of all our Commanders-in-Chief, put up every reason why the attack should be delayed till daylight reconnaissance was possible. Eventually he was persuaded that with the whole Canal Brigade on his heels no harm could result, even if his attack went astray. This same officer wrote to me after the war to say that the events of the Western Desert were greatly

influenced by this training. In the event I received a telegram:
'Have captured Cairo Army including a complete battalion of
infantry'.

Later on there was another very illuminating exercise, set by
Sir John Burnett-Stuart, in which I was the victim. He gave all the
tanks and armoured vehicles to my opponent and told me to
defend Cairo as best I could with cavalry and some lorried
infantry and if I was in danger of being overwhelmed to move out
to the nearest oasis fifty miles away. Liddell Hart had always
emphasized the difficulty of tank movement in a country inter-
sected by canals. So the Canal Brigade was dispersed behind a
very adequate water obstacle and all bridges carefully demolished.
Here we stayed for two days till Burnett-Stuart said the manœuvres were being ruined, and he waited to see what happened
when we left for the oasis. So in the dead of night on the third
day I made a furious attack on the left of the enemy's position
with my lorried infantry and escaped from the right of the position with all the cavalry. We made a fifty-mile march that night
through the desert to another haven, an oasis where we could lie
up, and there we waited for our lorry infantry to follow us and for
the enemy to attack us. It was some time, perhaps twenty-four
hours, before the enemy's armoured cars were knocking at our
door; they had not followed me till dawn. Then it took them no
more than six hours to bring up their tanks and overrun us.
And once more Liddell Hart's conception was proved wholly
justified. You cannot hold infantry positions if they are attacked
by masses of tanks unless you have some obstacle in front of you.
We had none.

Liddell Hart was always advocating the use of parachute
troops and here again he met great opposition from the General
Staff. It was even said that our men would not like jumping in
parachutes, but it was found later on during the war that the
numbers volunteering for the parachute brigade were very great.
At the time, the Russians were experimenting with parachute
troops and obviously were having great success in their manœuvres. Liddell Hart urged that our Army should have such troops
for seizing posts in the enemy's rear. At the time he had little

success, but later on the use of parachute troops became a commonplace. I don't think anyone will forget the Arnhem battle which was entirely a parachute affair and, though from our point of view it was not the success it should have been, it showed what could be done by parachuting well-trained troops. If that parachute drop had been properly supported by fast tanks the result must have been a great success.

The battles in the desert are probably the best advertisement for all Liddell Hart's work. General Montgomery was trained in the old style of tactics and strategy. Thanks to Liddell Hart's preaching he had begun to see the light, and his use of the hours of darkness at the beginning of Alamein and all the battles after Alamein was exactly as Liddell Hart had preached. Later, Montgomery used artificial moonlight. He accepted scientific advisers. He used his tanks to break through and then his infantry to mop up; then he used the tanks again, as a spearhead to disorganize well behind the enemy's lines.

Liddell Hart's influence on the thoughts of the German Army is well known but his influence on the British Army was ten times greater. We have always been a very conservative body of people, we regular soldiers. However, there is not an officer now, there is no training in the Staff College, that does not preach the use of night attacks; the use of concealment; the attack by indirect methods; the exploitation far behind the enemy's lines; and the use of scientists to show us better ways of winning battles. All these things are the direct results of Liddell Hart's teaching.

Perhaps it would be best to describe the changes in British Army tactics up to the end of the war as follows. First and foremost, the massed use of tanks. Secondly, support of tanks by infantry instead of vice versa. Thirdly, the complete abandonment of the horse cavalry. Fourthly, concealment as the main weapon in attack—this concealment to be by fog or smoke or by night attack. Fifthly, the use of artificial moonlight. And finally the acceptance of scientists to analyse our results and our failures. It is no mean achievement. For most of the time between the wars Liddell Hart was the sole prophet.

NOTES

1. This definition was first formulated in 1920 and embodied in various revised forms in several of Liddell Hart's works. It is here quoted from B. H. Liddell Hart, *The Tanks: the History of the Royal Tank Regiment and its Predecessors* (London 1959), ii. 453-454.
2. Heinz Guderian, *Panzer Leader* (English edn., London 1952), p. 20.
3. J. F. C. Fuller, *The Reformation of War* (London 1923), pp. 157-163.
4. J. F. C. Fuller, *On the Future of Warfare* (London 1926), p. 367.

§9§
British Strategic Doctrine
1918-1939

NORMAN GIBBS

Two general points should be made at the outset of an account of British strategic doctrine in the inter-war years. First, that the active public interest and participation in the enunciation of such a doctrine was, compared with postwar years, limited. There were undoubtedly some influential writers, the most important of whom was Liddell Hart himself, but that circle was small. As a result, then much more than now, strategic doctrine tended to be formed from the views of Ministers advised by the Chiefs of Staff. In the present state of historical research it is extremely difficult to know just how much Ministers were influenced by non-official views; the evidence of relevant published work to date suggests that the influence was limited. This chapter will, therefore, concentrate mainly on the official approach to strategic problems, insofar as that approach has been made public. Secondly, such strategic doctrine as was developed in this period was deeply affected, whether consciously or not, by opinions about the conduct of the first World War. If the public at large was mainly guided by its emotions in so strongly rejecting the thought of any more trench-warfare, others argued more cogently that the fighting of the years 1914-18 was a mistake from Britain's point of view because she had, in the process, deserted her traditional strategy. Liddell Hart, in his book, *The British Way in Warfare*, summed up this latter approach when he wrote 'I can see no convincing reason why we should have abandoned [a traditional strategy] proved by three centuries' experience of warfare'.[1] Governments, perhaps mistakenly, do not appear to have based their arguments overtly on such an historical approach. But, in the middle 1930's, when the shape of a future war was at last being planned in detail, they rejected just as firmly the view that Britain either should or could fight another major land war on the mainland of Europe.

Because of those reactions to the first World War as a betrayal of Britain's traditional strategy and the effect of those reactions in determining views after the war, it is important to try to summarize the essentials of that strategy and their relevance to twentieth-century conditions. Looked at exclusively from a national point of view, British strategy in modern times (i.e. since the emergence of a Europe of sovereign nation states and the expansion of those states in colonial areas) has been to command the sea. The successful establishment of that command rested upon a combination of two main factors: the maintenance of a powerful navy, often conforming to a 'two-power standard'; and the deployment of that navy in positions to control the sea-ways in and out of Europe. The latter was, of course, made possible by Britain's favoured geographical position. Thus deployed, the Royal Navy could protect Britain herself from invasion, guard British overseas trade, and also exercise a controlling hand over the use of the seas by her enemies. From all this, and particularly during the wars of the eighteenth century, came the growth of Empire and the establishment of Britain as the world's greatest trading nation.

If we look, however, at the detailed terms of this broad national strategy the picture becomes more complicated. Did Britain conduct this strategy alone against her enemies and, if not, how did she conduct coalition warfare with her allies? The first question clearly raises the issue of isolation. The general argument against an alliance strategy for Britain was perhaps best put by Lord Salisbury when opposing the German attempt to persuade England to join the Triple Alliance in 1901. During those negotiations Count Hatzfeldt, the German ambassador in London, urged upon H.M. Government the danger of remaining isolated in a world of alliances.

Count Hatzfeldt [wrote Salisbury] speaks of our *isolation* as constituting a serious danger for us. *Have we ever felt that danger practically?* If we had succumbed in the revolutionary war, our fall would not have been due to our isolation. We had many allies, but they would not have saved us if the French Emperor had been able to command the Channel. Except during his reign we have never even been in danger; and, therefore, it is impossible for us to judge whether the 'isolation' under which we are supposed to suffer, does or does not contain in it any elements of peril. It would hardly be wise to incur novel and most onerous obligations, in order to guard against *a danger in whose existence we have no historical reason for believing.*[2]

Salisbury's remarks should not be loosely interpreted outside their specific context. Nevertheless, there are historical reasons for thinking not so much that he was actually wrong as that many of his predecessors as well as his contemporaries quite clearly considered that he was. British Governments for many generations have taken the view that the emergence of a dominant land power on the continent of Europe, successfully upsetting the balance of power there, might, if in possession of the Low Countries and the Channel ports, be in a position to threaten Britain's trade in its terminal areas and perhaps even the security of Britain herself. 'If the nation of Spain', wrote Queen Elizabeth I, 'should make a conquest of those countries . . . in that danger ourself, our countries and people might shortly be.' It followed, therefore, for her and her Ministers, that it was vital to prevent 'the access and planting of the great force of the Spaniards so near to our countries'.[3]

That motive has strongly influenced Britain's foreign and defence policy ever since. And it has normally appeared to be unavoidable that if the European balance of power, particularly as it affected the Low Countries, was to be preserved, then Britain must find allies to help her in the process. To that extent the defence of this country has long been treated as a part of collective defence. Hence the Grand Alliance of William III and Marlborough. Hence, too, the efforts of the younger Pitt and his colleagues and successors to build four coalitions against France. In those alliances, and others like them, the British part, broadly speaking, was to use her sea-power against French shipping and French colonies, and to provide money and material to enable her allies to fight against France on land. That process involved some degree of specialization of function which was of value to all anti-French parties. Britain's allies in the end retained their independence, and Britain herself gained an Empire and became the centre of the world's trade.

The Liberal Government of 1914 declared war against Germany and fought together with Belgium, France and Russia basically in support of the long tradition, that the upsetting of the balance of power in Europe could directly threaten Britain's naval supremacy. Addressing his own colleagues and Dominion representatives at the reinforced meeting of the Committee of Imperial Defence on 26th May 1911, Sir Edward Grey forecast this position quite clearly. There was, he argued, 'no appreciable danger of our being involved in any considerable trouble in Europe, unless there is some Power, or group of Powers, in Europe which has the ambition of achieving what I would call the Napoleonic policy'. If Britain stood aside from such a process, however, watching other Powers being overcome one by one without going to their aid, then the result would be one great European combination outside which Britain would stand friendless. He went on:

If that was the result, then the naval situation would be this, that if we meant to keep the command of the sea we should have to estimate as a probable combination against us of fleets in Europe not of two Powers but five Powers. Now, that is the situation, and that is why I say, though I do not think there is any prospect that one can reasonably see at the present moment of our being involved in serious trouble in Europe, it is possible that under such extreme conditions as I have named the question might arise as to whether we ought to take part by force in European affairs, and if we did it would be solely because Sea Power, and the necessity of keeping the command of the sea, was the underlying cause and motive of our action.[4]

Again, in his speech to the House of Commons on 3rd August 1914, Grey emphasized that Britain's interest was in the preservation of the balance of power and that security, as well as honour, was involved in the decision to defend Belgium. It was, in principle, a denial of the point of view put forward by J. A. Spender, among others, that Britain's policy should be 'defensive and pacific', avoiding 'as far as possible, . . . entanglement in European quarrels'.[5] It was an affirmation of the view that avoidance of European entanglements could, sooner or later, endanger Britain herself. In anticipation, it should be said here that British Governments, between the wars, tended too often to forget this particular aspect of Britain's traditional strategy.

Given, however, that membership of alliances has been a normal feature of British strategy, there still remains the issue of what part

Britain has played in the strategy of alliances as a whole. Some things are clear. In the wars of the seventeenth and eighteenth centuries Britain's attacks upon Dutch, French and Spanish shipping and colonies absorbed a great deal of her war effort and were greatly to her advantage; it is not so clear whether, and if so to what extent, these same attacks directly benefited her friends in a narrow military sense. On the other hand, Britain's power to finance her allies, arising from command of the sea, was often a basic condition of success for the coalitions of which she was a member. Again—although this will be discussed in more detail later—Britain's direct participation on land sometimes proved of great value. The career of Marlborough bears witness to that. Finally, the presence or near location of an English fleet was sometimes an important condition of allied action, whether political or military, as in the Mediterranean during the build-up of the Second Coalition in 1798-99.

Beyond that it is not so easy to generalize about the value of Britain's contribution, however complete her maritime supremacy. The effect of economic pressure exerted from the sea, whether upon Louis XIV or upon Napoleon, is extremely difficult to assess accurately, not least because there was no generally accepted contemporary theory of the correct terms of economic warfare. It would certainly be dangerous to argue that, in either reign, France was defeated because of British sea-power applied in this particular way. Equally difficult to assess are the value and proper conditions of Britain's land contribution to the efforts of her allies upon the Continent. Did she help more by combining with the armies of her allies, as for so long under Marlborough and in the Waterloo campaign, or was her intervention more effective when she used her sea-power selectively to attack at the extremities of the enemy's position where it was most difficult and costly for the latter to reply? Opinions on this subject differ greatly, and this is not the place to analyse examples. But one thing is clear. In the period we have had under review Britain's allies had normally to attack the common enemy on land in major campaigns. Attacks on colonies, on shipping and on outlying areas by sea-borne raids were important; but alone they were not enough. Discussing this general problem in the light of the events of the War the Spanish Succession, Winston Churchill writes: 'The shipping resources of the two Maritime Powers [i.e. Holland and England], relatively large though they were, their harbours, quays, and port accommodation, were never sufficient to make the invasion of France possible by any sea-borne army likely to overcome so mighty and war-like a state. Raids and diversions of all kinds could be considered in their place, but our ancestors never believed that a grand and decisive stroke would be launched upon France from the sea.'[6]

The differing circumstances of wars over a period of 200 years make dogmatic generalizations about them dangerous. In the opinion of the present writer, however, Britain's highly successful concentration upon maritime warfare until the twentieth century was possible partly because she was opposed by enemies who could profitably be attacked in that way, and partly because those same enemies could be diverted from the defence of their own maritime interests by being made to conduct major land campaigns in Europe. In other words, war on land and at sea complemented each other. But if that is so, then is it valid to label maritime strategy 'right' and a continental strategy 'wrong'?

The twentieth century introduced some new features which complicated the details of British strategy but which did not change its underlying principles. First, at sea. Until late in the nineteenth century Britain, by her control of the sea-ways into and out of Europe, was able to use her command of the sea to ensure the security of the British Isles themselves, the freedom of Britain's trade, and the safety of her colonies. Britain could exercise naval command as far afield as the Pacific because there, in all normal circumstances, a challenge to her authority could come only from the navies of Europe. But by 1900 that situation had changed. New naval powers were emerging, and existing naval powers were establishing themselves permanently in the Far East in a way which rendered Britain's traditional naval strategy no longer valid. If she was to protect her Pacific interests she either would have to build up her navy in order to have a battle fleet permanently in that area, or else find an ally there who would protect those interests for her. Finance and the more urgent need to concentrate in Mediterranean and home waters precluded the first. She therefore chose the second. And the Anglo-Japanese alliance of 1902 heavily underlined that basic strategic problem which Britain has always faced: how, as a comparatively small island power, is she to defend herself and her Empire without allies?

In Europe the picture was dominated by the rise to power of Germany. As Grey's speech to the Committee of Imperial Defence on 26th May 1911 clearly implied, the problem of Germany was in many ways a traditional one. A Germany predominant on land in Europe, and determined to build a large navy, would pose a serious threat to Britain's own security. But there were also some new features which Grey, in his attempt to reassure the Imperial representatives about the prospects of peace, could clearly not enlarge upon. First, could Germany—a growing but certainly not a great colonial power—be as usefully diverted by attacking her colonies as, on occasion, France had been? In any case, was Britain herself any longer as anxious to acquire new colonial areas as she had been 200 years before? Second, how successfully could Germany's strength be sapped by action at sea, either against her navy or against her trade? And where trade was concerned, would it be possible in modern conditions to control the trading relations of a great neutral power such as the ·United States? Again, if, as always in the past, the aggressive power in Europe had to be made to fight on land, were France and Russia equal to that task without Britain's co-operation? And, if Britain co-operated on land, was it possible to find some peripheral theatre—as in the Peninsular war against Napoleon—where the Central Powers could be made to fight at great disadvantage while at the same time the allies used their resources economically? It is worth remembering that these questions had to be answered in a period when, despite the writings of Mahan, the military significance of land power was beginning to reassert itself against the nineteenth-century predominance of the sea.

These matters are not put forward in order to justify any particular aspect of the actual conduct of the first World War.

Certainly they are not an attempt, by implication, to justify the trench-warfare that actually occurred or to support a 'Western' as against an 'Eastern' thesis. They are advanced because postwar differences of view about how the fighting was actually conducted tended, even if unintentionally, to obscure the basically correct reasons which took Britain into that war in the first place. Her involvement was a continuation of, not a break with, a proper tradition of self-interest. To go farther, there was every reason to believe, from the examples of the past, that Germany would have to be fought on land and that, in that process, sea-borne raids as distinct from major campaigns mounted from the sea, would at the best divert not destroy. And, beyond that, there were already some reasons to think that Britain could no longer, even in her own interest, engage in alliance warfare on the somewhat preferential conditions which had characterized her efforts in the past. Traditions in themselves are neither right nor wrong. What makes them so is their relevance to changing circumstances.

British official strategic doctrine throughout the 1920's was essentially a negative one. Immediately after an unprecedentedly expensive war, in terms both of men and of money, it was understandable that economy became the order of the day and that economy was sought primarily in the area of expenditure on defence. In any case, the defeat of Germany and her allies, the setting up of the League of Nations, and the naval and Pacific settlements reached at Washington in 1921-22, all suggested a period, if not of complete international peace, then at least one unlikely to be disturbed by major quarrels. Hence the Ten-Year Rule.

Already, it seems, in the summer of 1919, Lloyd George's Coalition Cabinet had instructed Departments to plan on the assumption that Great Britain would not be involved in a major war during the next ten years, and that no expeditionary force would be required for this purpose.[7] This 'peace hypothesis' was then, at intervals, reaffirmed in relation to separate Service programmes, each time delaying the proposed date of completion of whatever plan was under discussion. Thus the fifty-two-squadron plan for the Royal Air Force, laid down in 1923 and originally due for completion in 1928, was so restricted by this negative planning hypothesis that by 1934 the R.A.F. was still ten squadrons short of its minimum objective. As Professor Postan has pointed out, the Army was the main victim of this financial stringency:[8] allocations for the purchase and maintenance of army weapons and war stores in the years between 1923 and 1933 averaged only about £2 million per year, or less than nine per cent of the already small sums spent on armaments.

In 1928, with Winston Churchill as Chancellor of the Exchequer, the Ten-Year Rule was reaffirmed more stringently than ever before. Failing an explicit rejection at any given point, then the rule was to be taken as applicable on a continuing basis. In other words, if not cancelled in 1931, then the planning basis would be that no major war was to be expected before 1941, and so on. True, provision was made at the same time for regular review, but, as experience was to show, in these new circumstances cancellation would be called for and approved only in a crisis, just at a time when the cumulative effects of the rule would need to be counteracted most speedily. Moreover, and from the point of view of strategic doctrine just as important, it was extremely difficult (indeed, quite impossible) for the Chiefs of Staff to give the Cabinet any realistic advice and any detailed appreciations of the war that might arise so long as the Ten-Year Rule governed all their thinking. In each of their annual reviews of strategic policy from 1928 onwards they gave expression to their anxiety about the rule and, in 1931, they were supported by a Foreign Office opinion that the rule had gradually become 'a speculation with hope still predominant, but with doubt shadowing the prospect'. Finally, driven beyond endurance by the imminent dangers of the crisis in Manchuria and then in Shanghai, the Chiefs of Staff in February 1932, according to Hancock, 'exploded into a full-throated denunciation of the rule', arguing that 'it had produced terrible deficiencies of all Service requirements, had thrown the British armaments industry into decay, and had produced a state of military ineffectiveness which would make it impossible for the United Kingdom to honour its obligations under the Locarno Treaties and the Covenant of the League of Nations or to fulfil its responsibilities of imperial defence.'

In this setting it is not surprising that there was no positive official strategic doctrine for Britain and her Empire before Hitler's advent to power. There is, however, more detailed evidence of doctrine on particular topics, and it will be convenient to group these under policies in relation to Europe and those concerned with the Far East.

In Europe, during the negotiations on the Versailles settlement, France had withdrawn her original demand for a permanent occupation of the Rhineland on condition that the United States and Great Britain would promise to go immediately to her help in the event of an unprovoked act of aggression against her by Germany. Those treaties were never ratified, although one Minister later argued that Britain would have done well to maintain her own guarantee even though the United States 'ran out'. The result was that France was left with a sense of insecurity *vis-à-vis* Germany which it proved impossible to dispel. In the middle 1920's several schemes were put forward which might have filled the gap; but both the proposals for a Treaty of Mutual Assistance and the Geneva Protocol of 1924 were successfully opposed by H.M. Government, who feared the threat to national sovereignty implied in compulsory arbitration and who objected to putting British fighting forces at the disposal of a League of Nations' General Staff. L. S. Amery later wrote that the Geneva Protocol proposals were strongly opposed by the Chiefs of Staff, and were 'even more in conflict with the views of the Dominions, who were all opposed to additional European commitments, whether under the aegis of the League or otherwise'.[9] What Amery says of the Dominions could surely be taken as true of public opinion in the United Kingdom itself at that time. On the other hand, it is difficult to believe, in view of their later insistence on the traditional strategy of preventing the occupation of all the Channel and North Sea ports by one potentially hostile power, that the Chiefs of Staff were, in 1925, totally unsympathetic to French fears or totally unwilling to advocate some altogether more restricted method of ensuring French security. Indeed, the speed with which the Locarno proposals followed on the rejection of the Geneva Protocol in 1925 suggests that this was so.

The Locarno Treaties were signed on 16th October 1925. They included certain agreements about Germany's eastern frontiers in which Britain was not involved. The main treaty, however, was one of mutual guarantee of the Franco-German and Belgo-German frontiers signed by Belgium, France, Germany, Great Britain and Italy. Article I of the treaty declared: 'The high contracting parties collectively and severally guarantee, . . . the maintenance of the territorial *status quo* resulting from the frontier between Germany and Belgium and between Germany and France and the inviolability of the said frontiers as fixed by or in pursuance of the Treaty of Peace signed at Versailles on 28th June 1919, and also the observance of the stipulations of Articles 42 and 43 of the said treaty concerning the demilitarized zone.'[10]

Sir Austen Chamberlain later declared that Locarno marked 'the real dividing line between the years of war and the years of peace'. Politically it was a statesmanlike achievement. Emotionally, it surely set, in Britain at least, the high watermark of that feeling of postwar forgiveness and good fellowship which welcomed Germany back into the family of nations. But militarily it was of no account. It did not signify on the part of the British Government or the British people a firm determination to defend those strategic interests the threat to which had so often engaged Britain in Europe's wars. As a result it is clear from the evidence of the 1930's that there were no plans or preparations on Britain's part at any stage to 'put teeth into Locarno'. Indeed, it is surely not too harsh to argue that, however laudable the motives which inspired people to see in Locarno a settlement of Europe's major political problem, those same motives were not entirely free from the less worthy hope that, because Europe's problems were solved, Britain could regard her part there as being happily completed.

This part of the story, at the risk of anticipating later events, can well be continued to 1936. One of the Versailles provisions designed to guarantee French security was that which ordered the permanent demilitarization of German territory on the left bank of the Rhine and also of an area fifty kilometres broad on the right bank. Any violation by Germany of the demilitarization clauses would be regarded as a hostile act against the signatories of the Treaty. The demilitarization clauses were later, as we have seen, guaranteed by Locarno. On 7th March 1936, the zone was occupied by German troops.

No doubt, as ex-Ministers have since argued, the demilitarized zone was primarily the problem of France and Belgium. If they saw their security threatened by Hitler's action, then it was, initially, their responsibility to respond by force. Nevertheless, if the security of France was part of the security of Britain herself, then the latter had strong reasons of national self-interest to intervene. The demilitarized zone was designed specifically to protect France against invasion. Yet it is now clear that British Ministers had for some time past admitted to themselves that they could not agree to protect the zone by force—at Stresa the whole matter was dealt with in the most perfunctory way—and when it was remilitarized by Hitler the response of British public opinion was to regard this as virtually a domestic German affair. The military hollowness of Locarno, at least to this extent, was amply demonstrated. It is true that the zone and the frontier were not identical. But it is far from evident that the implications of Eden's subsequent assurance that the inviolability of the French and Belgian frontiers was still 'a vital interest to the country', and the accompanying Staff talks, were, in fact, taken any more seriously than Locarno either by his colleagues or by the country at large.[11] There was still a wide gap between a statement of principles and an acceptance of the implications of those principles in practice.

Second, the Far East and naval defence. Throughout the inter-war years the Royal Navy was regarded, as it always had been, as the front line of national defence. The middle paragraphs of the 1935 Statement Relating to Defence put this quite clearly. The same Statement also went on to say that: 'The Main Fleet is the basis upon which our naval strategy rests', and 'In the Main Fleet the capital ship remains the essential element upon which the whole structure of our naval strategy depends.'[12]

There were several reasons, in the 1920's at any rate, why views about naval strategy should have been more widely discussed and more fully formed than those concerning either the Army or the Royal Air Force. In the immediate postwar years H.M. Government was faced by the inter-related problems of the danger of a naval arms race and the future of the Anglo-Japanese alliance. Those problems were solved, at any rate temporarily, by the Washington Treaty of 1922. But although Japan herself was a major signatory of that treaty, it was natural that the Admiralty— on the assumption that war against the United States was virtually impossible—should then develop their broad plans for the conduct of a major war on the basis of Japan as the potential enemy. During the 1920's the risk remained largely theoretical; after 1931 plans acquired a good deal more reality.

After Washington the desirable standard of naval strength was defined by the Admiralty as the 'one-power standard'. This standard would be satisfied, it was argued, if the British fleet, wherever situated, was equal to the fleet of any other nation, wherever situated, on condition that arrangements would be made in different parts of the world for local provision to keep the situation under control until the main fleet arrived, and also to provide the fleet, on its arrival, with sufficient mobility.[13] Given the Washington 5 : 5 : 3 ratio, then the Royal Navy should be able to meet the Japanese Navy in the Far East at its selected moment, still leaving behind in home waters a fleet capable of dealing with the then strongest European naval power. The only important qualification here was that the fleet needed an adequate base for maintenance and repairs on arrival in the Far East. In June 1921, therefore, it was decided to develop Singapore for that purpose.

Although the capital ship ratios agreed upon at Washington satisfied Britain's strategic needs as defined by the one-power standard, nevertheless the ten-year capital ship holiday agreed upon at the same time was vigorously opposed by the Admiralty.[14] It was a provision which, in spirit at least, was well in tune with the Ten-Year Rule; but it clearly suffered from the latter's most obvious defect: it was bound to create the need for a very large building programme when it ceased to operate, particularly for a power like Great Britain, whose ships were subject to unusually high rates of wear and tear in the normal course of duty. The drawbacks, from the Admiralty's point of view, of the Washington Treaty were greatly worsened by the terms of the London Naval Treaty of 1930. The latter agreement not only postponed the replacement of capital ships until after 1936; it also imposed on Britain parity in cruisers and destroyers on United States terms and involved an acceptance by Britain of a fifty-cruiser limit when the Admiralty argued that the minimum need was for seventy ships.[15] This was all the more serious since France and Italy did not accept the same limitations. The anxieties of later years were bound to be made keener if the political hopes upon which these arguments were based proved to be ill-founded. In the end the Admiralty was left with no room for manœuvre in the worsening conditions of the middle and late 1930's.

This accumulation of restrictions considered dangerous on purely military grounds probably explains the Admiralty wish to come to terms with a rearming Germany in 1935. The Anglo-German naval agreement of that year restricted Germany to a thirty-five per cent ratio in each category of vessels with the exception of submarines.[16] Politically this was an inept move on Britain's part. It did nothing to earn her favour with either Italy or France. On the other hand, it was not unreasonable to argue that it was best to come to terms with Germany while Hitler was still willing, in the hope of averting another naval arms race comparable to that which preceded the first World War. Nevertheless, it is difficult to understand such strong Admiralty approval for a treaty which did not provide an adequate margin —as Washington had done—for current needs. It was an important part of the traditional Admiralty approach to such problems that the standard of strength thought desirable should include a 'plus' element above the literal one-power or two-power measurement. Even assuming a continuation of the Washington 5 : 5 : 3 ratios after 1936—and in mid-1935 this was already extremely doubtful—it now looked as' though Britain must, at best, plan on the basis of equality with Germany and Japan combined, and that in two theatres as widely separated as they possibly could be.

The selection of inter-war issues so far discussed has not been made in order to suggest an overall pattern of official strategic doctrine. There was, and indeed could be, no such pattern, despite the newly established Chiefs of Staff Committee, so long as the Ten-Year Rule continued to exercise its negative influence. In the early 1930's, however, a change began. As we have already seen, the Chiefs of Staff expressed their anxiety about the operation of the Rule in each of their annual reports after 1928 until, in 1932, they were stung by events in the Far East into condemning it outright.[17] The Cabinet accepted their advice, and, in March 1932, the Rule was revoked. No positive action ensued, however, doubtless largely because of the National Government's view that the immediate and pressing problem to be dealt with was that of economic recovery.[18] It was not until eighteen months later that the Cabinet appointed a Defence Requirements Committee with instructions to 'prepare a programme for meeting our worst deficiencies'.[19]

The deficiency programme, accepted on its own revised basis by the Government in the summer of 1934, was, however, no more than a first attempt to correct the restrictive influence of the Ten-Year Rule and to implement programmes originally sanctioned in the early or middle 1920's. It bore little relation to the actually developing conditions of the 1930's, and particularly to the roughly simultaneous appearance of aggressive plans on the part of both Germany and Japan and the further threat to peace on the part of Italy—hitherto considered a friend. Not surprisingly, therefore, the Government appointed a Defence Policy and Requirements Committee in July 1935 which was instructed to go farther than its predecessor and 'to keep the defensive situation as a whole constantly under review so as to ensure that our defensive arrangements and our foreign policy are in line'.[20]

In November 1935 the Cabinet accepted a new report on which it proceeded to base its first major rearmament as distinct from deficiency programme, a programme outlined in the Statement Relating to Defence for 1936.[21] From then on the formal development of the rearmament programmes was nominally under the control of the newly created Minister for the Co-ordination of Defence, Sir Thomas Inskip. In the face of constantly increasing need and cost Inskip, in the autumn of 1937, instituted a major investigation into the rearmament programmes designed to lay down an overall strategic pattern for the three Services within the limits dictated by the nation's resources. That pattern, agreed upon in the spring of 1938, was then altered, indeed in some important respects completely discarded, under the impact of Munich and further Axis aggression in the spring of 1939. The onlooker, thirty years later, could forgivably find in all this a picture of confusion. But there were strategic doctrines involved, even if changing ones.

The political assumptions underlying the deficiency and rearmament programmes were, on the whole, simpler and more stable than the military ones. War against either the United States or France appears to have been ruled out from the beginning. From the beginning, also, the potential enemies were assumed to be Japan and Germany. The difficulty here was to assess from which quarter danger threatened most, and when. In 1933 Japan seemed to be the more immediate source of trouble; Germany, once she rearmed, the more dangerous one. Even at that time, or at any rate soon after, it is clear that Neville Chamberlain was of the view 'that we cannot provide simultaneously for hostilities with Japan and Germany, and that the latter is the problem to which we must now address ourselves.'[22] Chamberlain's view became generally accepted in practice once it became clear that Germany would be ready for war not in 1942, as originally anticipated, but most probably by 1939.[23] And by the spring of 1939 Anglo-French Staff talks were clearly conducted on the assumption that Germany was the main enemy and Japan, whatever the recurrent danger from her, the one whose hostile action might be postponed for the time being.[24]

So far as Italy was concerned, early plans had been drawn up on the assumption of her friendship: Abyssinia changed that. In 1937 the Cabinet felt compelled to instruct the Chiefs of Staff 'to include Italy alongside Germany and Japan in the list of possible aggressors, and to plan their defensive preparations accordingly'.[25] As a result, the detailed plans drawn up by the French and British Staffs in 1939 not merely included Italy, but involved the assumption that, if she entered the war, the first general allied offensive would be made against her.[26] But the Chiefs of Staff were never in any doubt that in the time thought to be available it would be quite impossible for Britain to make adequate preparations for a war on three fronts.[27] And there is therefore ample evidence that not only Ministers but also their professional advisers remained anxious to come to some sort of understanding with Italy which would encourage her to remain neutral. The quarrel between Chamberlain and Eden was not over this basic need but rather about the method by which the need should be satisfied.

With a growing menace from Germany and an uncertain one— at least in terms of degree—from Italy and Japan, it is not surprising that strategic plans changed during the period 1934-39. An attempt to analyse those plans and the doctrine underlying them will be made by examining the programmes for the three Services separately, and then seeing to what extent they complemented one another.

Despite tradition there is a strong case for dealing with the Royal Air Force first. In the spring of 1922 the Coalition Government formally decided that the Air Ministry should be responsible for the air defence of the United Kingdom, thus giving the new Service a specific place in national strategy. In June 1923 the Conservative Government went a stage farther and approved plans for a metropolitan air force of fifty-two squadrons designed to provide rough numerical equality with the French air striking force.[28] This was done at a time of some political strain between

Britain and France, and is the first clear sign of that principle of 'parity' which was to be referred to so often in the 1930's. In March 1934, Mr Baldwin assured the House of Commons that the Government would not accept in airpower 'a position inferior to any country within striking distance of our shores'.[29]

For ten years the Royal Air Force languished under successive economy restrictions. But with the first report of the Defence Requirements Committee, and subsequent Government action upon it, the R.A.F. sprang into a prominence which it never lost in the prewar years. The reason for this was that most Ministers believed (and thought they faithfully represented public opinion in so believing) that the most serious and likely danger Britain would have to face in a major war of the future was a direct air attack upon her cities.[30] From now on it is fair to say that the R.A.F. received 'preferential' treatment.[31] The first Report of the Defence Requirements Committee had been a balanced tri-Service programme based on the strategic doctrine, more than once enunciated by the Chiefs of Staff in these years, that if war came it would have to be fought out in all three elements. Ministers in 1934 took a different view. They not only cut the whole deficiency programme by one-third; they also cut the army's share by one-half and decided to 'rely largely on the deterrent effect of a larger air force than that suggested'.[32] This same concentration of thought was revealed in May 1935 when the R.A.F. was once again expanded unilaterally,[33] and throughout these years down to the spring of 1939.

The R.A.F. programmes of these years reveal some strategic arguments and assumptions of considerable importance.[34] First, the Air Staff planned very largely on the supposition of war against Germany. Successive expansion programmes were planned on that basis and under pressure from the popular demand for parity with the rapidly expanding German air force. As a result, when financial restrictions later became unavoidable, expansion for overseas commitments was sacrificed in the interests of the metropolitan force. Second, ever since the first World War, air-force thinking had been shaped by Trenchard according to the offensive bomber doctrine. Air defence meant primarily air attack.

Therefore, air expansion programmes, certainly until the spring of 1938, were weighted in the bomber's favour. In the last eighteen months of peace, however, Ministerial fears and doubts about the wisdom of this course imposed some check on airmen—in practice if not in theory.[35] One result of this emphasis on the independent or strategic function of bomber forces was to lead many airmen to see their own place in national strategy as competitive with rather than complementary to those of the other Services. The Royal Air Force was, so they sometimes argued, the means which 'alone could provide the necessary deterrent against war or the means by which victory could be won, if war came'.[36] Thirdly, it is in the present writer's view misleading, at least in some respects, to equate this particular strategic approach of airmen before 1939 with the traditional 'continental' as opposed to the 'maritime' school of thought.[37] Whatever the particular circumstances before the outbreak of war in 1914 this difference of strategic doctrine was based, traditionally, on political and economic as well as military arguments. It was not in any serious sense a reflection of professional rivalry between sailors and soldiers. Airmen between the wars were concerned largely with military arguments alone. The element of Service rivalry was strong. From the point of view of Ministers, however, the comparison is more just. For them, concentration upon the air and the sea was both enough to absorb the major part of Britain's resources and a political as well as a military justification for her refusal to contemplate a large army for major continental war.

One final significant item is in the development of air expansion programmes. From the time of the first deficiency programme Ministers had made it clear that defence programmes were in no way to interfere with the normal course of trade and business. The country's fourth arm of defence was its financial stability which, in turn, depended upon full industrial recovery and the export trade. More than once the Chiefs of Staff argued that delays in executing approved programmes were primarily the result of this decision to adhere to the principle of 'business as usual'. Finally, in March 1938 the Air Ministry argument that the limiting factor in the air expansion programmes was the productive capacity of the aircraft industry, itself dependent on the industry's ability to procure the necessary resources in skilled man-power and materials, led the Government to cancel its long-established rule. From now on plans must be accelerated at all costs. Therefore 'men and materials will be required, and rearmament work must have first priority in the nation's effort. The full and rapid equipment of the nation for self-defence must be its primary aim.'[38] The first major step in the adoption of a wartime economy had been taken, and it is not without significance that it was the demands of the air programmes which were the immediate cause of this major change of policy.

Throughout the period down to the Abyssinian and Rhineland crises of 1935-36, it had been assumed by the Admiralty that the only serious naval danger lay in the Far East.[39] Indeed, it has already been argued that the Anglo-German Naval Treaty should be seen, at any rate partly, as the product of wishful thinking on that hypothesis. On the basis of that assumption a one-power naval standard seemed sufficient. But by the winter of 1935-36 the situation demanded review. It now became increasingly clear that the danger in European waters was not one which, for planning purposes, could be relegated to second place; Britain now faced the possibility of war against two first-class naval powers, if not three. In these circumstances the Defence Requirements Sub-Committee of the Committee of Imperial Defence, in its third report drawn up in November 1935, recommended what came to be called the 'D.R.C. standard' of naval strength which planned on 'a force sufficient to prevent the strongest European naval power from obtaining control of Britain's vital home terminal centres while the Navy was making the disposition for war in the Far East'. This new standard involved mainly additions to cruiser, destroyer and escort vessel strength.[40]

Within the next year, however, Germany's rapidly developing rearmament compelled the Admiralty formally to rate the European danger first and also to ask for large additions to all classes of vessel so that a modern 'two-power standard' could be achieved. Such a standard became, from now on, 'the ruling strategic concept'. The naval strength of such a standard was defined as sufficient: '1. to enable us to place a fleet in the Far East fully adequate to act on the defensive and to serve as a strong deterrent against any threat to our interests in that part of the globe; 2. to maintain in all circumstances in Home Waters a force able to meet the requirements of a war with Germany at the same time.'[41]

The Government, on financial grounds, refused to sanction such a standard when it was first proposed although (and despite some sharp debate) the building programmes of 1937 and 1938 assumed the standard in practice if not in principle. After Munich, however, and in the emergency programme period of 1939, the Admiralty began to get its way. But the priority of small-ship building then decided upon emphasized yet further that Germany was the main prospective enemy.[42]

What of calculations about Italy in this developing naval strategy? War on three fronts was never planned for in detail; the programmes of naval expansion in the prewar years were prohibited by financial limitations from envisaging such a possibility. The practical result, as well as part cause, was that friendly terms with Italy were argued to be again essential. Japan and Germany were the two potential enemies against whom preparations must and could be made. Therefore, in a major strategic appreciation prepared in 1937, the Chiefs of Staff made it plain that, 'in their opinion Japan ranked second to Germany as a possible enemy and Italy ranked third'. Risks must be accepted in the Mediterranean in order to provide adequate naval strength in home waters and in the Far East.[43] But with the inexorable pressure of events as war drew near, a major strategic change was discussed which represented a return to that strategy of concentration at home and in the Mediterranean which had characterized the Admiralty's policy before 1914. In February 1939, the Chiefs of Staff advised that the strength of the fleet to be sent to the Far East in war 'must depend on our reserves and the state of the war in the European theatre'.[44] In May the C.I.D. went farther and stated that it was not possible to say when a fleet could be sent to the Far East after the outbreak of war or how large it could be.[45] Italy had supplanted Japan in the order of priority. This was not easy advice to give, nor was it fully and finally accepted before war began. Commonwealth protests were expected and were made. But it was a clear indication of that order of priorities which is bound to put home and near defence first when resources are inadequate for everything that may demand to be done.

In the 1930's, even if not before, the Army deserved the title of the 'Cinderella' Service.[46] The first report of the Defence Requirements Committee, which provided the basis for the deficiency programme of 1934, assumed that in addition to its normal imperial commitments the Army would provide a continental expeditionary force on the outbreak of a European war.[47] The current official strategic doctrine was that: '. . . the importance of the integrity of certain territories on the other side of the Channel and North Sea, which for centuries has been, and still remains, a vital interest to this country from a Naval point of view, looms larger than ever when air defence is also taken into consideration.'[48]

At this stage the issue was not whether there should be such an expeditionary force but simply what its size should be, particularly in terms of reinforcement after the original regular Field Force had been committed. But as the terms of reinforcement began to be discussed, particularly during the winter of 1936-37, a new and different strategic doctrine began to harden. During his last few months of office as Secretary of State for War, Mr Duff Cooper tried to persuade his Cabinet colleagues to provide equipment for the Army to sustain not merely an expeditionary force of five regular divisions but also a reinforcement strength of twelve divisions of the Territorial Army. Towards the end of 1936 the Cabinet instructed the Chiefs of Staff to investigate this problem, paying special attention to the 'relative merits as a deterrent of a land force and an air force to be provided at an equivalent expenditure'.[49]

The Chiefs of Staff, as often before and after, came back with recommendations in favour of a balanced programme; major war, if it came, would be fought by all three Services in conjunction. But the need to observe financial restrictions was being pressed upon the Cabinet by the Chancellor and by the Minister for Co-ordination of Defence, and air defences were assuming an increasingly prominent part in the Government's scheme of things. During the winter of 1937-38, therefore, a new view of the Army's responsibilities was accepted, based on the strategic doctrine of 'limited liability'.[50] The core of this doctrine was that Britain should concentrate her efforts on naval and air rearmament. This, as so often in the past, would leave the weight of land fighting to be borne by her allies. Within the Army's own range of responsibilities provision of anti-aircraft and balloon defences should come first, imperial commitments second, and an expeditionary force last. The rejection of a 'continental hypothesis' was the essence of the policy of 'limited liability'.[51] The equipment of the Field Force was to be planned on the concept of 'colonial warfare in operations in an Eastern theatre'.

It is true that, at least before Munich, there is no clear evidence of French pressure upon Britain to provide a large expeditionary force. Further, both then and later, Liddell Hart suggested that the current British approach to this problem should have been to supply a small specialized armoured force to strengthen French resistance and to counter German Blitzkrieg methods. This may well have been the right solution. But it could have been worked out only on the firm assumption of a continental commitment and it was precisely that commitment which was denied.

All this was changed in the spring of 1939. After Munich, whatever their attitude before, the French began to press for substantial help on land from the United Kingdom.[52] If, in the war that now seemed inevitable, great casualties were to be suffered, then the French could not accept the view that theirs alone was the burden of accepting them. In the spring of 1939 the continental commitment was accepted in full and plans set on foot for an army of thirty-two divisions. From this followed the increase in the size of the Territorial Army and the introduction, for the first occasion in Britain's history, of conscription in peace time. In strategic doctrine the Conservative Government, by the time of the Anglo-French Staff talks of the spring and summer of 1939, was back where its Liberal predecessors had been eight years before the outbreak of the first World War.

It is difficult, in attempting to summarize the trends of thought over twenty years, not to be unjust at times to individuals and to governments. But there are two points to be made in conclusion. First, that strategic doctrine in Britain between the two World Wars was largely based upon a return to the concept of independence or isolation implicit in Salisbury's words quoted at the beginning of this essay. Ministers and public alike were too often misled into confusing the methods by which the first World War was fought with the strategic reasons which prompted Britain to enter it in the first place. There were notable exceptions: Eden and, after 1933, Churchill. Second, although the advice of the Chiefs of Staff often warned Ministers of the dangers of that misconception, nevertheless the three Services for too long thought and planned for their separate wars rather than a common one. The sailors had their eyes fixed on Japan and the needs of a capital ship fleet; airmen focused on Europe, but too often their thinking was a part neither of inter-service nor inter-allied doctrine; and the soldiers were for too long concerned most with the needs of land fighting in the 'traditional' areas of Egypt and India. The difficulty here is to decide whether these differences of approach were more the product or the cause of the absence of a coherent national strategic doctrine.

With the advantage of hindsight at least one thing seems clear. The British people as a whole failed before 1939 to understand the implications for their national strategy of those changes in the world balance of power which had been developing over the past two generations. A more correct appreciation of the hidden and less obvious features of Britain's traditional strategy might have helped them to avoid this error and to see in adaptation not a refusal to learn the lessons of the past but a willingness to apply those lessons to the conditions of the mid-twentieth century.

NOTES

1. B. H. Liddell Hart, *The British Way in Warfare* (new edn., London 1942), p. 29.
2. G. P. Gooch and H. Temperley, *British Documents on the Origin of the War* (H.M.S.O., London 1927), ii. 68.
3. Quoted in Admiral Sir H. Richmond, *Statesmen and Sea Power* (Oxford 1947), p. 7.
4. Public Record Office, Cab. 38, 18/40, p. 11.
5. J. A. Spender, *The Foundations of British Foreign Policy* (London 1912), p. 56.
6. W. S. Churchill, *Marlborough, His Life and Times* (London 1955), i. 559.
7. W. K. Hancock and M. M. Gowing, *British War Economy* (H.M.S.O., London 1949), p. 45. Hereafter referred to as 'Hancock'.
8. M. M. Postan, *British War Production* (H.M.S.O., London 1952), p. 6.
9. L. S. Amery, *My Political Life* (London 1953), p. 301.
10. Cmd. 2525.
11. Earl of Avon, *The Eden Memoirs: Facing the Dictators* (London 1962), pp. 330 ff.
12. Cmd. 4827, Sec. IV.
13. See Postan, op. cit., p. 3; Lord Chatfield, *It Might Happen Again* (London 1947), ii. 80.
14. Chatfield, op. cit., ii. 3.
15. Ibid., pp. 41-44.
16. For account of this treaty see Chatfield, op. cit., chap. LX; Earl of Avon, op. cit., chap. XII; Viscount Templewood, *Nine Troubled Years* (London 1954), chap. X.
17. Hancock, op. cit., p. 63.
18. The effect of this preoccupation, despite the acceptance of the Chiefs of Staff's advice, can be seen in the yet further reduced Air Estimates for 1933; see the speech of the Under-Secretary of State for Air to the House of Commons on 14th March 1933. (275 H.C. Deb., 5s, 1795.)
19. Hancock, op. cit., p. 63.
20. Hancock, loc. cit.
21. Cmd. 5107.
22. Keith Feiling, *Life of Neville Chamberlain* (London 1946), p. 253.
23. Hancock, op. cit., p. 64.
24. This view is implicit in the account of the Staff talks given by J. M. Butler, *Grand Strategy II* (H.M.S.O., London 1957), chap. I.
25. Hancock, op. cit., p. 64.

26. Butler, loc. cit.
27. Hancock, op. cit., p. 64.
28. Basil Collier, *The Defence of the United Kingdom* (H.M.S.O., London 1957), pp. 12-15.
29. 286 H.C. Deb., 5s, 2078.
30. Hancock, op. cit., p. 65; Collier, op. cit., p. 27; Sir Charles Webster and N. Frankland, *The Strategic Air Offensive Against Germany, 1939-1945* (H.M.S.O , London 1961), i. 67.
31. Cmd. 5107, para. 36.
32. Collier, op. cit., p. 27.
33. Webster and Frankland, op. cit., i. 70.
34. The authoritative account of these matters is to be found in Webster and Frankland, op. cit., i, chap. II.
35. Ibid., pp. 77 ff.
36. Ibid., p. 76.
37. For an argument on these lines see Richmond, op. cit., p. 314.
38. 333 H.C. Deb., 5s, 1410-1411.
39. For this section on the Royal Navy see Postan, op. cit., chaps. ii and iii.
40. For some of the details see Cmd. 5107, Sec. II, and Cmd. 5374, Sec. III.
41. Postan, op. cit., p. 25.
42. Ibid., p. 58.
43. Maj.-Gen. S. W. Kirby, *The War Against Japan* (H.M.S.O., London 1957), i. 17.
44. Ibid., p. 19.
45. Ibid. See also Butler, op. cit., p. 13.
46. Postan, op. cit., p. 27.
47. Postan, op. cit., p. 28.
48. Cmd. 4827 (March 1935), para. 24.
49. Postan, op. cit., p. 29.
50. See Duff Cooper, *Old Men Forget* (London 1954), p. 205, for an early mention of this.
51. Postan, op. cit., p. 29; R. J. Minney, *The Private Papers of Hore-Belisha* (London 1960), chaps. VII, IX and X *passim*; Hancock, op. cit., p. 66.
52. Feiling, op. cit., chaps. xxx and xxxi *passim*.

§ *10* §

The American Approach
to War, 1919-1945

MAURICE MATLOFF

*I*N the twenty years that followed the first World War, few Americans concerned themselves with war. Only a handful of officers in Washington and at the service schools were interested in war plans, military theory and strategic doctrine. Yet in the second World War, in contrast with its limited role in the first World War, the United States played a leading part in forging allied strategy. What brought about the great change? What were the intellectual foundations of that transformation and how did they develop? Did the Americans enter the second World War with a coherent strategy? Did American wartime strategy follow peacetime theory? How well did prewar doctrines and concepts stand the test of actual warfare? Behind the American strategy in the second World War that has aroused so much postwar controversy lies a story of changing currents in thinking and planning that has only begun to be explored.

For American strategists, as for the nation at large, the first World War was an aberration. Since the turn of the century American military planning had been geared to two dominant themes: continental defence and protection of possessions in the Pacific. The first interest was traditional; the second had come to the fore with America's rise to world power and acquisition of an overseas empire in 1898. To defend territorial United States was the Army's basic objective and War Department plans were based primarily on that goal; beyond that, its mission was vague and unpredictable. Familiarity with trends in land warfare rather than strategic dogma determined its major prewar policies.[1] The Navy, the traditional first line of defence, was preoccupied with the Pacific. Its thinking was dominated by Alfred Thayer Mahan's strategic doctrine of sea-power built about a big navy, capital ships, command of the sea, and overseas bases. Joint Army–Navy planning, still in its infancy, was also focused on the Pacific.

American participation in the first World War provided no real test of American strategic doctrine. Entering late and, as usual, unprepared, the Americans had limited strategic influence on the conduct of the war. The important questions—which enemy to defeat first, and where and how to go about it—had already been decided.

Yet participation set important precedents and gave new direction to American planning. However much public opinion and national policy in the post-first World War years would recoil from future involvement in Europe, the war rooted in the subconscious of the military planners the idea of a major American effort across the Atlantic. The Americans had proved that they could, with allied help, send a force of two million men to Europe and sustain it. Tied to this concept was the importance of Anglo-American control of the Atlantic in order to link the new and old worlds in a common war effort. The idea that the imbalance of power on the European continent might threaten the long-range national security of the United States and require overseas ground combat operations in Europe was a revolutionary principle. This extra-continental role of American land forces went far beyond earlier, simple concepts of defence of the homeland that had hitherto dominated military strategic thinking. In this sense the first World War foreshadowed the rise of the Army on the strategic scales, much as the war of 1898 had led to the Navy's elevation. The possibility that the nation might have to rely on a new strategy, based on large land forces prepared to fight for national security abroad and in advance of a direct threat to the U.S. continent, was not immediately and squarely faced. But a European note had been put into the American strategic bank and would be drawn upon later.

The first World War set other important landmarks for future American strategy. It marked U.S. participation in a war of allies and exposed the U.S. to the first of its major experiences in twentieth-century coalition warfare. Though setting no major lines of allied strategy, and having no well-worked-out plan of its own, the United States from the beginning held to certain principles: the integrity of American forces in combat, unity of command, concentrated effort, and the offensive spirit. When General Pershing insisted from the outset that U.S. troops must be trained for offensive combat in open warfare in order to prompt a break-through of the stalemated Western Front, he was reflecting American impatience with long-drawn-out wars; he was restating the traditional desire for 'sharp and decisive' wars. American leaders cautioned against 'side-shows' and called for a war of mass and concentration; and national policy, with the exception of the Siberian and Murmansk expeditions, backed the military. As in the nation's earlier wars, the military goal from the beginning was total victory, and President Wilson's 'peace without victory' remained a slogan that did not become part of military doctrine.

Though the Army had not evolved a strategic doctrine to match the Navy's (that is, on the broad scale of sea-power and national strategy in the sense of Mahan), by the end of the first World War the Army had been successful in executing what could later be termed 'theatre strategy'. The European experience of the first World War provided a significant part of the strategic education of the future military leaders of the second World War, for example, General George C. Marshall. Many of the strategic principles by which American troops were deployed in Europe were later reasserted by American leaders in the multi-theatre context of the second World War and given a global application. Out of the experience of American combat on the battlefields of Europe came the foundations of future strategic faith.

1919–38: The Retreat from Reality

After the Armistice, the pendulum swung back. In typical American reaction to war, the nation rushed to get its boys home and forget the aberration. More important, the United States rejected an active world role. Nor was there any obvious or immediate reason after the war for the United States to feel insecure. Presumably a balance of power had been restored abroad and along with it a measure of normality. In the twenty years that followed the close of hostilities—to the Munich Pact in September 1938—the United States sought to protect its national security in extra-military ways. Disillusioned with the outcome of the first World War, it put its hopes in its geographic barriers, in international agreements to outlaw war and limit naval armaments, in diplomatic and economic sanctions to discourage aggression and in legislation to keep the United States out of foreign wars.

During these years the national policy was deeply influenced by popular belief that the United States should neither enter into military alliances nor maintain military forces capable of offensive action. Under these circumstances and in the interest of domestic economy, national policy opposed a large and expensive military establishment. The twenty lean years of economy during the truce between the first World War and the second World War sapped the strength of the military establishment. By 1939 the Army had been reduced, as General Marshall put it, to that of a 'third-rate power'. The air arm, as General Henry H. Arnold later stated, had 'plans but not planes'. Even the traditional first line of defence was still essentially a one-ocean Navy.

As the size and strength of the military establishment lagged behind those of other great powers, American war plans also withdrew from reality. War planning in the 1920's and 1930's centred about the so-called 'colour plans' fashioned by planners in the War and Navy Departments. Of the dozen or so colour plans, in which each colour was a code name denoting a particular emergency situation or a particular nation envisaged as an enemy in the situation, all represented little more than abstract academic exercises. These early war plans conformed with the philosophy derived from the classic General Staff ideal of being prepared for action in any conceivable emergency. But the peacetime atmosphere in which they were drafted made it difficult to attain practicality. There was no real anticipation of hostilities. The emergency situations visualized were, therefore, highly improbable or of relatively minor importance. Limited in scope, the plans envisaged neither global nor total war. Instead, they represented the types of war that the planners believed Congress and the public might support. The keynote of all the colour planning as late as 1939 was the strategic concept, imposed by national policy, of defending, against any foreign threat, the continental United States and its interests by the United States alone. With the exception of Plan Orange, signifying Japan, these plans bore little relation to contemporary political and military alignments.

Interestingly enough, no colour plan was developed against Germany, the foe in the first World War.[2]

In retrospect, American war planning before 1939 represented a reversion, after the interlude of the first World War, to pre-occupation with defence of the continent and the Pacific. National policy, the public mood and starved budgets put constraints on strategic planning and returned it to earlier channels. Implicit in the colour plans was a concept of limited war—limited in participants, areas and forces—but no doctrine was developed for it.

Beneath the quiet surface of war planning between 1919 and 1938, however, strategic theory was in flux. New weapons introduced in the first World War were being further developed and refined, while European theorists argued over their potential and over the meaning of the war. As an outgrowth of the first World War experience, strategy in Europe, as well as in the United States, came largely to mean defence. Indeed, one of the principal strategic lessons derived from that conflict was the paramount importance of defence over offensive power on the battlefield. But counter-trends in European theory soon disputed this prevalent emphasis. A strong challenge came from the new school of thought—the exponents of airpower, led by Giulio Douhet; another came from champions of mechanization and motorization, among them J. F. C. Fuller and B. H. Liddell Hart in England and Charles de Gaulle in France.

The debate over strategy was livelier in Europe because of its older and stronger traditions of strategic theory. But reverberations were soon echoing among the American theorists, not only those in the higher military schools but those who were relatively isolated thinkers. Gradually the offensive overtones in European theory came to be seen as reinforcing American experience and began to seep through the constraints imposed on war planning and on official doctrinal writings. While each military service presented its strategic case in the language of defence, a requirement in the 1920's and 1930's, in one way or another the spirit of the offensive entered strategic thought and became embodied in planning.

Nowhere was the preference for the offensive more apparent

than in the case of the Navy and its planning for a war against Japan. Because the first World War had drastically changed the strategic position of the United States in the far Pacific, U.S. strategic thought from 1919 to 1938 was largely oriented towards the Pacific and the problems arising out of possible Japanese aggression against American interests or territory there. When the Navy planners pre-eminently concerned with the defence of the area resumed the Pacific strategic theme after the war, they were fortunate to be able to build on the theoretical foundations laid in the prewar period by Mahan. They sought to adapt his strategic legacy to the new technology and tactics, to the changing international situation, and to the need to compromise with the sister service, the U.S. Army.

Even before the first World War the Navy, in accord with Mahan, had argued that the defence of an insular position rested on sea-power and that a land defence was doomed to failure without naval supremacy. Central to the protection of American interests in the Pacific was the supremacy of the U.S. fleet. Believing that the only real threat in the Atlantic could come from the British fleet and that England was best fitted to maintain American security in that ocean, Mahan reasoned that America's insular possessions in the Pacific had to be converted to naval bases in order to ensure the supremacy of the American fleet, which could be held in the Caribbean and sent to the Pacific. This foreshadowed a holding role for the Army in the Philippines until the fleet arrived. But the precise locations and defences of the vital bases in the Pacific were problems that would long be debated by the Army and Navy.

From the early 1920's, Army and Navy planners in Washington gave precedence over other planning exercises to the study of operations against Japan embodied in the Orange plan.[3] Between 1924 and 1938 they revised the Orange plan, which envisaged primarily a naval conflict, many times. Out of these revisions emerged basic strategic concepts to guide American forces in a war with Japan. By the mid-1930's the American military planners concluded that Japan could be defeated only after a long and costly war in which the Philippines would early be lost. By then the naval planners were calling for American offensive operations to take the form of an advance across the Pacific through the mandated islands, beginning with the Marshalls and Carolines, and establishing a secure line of communications to the western Pacific. This new naval concept of a progressive movement through the mandates became embedded in naval thinking.

The War Department had serious doubts as to whether the United States should run the risk of fighting the Japanese in the western Pacific. In autumn 1935, Army planners took the position that the United States should no longer remain liable for a fruitless attempt to defend and relieve the Philippines and the costly attempt to retake them. To rely on a base that was not adequately defended would invite disaster. Brigadier-General Stanley D. Embick, the senior Army planner, insisted that U.S. strategy in the Pacific ought to concentrate instead on holding what was called 'the strategic triangle', Alaska–Hawaii–Panama. The Navy planners rejected this view, for the whole basis of the Navy's peacetime planning rested on the assumption that the Navy must be ready to take the offensive in the Pacific in the event of war. It was out of the question for the Navy planners to give up planning to use the fleet in offensive operations west of Hawaii.

For two years the Army and Navy planners were unable to resolve their differences over Pacific strategy. Early in 1938 they finally came to agreement. They did so by avoiding the issues in dispute. In the revised Orange plan of 1938, the Navy planners agreed to eliminate references to an offensive war, the destruction of the Japanese forces, and the early movement of the fleet into the western Pacific. In return, the Army planners agreed to remove the proviso that operations west of the Hawaiian Islands would require Presidential authorization. The revised plan did not indicate how long it should take the Navy to advance into the western Pacific and tacitly recognized the hopeless position of the American forces in the Philippines, which were to retain their mission of holding the entrance to Manila Bay but with little hope of reinforcement.

Though neither service won all it wanted, each gained recognition of principles it considered important. The Army had written into the plan the primary importance of the strategic triangle, Alaska–Hawaii–Panama, to the defence of the United States. The Navy had secured the principle of an offensive war, which was implicit in the concept of a progressive advance across the Pacific, and had avoided committing itself on the length of time required for the move—a basic element in any plan for defence of the Philippines. The Orange plan of 1938, a compromise between offensive and defensive strategy, reflected the contradictions and restrictions of national policy and public opinion under which the planners laboured. The nation would neither give up the Philippines nor provide the means to guarantee their defence; nor would it fortify Guam as an alternative base.

Meanwhile, despite the restrictions in budget in the era between the world wars, the Navy perfected techniques, tactics, equipment and doctrine in support of the offensive. It began to develop the aircraft carrier as a striking weapon. To wed aviation to the fleet, enthusiasts of the naval air arm had to overcome the resistance of battleship admirals and the exponents of a single air force. At the same time, the Navy improved submarines, and Navy and Marine Corps officers worked with civilian manufacturers to develop new types of landing craft and vehicles for amphibious warfare. The Marine Corps base at Quantico, Virginia, became the dynamic centre for the evolving art of landing operations, and by the mid-1930's, after years of study and experimentation, the Marine Corps formulated a new body of amphibious doctrine that was to lead to one of the most far-reaching tactical innovations in the second World War. By the end of the 1930's the Navy was advancing techniques of refuelling the fleet at sea and had made progress towards the fast carrier task force that was to reach its culmination after Pearl Harbour. Before Pearl Harbour, the Navy was already thinking of advanced concepts in sea-power, particularly with respect to war in the Pacific.

While the Navy was concentrating on problems of trans-oceanic warfare in the Pacific, the Army was preoccupied with ground warfare and defence of the continent. In the language of defence, the Army spoke in terms of preventing European powers from gaining a foothold on the continent. General Peyton C. March, the Chief of Staff in 1919, had sounded the keynote: 'It is, accordingly,' he wrote, 'one of the very important lessons of this war that responsible prevision and a sound military policy demand that there shall be at all times available for immediate use a sufficient trained and organized force to insure, in connection with our fixed coast defences, that no probable or possible enemy can ever seize a great strategic base on our coast.'[4]

Beneath the surface of the Army's concern for continental defence, however, offensive aspirations were also stirring in response to the impact which the first World War had on Army strategic thought and doctrine. General Pershing's victories in France appeared to confirm the traditional principles of achieving victory on the battlefield in accordance with Clausewitz's idea. But official postwar precepts made no reference to allies. This was clearly apparent in the authoritative doctrine incorporated into the U.S. Army Field Service Regulations, revised by the General Staff in 1923, which paraphrased an axiom taken from Clausewitz: 'The ultimate objective of all military operations is the destruction of the enemy's armed forces by battle. Decisive defeat in battle breaks the enemy's will to war and forces him to sue for peace.'[5] Only an offensive would obtain decisive results. To be successful, an offensive required not only concentration of superior forces at the decisive place and time but also co-operation of ground and air forces. 'No one arm wins battles,' the Regulations stated, but the 'co-ordinating principle which underlies the employment of the combined arms is that the mission of the infantry is the general mission of the entire force. The special missions of the other arms are derived from their powers to contribute to the execution of the infantry mission.'[6] In this interpretation infantry was still 'queen of battles'.[7]

This theory of war, largely borrowed from European theorists and from the first World War experience on the European continent, remained essentially the American Army's approach to war. Where and how ground and airpower would come to grips with an enemy was not clear. The modifications in Army doctrine before the second World War were nods in the direction of new currents affecting armoured and air warfare. At the risk of

223

over-simplification, the Army's doctrine in the inter-war period might be epitomized as Clausewitz with refinements.

Meanwhile, the first World War experience left its imprint in other areas of the Army's postwar thinking, specifically in organization, tactics, manpower requirements and equipment. Because the war had taken place for the American Army essentially in a single operational environment, the European theatre, the Army was especially interested in the General Headquarters concept and its implicit assumption about war abroad. In the minds of General Pershing and his advisers, the war confirmed the idea that strategic planning in Washington and the conduct of operations in the field had to be more closely linked. The institutional machinery for raising and deploying a force for a major overseas effort had to be strengthened. Since it was not fashionable in the 1920's and 1930's to put forward such thoughts in strictly offensive strategic terms—any more than it was politic to talk of allies and expeditionary forces—Army thinkers tended to carry forward the precepts of Elihu Root, who had brought the General Staff idea to fruition in 1903. Building on the General Staff concept, they dressed their strategic thinking partly in terms of organization. This found its expression in the G.H.Q. plan advocated by General Pershing and his advisers upon their return to the United States. A special group of officers on the General Staff, they proposed, was to draw strategic plans in time of peace and carry them out in the field in time of war. This group would assist the Chief of Staff, who would move to the theatre of war as the Commanding General, Field Forces. Accordingly, the War Plans Division was constituted in 1921 as the fifth division of the General Staff and charged with the duty of strategic planning and of furnishing the nucleus for a G.H.Q. in the event of war. Reminiscent of A.E.F. experience in the first World War, the G.H.Q. concept of 1921 assumed a major effort in a main theatre —a single front—overseas. Significantly, there was no thought of huge forces deployed overseas in a global war waged in many theatres. When war broke out in Europe in 1939, the G.H.Q. concept was still accepted Army institutional doctrine.

Vague as the Army necessarily was in terms of the possible foe or overseas theatre in which it might some day have to fight, its leaders and planners pondered the dilemmas of a national policy that demanded a small army in time of peace and the national habit that demanded a 'sharp and decisive' offensive on the outbreak of war. Limited though its staff contacts abroad were, the Army sought also to keep up with trends in land warfare and technology. It wrestled with new ways of overcoming the strategic stalemate that had stalled the first World War for so long. Lecturers at the Army War College and other Army schools anticipated a future war of movement and favoured mechanization and motorization—currents that were stirring in European combat theory. They emphasized that time and space factors were being changed by aviation and motor vehicles and by innovations and experiments with tanks. In the quiet of service schools and garrison posts, officers were studying European classical theorists and the campaigns of the Civil War and the first World War. Meanwhile, at isolated posts, the leaders who were later to direct huge allied forces in the second World War—the Eisenhowers, Clarks, Bradleys, and Pattons—were, at most, commanding battalions.

By the close of the inter-war period there were signs of increasing ferment in military thinking. But the still-starved Army had evolved no theory of grand strategy—no coherent design built about ground power as an instrument of national policy—to match the Navy's, or even that of the apostles of airpower. The Army had found neither its own Mahan nor its own Clausewitz. Nor, for that matter, its own Douhet.

While the Navy and War Departments in the inter-war period were formulating concepts of warfare built around sea and ground forces respectively, thinkers in and out of the Army air arm advanced a third and more revolutionary approach to war: the theory of air warfare. This new concept of war and the doctrine that grew up with it were built around the air weapon and strategic bombardment. The detailed story of the evolution of the strategic bombardment doctrine and of the related struggles for service independence and for the long-range heavy bomber, has been well told elsewhere. Nor is there need to dwell on the public debates and controversies stemming from the crusade for air-power waged by the colourful Billy Mitchell, forced to resign from the Army in 1926. What should be noted are the influences playing upon this pioneering American airman's thought and the impact he had on American air theory evolving in the Air Corps Tactical School.[8]

Mitchell's ideas derived in part from foreign influences, in part from his own wartime experience in France, and in part from the American milieu after his return. The views of Sir Hugh Trench-ard, commander of the Royal Flying Corps in France, whom he met in 1917, especially impressed him. Trenchard, he was aware, espoused the aeroplane as essentially an offensive weapon and had advanced a programme of strategic bombardment—prin-ciples which he himself adopted. But Mitchell also believed that each nation, as a result of differing patterns of geography and habits of thought in national defence, required a different air policy. After the war he developed and advanced his own ideas in an American context.

Upon his return to the United States, Mitchell found the Navy still regarded as the first line of defence. The role of airpower, according to the dominant notion then accepted in the Army, was close support of the infantry. Indeed the General Staff, which con-trolled the formulation of doctrine in the Army, wrote this thesis into the Field Regulations of 1923. As Mitchell developed his counter-theses, he began by challenging the Navy as the first line of defence and ended by disputing the infantry as queen of battles.

In his last book, *Skyways*, published in 1930, Mitchell summed up his theory of war most succinctly. 'War', he stated in the familiar vein of Clausewitz, 'is the attempt of one nation to impress its will on another nation by force after all other means . . . have failed. The attempt of one combatant, therefore, is to so control the vital centres of the other that it will be powerless to defend itself.'[9] He defined the vital areas as cities, centres of pro-duction and transport lines. But then he sharply diverged from the old master. Armies and navies, he asserted, had been organ-ized to prevent an enemy from attacking those strategic areas. War had become a drawn-out blood-letting between opposing

226

military forces as modern weapons had swung the advantages to the defence. Therefore, his main point, 'The advent of airpower which can go to the vital centres and entirely neutralize or destroy them has put a completely new complexion on the old system of war. It is now realized that the hostile main army in the field is a false objective and the real objectives are the vital centres. The old theory that victory meant the destruction of the hostile main army is untenable. Armies themselves can be disregarded by airpower if a rapid strike is made against the opposing centres. . . .'[10]

By the early 1930's Mitchell's ideas had permeated the thinking of the instructors at the Air Corps' most advanced school, the Air Corps Tactical School (A.C.T.S.) at Maxwell Field, Alabama. That faculty comprised a high proportion of officers, many still captains or majors, who were later to emerge in influential positions in the Air Forces hierarchy in the second World War. In addition to Mitchell, the instructors turned to such other theorists and writers as they could find, some classical, some contemporary: to Clausewitz, Liddell Hart, Goering and Douhet. The lecturers emphasized an offensive type of warfare aimed at breaking the enemy's will and power to resist. The three arms—air, ground and naval—were to co-operate, but each had a special function. The role of the air arm was to attack the whole enemy national structure. The real target was the industrial complex, so important to modern war and to national strength. In at least two important respects the lecturers went farther than Mitchell. He had spoken of seizing off-shore island bases leading away from the United States to extend the air range; instructors at the A.C.T.S., in a changing international context, even in the mid-1930's, were looking to allies to provide bases in the event of a major war. They were also more conscious than Mitchell of the need in peacetime to study systematically profitable targets in possible enemy territory for air bombardment in war. Out of the teachings at the Air Corps Tactical School came, in effect, a concept of total war, American style.

The theory of war taught at the advanced Army air school, closely related to Mitchell and Douhet, clearly differed from official Army doctrine dominated in the inter-war years by ground force officers on the General Staff. Even in the air arm these teachings represented the thought of the 'radicals'.[11] Indeed the air doctrine represented a revolution in thought, the full impact of which would be felt later at air corps, service and national levels. By the close of the inter-war period American air enthusiasts were still far from completely achieving other related articles of strategic faith: the organization and weapons to apply that doctrine. Nor had they achieved the goal of a separate Air Force. But they had scored gains in the Air Corps Act of 1926 and in the formation of the G.H.Q. Air Force in 1935. The G.H.Q. Air Force, a consolidation of several tactical air units, represented the makings of a striking force. It was limited by Army and joint Army–Navy doctrine to quasi-independent but largely defensive functions, in which strategic bombardment was subordinated to counter-air and over-water operations. Meanwhile the air arm developed the 'most advanced bomber in the world'—the B-17, delivered in 1937. The Army War College and the Joint Board were still inclined to regard the principal function of aviation as the close support of the ground forces and Navy. But by the time war broke out in 1939 the Army Air Corps had a well-defined doctrine built around the bomber as a long-range offensive weapon in war. The heresy of 1919-38 was soon to become dogma.

Thus, American strategic theory and planning in the 1919-38 period developed essentially along individual service lines. There was no serious attempt by any of the Presidents of the period to evolve a national strategic doctrine. The disillusionment with war, the retreat to isolation, and the Great Depression tended to turn the eyes of the Commanders-in-Chief inward to domestic affairs. The Presidents, therefore, maintained the traditional separation between the political and military spheres and made no real effort to link foreign policy and military planning. Nor were joint service mechanisms perfected that might have developed a coherent and authoritative body of strategic theory. The Joint Board, not an altogether effective instrument of control, chose to straddle strategic issues between the services. Most of the plans evolved by the joint service planners were academic exercises. As a result of the lack of guidance from above and the absence of strong lateral co-ordination between the services, still co-equal sovereignties, a *laissez-faire* policy on the part of each service towards the other was inevitable.

Despite the emphasis in official policy on the defensive, offensive notes had crept into service strategic thought. On the eve of the Munich conference, late in 1938, the Army built its theory of war around the infantry and a heavy concentration of ground forces against an enemy; the Navy put its faith in the capital ship and a powerful sea offensive, especially in the Pacific; and a rising group of theorists in the fledgeling air force envisaged its future against a background of strategic air bombardment. From late 1938 on, however, the winds of impending war began to have their impact on American military policy and planning. Out of the new and old strands, in the three years of peace that remained for the United States, were to come new concepts and patterns in American strategic thought.

1939-41: *The Quickening Environment*

Between Munich and Pearl Harbour the environment of American strategic planning changed and the pace quickened. Under the leadership of President Roosevelt, the country gradually awakened to the dangers from without and began to mobilize. In 1940 the Selective Service Act was passed and aid to Britain became official national policy. Lend-lease to Britain and to other friendly powers began in 1941. Laying aside their earlier academic exercises, the strategic planners in Washington widened their horizons and began to think in terms of global and coalition warfare, to take into account not only the rising danger of war with Japan but also the reassertion of German imperialist aims.

In the uneasy transition between peace and war—perhaps the most difficult of all periods for strategic planners—the planning staffs in Washington were faced with many unknowns. They could not be certain about the status of foreign powers—potential enemies as well as friendly nations. On the eve of Pearl Harbour, for example, the American staff seriously doubted that the Russians would be able to continue to fight actively against Germany. Nor could the American staff be sure of the course of

American national policy and of the future temper of the American people towards war. In accord with their traditions, the staffs kept aloof from controversies over national policies. On his part, the President broadened his knowledge of service affairs to include Army and Air plans, as well as Navy strategy more familiar to him in the past. But he did not commit himself irrevocably to their war plans nor did he try immediately to influence their strategic ideas. As a result, American war plans were still partially dissociated from national policy. But the loose relationship between the President and the military had important by-products. It permitted the American military planners a good deal of freedom to discuss with British officers the use of American forces in coalition strategy without seriously committing the Administration. This time, unlike before the first World War, the American staffs had a chance, in advance of war, to compare theories and concert plans with a potential ally, and to shape global coalition strategy.

In this changing milieu of 1939-41, the planners laboured to bring their theories up to date, and to incorporate them into tangible, realistic form in new service, joint (inter-service) and even tentative Anglo-American plans. As war clouds gathered over Europe and Asia, new trends emerged in American strategic doctrine and planning. The character and content of American strategic thought began to be transformed. Four developments had special significance: first, the change from Colour to Rainbow plans; second, the shift in concept from continental to hemisphere defence; third, the adoption of the 'Europe first' principle; and fourth, the emergence of theories on how to defeat Germany.

The progression from Colour to Rainbow planning stemmed from the trend in strategic thinking that began in the fall of 1938, when the military and civilian leaders first began to work on the assumption that Axis aggression might jeopardize American security. The course of events abroad and the President's concern licensed the planners to study the impact of concerted action by Germany, Italy and Japan. In the summer of 1939, the Joint Board, which the President drew closer to him, authorized the preparation of five new basic war plans. Unlike the Colour plans, aimed at one or another single power, these five new plans envisaged war against more than one enemy and in more than one theatre. Receiving appropriate code names of Rainbow Nos 1, 2, 3, 4, and 5, they were the first inter-service plans to envisage a global coalition war—an important step in re-establishing contact with reality in war planning. As Army and Navy planners worked on the five sets of contingencies and developed both inter-service and service plans after the summer of 1939, they incorporated for the first time the idea that the United States would fight alongside allies.[12]

Along with the change in the character of war planning after Munich, the concept of continental defence was broadened into hemisphere defence. After Germany's lightning victories and the fall of France in the spring of 1940, American concern grew over a possible Axis threat to eastern Brazil and the 'soft underbelly' of the United States. The President became convinced, moreover, that Britain's survival was essential to hemisphere and national security.[13] Before the United States entered the war, the perimeters of defence for the continent and hemisphere were gradually extended. The United States committed itself to defend the whole Western Hemisphere by force against external attack. For planning purposes, the Western Hemisphere was defined to include the land masses of North and South America, Greenland, Bermuda, and the Falklands in the Atlantic area, and the Pacific islands east of the 180th meridian, including the Aleutians. This broad commitment represented a radical extension of the historic mission of the armed forces to defend the homeland. It resulted in the United States entering into close military relations with most of the other nations of the Western Hemisphere—also a radical departure in U.S. history. The new concept of hemisphere defence had great influence over American military planning in the emergency period 1939-41. Written into Rainbows 1 and 4, it was also incorporated in Rainbow 5. Under this concept, the primary air role was conceived as defence against hostile action from air bases established in the Americas—a counter-air rather than strategic bombardment mission. And the linking of the security of the Western Hemisphere with Britain's survival brought the

U.S. Navy into Atlantic action, months before Pearl Harbour.[14]

While the concept of national defence was broadening to include the whole hemisphere, the strategic pendulum swung once again, after a lapse of twenty years, from the Pacific to the Atlantic, from preoccupation with Japan to concern over Germany.[15] In the revised Orange plan of 1938 the Army was beginning to look anxiously towards Europe. And after 1938 the Atlantic occupied American strategists increasingly. In June 1940 General Marshall, concerned over the possible loss of the French Navy, raised the question of reframing U.S. naval policy to 'purely defensive action in the Pacific, with a main effort on the Atlantic side'.[16] By the summer of 1940 American strategy and hemisphere security had come to be linked to the fate of Britain and its fleet. Two key documents marked the shift to the Atlantic.

One was a study by Admiral Harold R. Stark, Chief of Naval Operations, the Plan Dog Memorandum of November 1940—a landmark in the evolution of American strategy of the second World War. In his study Admiral Stark affirmed the close link between American security and British fortunes in the Atlantic and Europe: '. . . if Britain wins decisively against Germany we could win everywhere; but that if she loses the problem confronting us would be very great; and, while we might not *lose everywhere*, we might, possibly, not *win* anywhere.'[17] He concluded that the United States must prepare, in case of war, for great land operations across the Atlantic. The defence of the Western Hemisphere and the survival of the British Empire required that the United States remain on a 'strict defensive' in the Pacific. He rejected the idea of an unlimited commitment in the Pacific and believed that it might prove very difficult to prevent a limited war against Japan from becoming unlimited. He foresaw that large American land and air forces would have to be sent across the Atlantic to participate in the land offensive.

Plan Dog was the first attempt to deal with American military strategy as a whole on the assumption of concerted British and American operations. Interestingly enough, it was the Navy rather than the Army staff that first tried to think through the relation between British and American plans and to talk in terms of big expeditionary forces and large-scale land operations. This was perfectly natural. The Navy had had more continuous staff contacts with the British, whose fleet dispositions were generally complementary to those of the American fleet. The Navy, moreover, could view with detachment the delicate issues with which the Army had to deal in raising and using huge conscript forces. It was therefore entirely in character for the Navy, still the recognized pre-eminent 'strategic' service in the prewar period, to take the lead. Nor was it unnatural for the Army to rally to Stark's proposals. Plan Dog promised to meet the old military axiom of concentration of force in a single direction.

Early in 1941 the primacy of the Atlantic was embodied in another important document of prewar strategy, the British-American report known as ABC-1. This report issued from British-American staff talks (the ABC Conversations) held in Washington from 29th January to 29th March 1941. ABC-1 represented no binding commitment upon the United States to enter the war. But it did lay down the principles of Anglo-American co-operation if the United States had to resort to war. On the assumption that Germany was the predominant member of the hostile coalition, the main Anglo-American effort was to be exerted in the Atlantic and European area. If Japan entered the war, military strategy in the Far East would be defensive. The principle that the first aim had to be the defeat of Germany—the single most important strategic decision for coalition strategy in the second World War —thus emerged on the Anglo-American level.

Of the five basic war plans on which the American staff had been working since the summer of 1939, Rainbow 5 fitted most closely the strategy outlined in ABC-1. On 14th May 1941, the Joint Board approved Rainbow 5 and ABC-1. In early June the documents were sent to the President. When war came, the overall strategy adopted was essentially that of ABC-1 and Rainbow 5.

By the time of Pearl Harbour, the United States and Great Britain, linked by common interests in the North Atlantic, had drawn closely together. Indeed, by then, the United States was a non-belligerent ally. But agreed as they were on the need to defeat Germany first, they still had no agreed theory or plan on how to

233

go about defeating her and liberating Europe. Nor, indeed, were the American services in complete agreement among themselves on how, when and where to defeat Germany.

The divergency of British and American concepts in strategic theory began to emerge early. Even at the ABC Conference in early 1941, the British put forward Italy and the Mediterranean as the proper line of attack on Germany. In the summer of 1941 during the Atlantic Conference the British Chiefs proposed reliance on blockade, bombing, subversive activities and propaganda to weaken the will and ability of Germany to resist. They emphasized a theory of probing soft spots by mobile, hard-hitting armoured forces operating on the periphery of German-controlled territory and eventually striking into Germany itself, rather than large-scale ground action to meet the full power of the German military machine. Envisaging, from the beginning, a cross-Channel operation in force as the climactic blow against a Germany already in process of collapse, the British were much concerned with preparatory operations—with what would later be termed 'complementary operations'—in the Mediterranean. The British concept was in harmony with its insular position, its maritime traditions and its experiences in continental wars—with wars of opportunity and attrition. It was a compound of military and political factors, of British experience in the first World War and Dunkirk, and of the Prime Minister Winston Churchill's predilections. It was tailored to suit scattered interests, a small-scale economy and limited manpower for ground armies, and to exploit sea- and air-power.

The American outlook and ideas were quite different. As far back as November 1940, Admiral Stark had suggested that large-scale land operations would be needed to defeat Germany. In the summer of 1941 the Army strategic planners, estimating potential requirements for the President's Victory Programme, made the most thorough examination of long-range problems of strategy the Army had hitherto made: studying size and composition of task forces, theatres of operation, dates of commitment. They concluded, 'we must prepare to fight Germany by actually coming to grips with and defeating her ground forces

234

and definitely breaking her will to combat'.[18] Vague as they were about preliminary operations, they were already disposed to think in terms of meeting the German armies head on—and the sooner the better. Here was the kernel of the American theory of a war of mass and concentration, in keeping with the traditional 'sharp and decisive' war leading to the defeat of the enemy's armies. It reflected American optimism, confidence in its industrial machine and material resources, disinclination to wage a long war of attrition, and faith of the military in quickly preparing a large citizen army for offensive purposes.

Significantly, the Army air arm, permitted to estimate its own requirements for a possible war, seized the opportunity to put forward its more revolutionary concept of strategic theory. Its newly formed Air War Plans Division in Washington, staffed almost entirely by former faculty members of the Air Corps Tactical School, wrote the doctrine of strategic bombardment into A.W.P.D./1, the first of the air plans for the second World War and a most unusual document.[19] Really a detailed blueprint for the war to come, A.W.P.D./1 had as its main feature the application of airpower to break down the industrial and economic structure of Germany. It relied on daylight precision bombing of selected strategic targets to paralyse the German war potential. Doubting that a large-scale invasion of Europe could be launched before the spring of 1944 (a remarkably accurate forecast), the air planners saw that date as coinciding with the climax of the programme of strategic bombing they envisaged against Germany. Significantly, they added: 'if the air offensive is successful, a land offensive may not be necessary'.[20] But provision was made for air support of an invasion and a subsequent land campaign. Though this qualified faith in victory by airpower was not completely consistent with the War Department position, A.W.P.D./1, the Air Forces' planning charter in the second World War, met with approval by the Army's War Plans Division (W.P.D.), General Arnold (Chief of the Army Air Forces), General Marshall, Mr Lovett (Assistant Secretary of War for Air), and Mr Stimson (Secretary of War), and was incorporated in the Joint Board's report of 11th September 1941. Thus, shortly before Pearl Harbour, the doctrine of the air apostles had at last gained recognition on a service and inter-service level. The European track opened by Admiral Stark in November 1940 had brought the Army back into the strategic picture. It also gave the Air Force an opportunity to make its strategic bid.

Pearl Harbour put an end to the three years of peacetime preparation for war. Yet military plans were still far from complete; the co-ordination of strategic plans with plans for industrial and man-power mobilization was only beginning;[21] a comprehensive strategic doctrine for a war fought by allies had not been developed; and no firm agreement had been reached on how to defeat Germany and Japan on either the inter-service or the Anglo-American level.

Still, the prolonged 'short of war' period had proved a boon to strategic planning. The handful of harried planners, struggling to keep their plans abreast of changing international developments and shifting national policy, thought increasingly in global and coalition terms, and sloughed off outmoded concepts inherited from an earlier era. Conflicting theory and practice could begin to be resolved. For example, when the Army tried in 1940 and 1941 to activate G.H.Q., it soon realized that this concept, designed for a single-front war of the first World War variety, would not meet the strategic needs of the multi-theatre war that was looming. The planners thereupon began to think of establishing an effective Army wartime high command post in Washington, a plan that was put into effect in March 1942.[22]

The planners had also learned that whatever their theories and plans, they would have to reckon with an active and forceful Commander-in-Chief bent on pursuing his own course. When, for example, the President had touched off the drive for rearmament in November 1938, his ideas on how to rearm came into conflict with those of the professional military staff.[23] His calls for planes 'now and lots of them' clashed with the staff's notions of an orderly development of a balanced force. Favouring U.S. aid for the immediate combat needs of allies over the needs to expand the American armed forces was a major prewar decision of F.D.R. Significantly, Presidential wish, not American strategic doctrine, determined this decision. By Pearl Harbour the planners had begun to appreciate what would become even more apparent later, that despite his relatively close working relationship with his military staff, F.D.R. would play an independent role in coalition policy and strategy.

Thus, by the time of Pearl Harbour the planners had gone a long way in adjusting to reality. The services, now virtually three, had incorporated their evolving theories into strategic plans that bore closer resemblance to the world at war. They had begun to reach compromises among themselves and a habit of inter-service co-operation was growing up in the joint planning committees. They had also started to brush up against British theory and to become aware of how it differed from theirs. For the first time in its history, the nation entered a war considerably advanced in its strategic thinking on how to fight it.

The Test of War

With war came new pulls and pressures and further compromises and adjustments in strategic theories and concepts. Despite the agreed primacy of Europe, the Japanese attack on Pearl Harbour and the need to stem the Japanese advance compromised the Germany-first concept from the outset. The Americans recognized the principle of fighting a strategically defensive war against Japan but had no doctrine on how to fight a limited war. Nor would public opinion condone a completely defensive, limited war against Japan, pending the defeat of Germany. As U.S. military resources poured swiftly into the Pacific, American strategists learned that forces in being had a way of generating their own strategy. Ground and air forces concentrated in Australia after the Japanese sweep through the Western Pacific area could not be left idle. Naval power in the Pacific recovered quickly from the disaster in Hawaii, and naval strategists began to push for the initiation of the old Orange Plan concept of a Central Pacific offensive. The President's decision to bolster China led to a further drain upon U.S. military resources. The limited war would not stay limited. For two years, the requirements of the war against Japan almost equalled those of the war against the European Axis. Not until 1944 did the preponderance of American military strength shift to the task of defeating Germany.

Since the war against Japan was almost exclusively an American affair, strategy was an inter-service concern. Because of the traditional naval interest in the Pacific and the heavy demands upon shipping there, particularly assault shipping, the Navy carried the main burden in developing the offensive strategy for that area. Yet naval plans for the Central Pacific had to be reconciled with General MacArthur's concept of creeping up on Japan via the New Guinea–Mindanao axis. Thus, a two-pronged strategy replaced the original single-axis approach, and this led to a strategy of opportunity, not unlike that urged by the British for the war in Europe. The critical question of whether Japan could be defeated by bombardment and blockade alone, or whether an invasion would be necessary, to which American prewar theory had not given a definitive answer, was debated until the Japanese surrender rendered the subject academic. In the end the war simply out-ran the theorists. The atomic bomb was used before a doctrine of atomic warfare had been developed.

European war strategy, on the other hand, was fashioned on the international level, with the United States contending with the diverse national interests and strategic concepts of Great Britain and Russia. In the process the Army, intent after Pearl Harbour on concentrating forces for an early cross-Channel operation, had to learn to adjust to British notions and to deal with permutations and combinations of cross-Channel, Mediterranean and strategic bombing operations. Through the doctrine of concentration, however, American strategists in the Pentagon eventually found common ground with Russian strategists in the Kremlin.

As for the air theorists, a decade of doctrine virtually disintegrated in the disastrous daylight raids over Schweinfurt, Germany, in October 1943. Indeed, without the hurried addition of long-range escort fighters, for which prewar doctrine had not provided, American strategic bombardment might have failed completely.[24] Despite the considerable damage inflicted upon both Germany and Japan through strategic bombardment, the experience in the second World War afforded no clear-cut answers on the ability of air power to defeat an enemy.

Institutionally, the second World War became for American strategists an organization war, a war of corporate leadership, of big planning staffs in national capitals and in theatre headquarters. The production of strategy became a regular industry in the big business that the huge American wartime military establishment came to represent. Plans were drawn on a day-to-day basis and agreement reached through a whole hierarchy of channels. The committee system blossomed on the service, inter-service and international levels and brought leaders and experts together to select courses of action. In the great international conferences, the chairmen of the board—Roosevelt, Churchill and sometimes Stalin—considered the committees' recommendations and made the final decisions.

Because of the constant struggle to adjust ends and means, compromise was the keynote of the international conferences. Despite attention to 'principles', allied strategy turned out to be a hybrid product, largely hammered out on the anvil of necessity. Events almost as often determined strategy as the reverse.

Through it all, the American planners had to reckon with a pragmatic President, who had served notice even before Pearl Harbour that he would play his own hand. Their task was not made easier by the fact that their Commander-in-Chief sometimes found himself more in agreement with Churchill than with his own staff. To the President, intent on keeping the coalition in harness for war as well as for postwar purposes, strategy, like politics, was the art of the possible. He was wedded, the planners were to learn, to no strategic doctrine except victory.[25]

The separation of the political and military spheres of American national policy continued throughout the war, reinforced by the President's unconditional surrender formula. No strategic doctrine to relate political and military objectives in a coherent pattern emerged before or during the conflict. American political and military strategy were not systematically meshed, a gap that was to arouse especially harsh criticism after the war.

The emerging maturity of the American strategic planners was hastened during the second World War, which added a significant chapter to their education. As General Marshall once put it, his military education as well as his experience in the first World War had been based on roads, rivers and railroads; in the second World War he had to acquire 'an education based on oceans and he had had to learn all over again'.[26] This first truly global conflict exposed American strategists to all kinds of theoretical and practical approaches to warfare now grown more total than ever. Their intellectual horizons were widened. The war enabled them, too, to exercise their ingenuity—by submarine warfare, amphibious assaults, island-hopping and 'leapfrogging' strategy, fast carrier task forces, armoured task forces—in tipping the scales once more in favour of the offensive.

The Americans had entered the war with a strategic framework fashioned out of bits and pieces of European theory and American experience and innovation. No Ralph Waldo Emerson arose to issue a dramatic call for an American declaration of independence from European doctrine. But the principles Americans chose to emphasize in the common body of strategic thought they shared with Europeans were entirely in harmony with their own traditions and national policies. Throughout they showed a penchant for quick, direct and total solutions. Though they still regarded war as an aberration, an interruption to normality to be ended as swiftly as possible, they imposed an American style and an American approach on war and on global strategy and forced the partners in the coalition to reckon with them. Becoming more skilful in advancing its own strategic case, the rising military power from the new world in effect asserted its strategic independence from the old.

As American power flowed into the field in overwhelming strength, the Americans came increasingly to dominate allied strategy. They gained confidence along with power. They were able to hold their own with allies in the councils over European strategy and also while directing freely the war in the Pacific. As a result, the second World War marked a reversal of the U.S. strategic experience in the first World War. In the first, the United States had had to conform to a strategy already set by the allies; in the second, the United States played a large part in moulding allied strategy, and in the Pacific fashioned an American strategy to which the allies had to conform.

In retrospect, American strategy appeared least successful where prewar strategic doctrine was least clear, in the relationship of warfare to politics and diplomacy, the area of grand strategy rather than military strategy. It proved most skilled in adapting the mass-production economy for war and in solving technical problems of warfare by improvisation on a grand scale. Building on the theories, plans, and experiments of the inter-war years, a nation of 'doers' showed an extraordinary ability to apply power on a massive scale and in the three dimensions of war. If American wartime strategy was not distinguished by a well-worked-out new grand design for war and peace, it was marked by a capacity to adapt to changing military needs. The Americans successfully harnessed the revolution in military technology and in tactics that had been developing in the years between the wars to the war of mass and mobility that the second World War turned out to be. By the end of the greatest test in war the nation had ever faced, the United States had emerged as the leading military power of the Western world. American strategists had come of age.

NOTES

1. Paul Y. Hammond, *Organizing for Defense* (Princeton 1961), pp. 67-68.
2. This point was recently discussed by Dr Stetson Conn, Chief Historian, Department of the Army, in a paper entitled 'Changing Concepts of National Defense in the United States', presented at the American Historical Association meeting in Philadelphia, December 1963.
3. The Orange Plan is discussed in a number of volumes in the official *U.S. Army in World War II* series, including Maurice Matloff and Edwin M. Snell, *Strategic Planning for Coalition Warfare, 1941-1942* (Washington 1953), chap. i; the fullest account appears in Louis Morton's illuminating study of Pacific strategy, *Strategy and Command: The First Two Years* (Washington 1962), chap. i, and the subject is also definitively treated in his article, 'War Plan Orange: Evolution of a Strategy,' *World Politics* (January 1959).

4. Report of the Chief of Staff, *War Department Annual Reports, 1919*, Vol. I, 476.
5. *Field Service Regulations, U.S. Army, 1923* (Washington 1924), p. 77.
6. Ibid., p. 11.
7. Wesley F. Craven and James L. Cate, *Plans and Early Operations, January 1939 to August 1942: The Army Air Forces in World War II* (Chicago 1948), p. 44.
8. The following summary of the evolution of air doctrine in and out of the Air Corps Tactical School in the inter-war period draws heavily on the definitive treatments contained in Craven and Cate, I. ii, and James L. Cate, 'Development of Air Doctrine, 1917-1941', *Air University Quarterly Review*, I (Winter 1947), and the author is greatly indebted to the pioneering work of these Air Force historians.
9. William Mitchell, *Skyways* (Philadelphia 1930), p. 253.
10. Ibid., p. 255.
11. James L. Cate, op. cit., p. 18.
12. Various aspects of the Rainbow plans are discussed in a number of accounts in the *U.S. Army in World War II* series: Mark S. Watson, *Chief of Staff: Prewar Plans and Preparations* (Washington 1950), chaps. IV, XII, XV; Matloff and Snell, op. cit., chaps. I-IV; Richard M. Leighton and Robert W. Coakley, *Global Logistics and Strategy, 1940-1943* (Washington 1955), Part I; Louis Morton, *Strategy and Command*, chaps. III, IV, VI; and Stetson Conn and Byron Fairchild, *The Framework of Hemisphere Defense* (Washington 1960), chaps. I, II, IV, XIV.
13. Conn and Fairchild, *The Framework of Hemisphere Defense*, p. 422.
14. The emergence of the concept of hemisphere defence and its impact on planning, 1939-41, are discussed in detail in ibid. Especially valuable is the concluding survey in chap. XVI.
15. The story of the emergence of the 'Germany First' principle is traced in the various accounts listed in note 12. A succinct summary has been presented by Louis Morton, in his essay entitled 'Germany First: The Basic Concept of Allied Strategy in World War II', *Command Decisions* (ed. K. R. Greenfield, New York 1959).
16. Matloff and Snell, op. cit., p. 17.
17. Ibid., p. 25.
18. Ibid., p. 61.
19. For a detailed discussion of A.W.P.D./1 see Craven and Cate, op. cit., pp. 131-132, 146-147, 149-150, 594, 599-600.
20. Ibid., p. 149.
21. For a review of American economic preparedness for war, see

Harry B. Yoshpe, 'Economic Mobilization Planning between the Two World Wars', Part I, *Military Affairs* (Winter 1951) and Part II, ibid. (Summer 1952).

22. The institutional evolution is traced in R. S. Cline, *Washington Command Post: The Operations Division* (Washington 1951), chaps. II, IV-VI.
23. Mark S. Watson, 'First Vigorous Steps in Re-Arming, 1938-39', *Military Affairs* (Summer 1948).
24. For a recent evaluation of American air theory and practice in the second World War, see William Emerson, 'Doctrine and Dogma: Operation Pointblank as Case History', *Army* (June 1963).
25. A recent discussion of F.D.R.'s wartime role appears in Maurice Matloff, 'Mr Roosevelt's Three Wars: F.D.R. as War Leader', Harmon Memorial Lecture Number Six, United States Air Force Academy, Colorado, 1964.
26. Maurice Matloff, *Strategic Planning for Coalition Warfare, 1943-1944* (Washington 1959), p. 363.

Part III

The Development of Soviet Military Doctrine since 1918

MALCOLM MACKINTOSH

THE Red Army of Workers and Peasants, to give the force which was founded in Russia on 23rd February 1918 its official title, came into being in the midst of revolution and political upheaval resulting from the defeat in war of the Russian Imperial Army and the political and economic collapse of the Government which it served. Although 'peace and no annexations' was one of the new Bolshevik administration's first aims on coming to power, it quickly discovered that it had to defend itself not only against the Central Powers bent on seizure of territory in the East, but also against armed rebellion by anti-Communist elements within Russia itself, supported in many cases by the Entente. The rough-and-ready irregulars, the 'Red Guards', who had provided the régime's armed force during the Revolution itself, were quite inadequate for this task, and Lenin soon realized that the creation of a large-scale army had become inevitable. This ultimately involved the conscription of up to five million peasant soldiers who had fought the Germans and Austrians for four years and were reluctant to volunteer for further active service; it also forced the Bolsheviks to employ a large number of ex-officers of the Imperial Army as 'military specialists', working in a professional capacity as commanders, staff officers and technical personnel under the control of trained Communist Political Commissars. In this way the Soviet Government acquired the forces necessary for the defeat of their internal and external enemies, though not without severe crises in morale and organization, and one major defeat at the hands of the Poles. With some measure of peace achieved in 1922, the Bolsheviks settled down to decide the nature and size of the armed forces of the world's first Marxist state.

The situation facing the Soviet Government and its military advisers was virtually unique. The vast military machine of the Imperial Government had foundered in the war against the Central Powers and, with the exception of the General Staff (which was highly professional and based on the Austro-Hungarian model) and some of the higher military academies, had virtually dissolved itself. The civil war of 1918-22 had been fought on an improvised basis, and while they had very little in the way of advanced weapons or equipment, the Red Army leaders were able to start their doctrinal work with something like a clean sheet. On some points of organization most of the new commanders were agreed: imperial traditions in the army were to be abandoned, officers' titles and ranks were to be abolished, all ranks were to wear the same uniforms and there were to be no privileges such as pay differentials or separate messes for commanders and staff officers. Formal discipline was to be kept at a minimum, and some elements in the forces were even anxious to retain the principles of election of commanders and discussion of orders in the new Communist Army.

Against this background the debate on the future form and military doctrine of the Red Army was a many-sided one. On one wing stood a group of ex-generals and colonels of the Imperial Army who pleaded for a regular army with good order and discipline. Led by the former Major-General Svechin, they declared that war is subject to certain permanent factors related to weapon development, economic power, man-power resources and qualities, and military traditions, and that a regular orthodox Red Army would be best suited to exploit these essential requirements. They argued against reliance on the experience of the civil war, with its successes for the cavalry and for armoured trains and far-ranging raids behind the enemy's lines, holding that it had been a conflict waged by improvised means; no future war in Europe would have this character, and therefore its lessons were of limited value. The War Commissar, Lev Trotski, agreed with Svechin on the universal nature of the factors governing the·waging of war, but rated the value of the experience of the civil war higher than did the military specialist. On the other side of the debate stood groups of successful field commanders in the civil war, some of them former junior officers of the Imperial Army and zealous converts to Communism like Mikhail Tukhachevski and Ieronim Uborevich, both of whom had commanded armies in their twenties. Others were self-made men like the ex-non-commissioned officer Semyon Budyonny, the former workers Mikhail Frunze, 'Klim' Voroshilov and Vassili Blyukher, who believed that the experience of the civil war was all-important, and that the concept of 'manœuvre' which they had practised would form the basis of any future war. Trench-warfare, static defences and fortifications were a thing of the past: moreover, Communism could provide the inspiration for a doctrine rooted in the spirit of the offensive, upon which all training and development of the Red Army should be based.

Trotski took special issue with the main spokesman of this group, Mikhail Frunze, on the place of the offensive in Soviet military thought. The War Commissar argued that this was good theory, but in the exhausted state in which Russia found herself in the mid-1920's the only possible outlook and doctrine for the Red Army was an orthodox and defensive one. All thought of indoctrinating the Red Army with the spirit of the offensive in the field of armed support for Communist revolutions abroad (as the fire-eating young Tukhachevski advocated) was ludicrous, said Trotski (and it should be remembered that he, Trotski, had opposed the march on Warsaw in 1920). Trotski called for the establishment of a regular covering force for the protection of the Soviet frontiers, and the conversion of the rest of the peacetime Army into a territorial force, stationed and recruited in the main industrial centres of the country, in order to maintain a proper balance in favour of the industrial proletariat. But the whole emphasis in training and doctrine should be defensive and, in general, based on the permanent factors inherent in large-scale warfare in the European theatre of operations.

While this debate was in progress—and indeed while Trotski was putting some of his ideas into practice—the War Commissar came under heavy fire from his rivals in the Party's political hierarchy, and was driven from office in January 1925. He was succeeded by Frunze, and in the reshuffle of military posts which followed, advocates of the offensive and of mobile warfare based on cavalry came to the fore. Frunze was also well aware of the poverty of the Soviet Union, and continued Trotski's division of the land Army into a covering force of thirty-one regular infantry or 'rifle' divisions at sixty-four per cent of their war strength. But he saw to it that his concept of a mobile striking force was retained in the peacetime Army by reorganizing the Red cavalry into eleven divisions, all but one of them with 'regular' status. While 'military specialists' such as the ex-Generals S. S. Kamenev and N. N. Petin were given secondary posts in the Commissariat of Defence in the field of administration and inspection, firm supporters of the offensive received key appointments such as Chief of Operations of the Army Staff (M. N. Tukhachevski) and Head of Military Training and Education (the brilliant Jewish civil war commander I. E. Yakir). Command of the Red Air Force went to P. I. Baranov, a particularly close adherent of Frunze, and it is interesting to note that the subsequent Air Force reorganization included the establishment of a long-range bomber element in addition to battlefield support squadrons.

Frunze died less than a year after becoming Defence Commissar and was succeeded in November 1925 by Voroshilov. Given the acceptance of the Frunze concept of military thought, which theorists and practitioners such as Tukhachevski, Uborevich, Shaposhnikov and Tryandafilov were elaborating in books and in the pages of Soviet military journals, it was natural that Voroshilov's search should have been for weapons and vehicles with which to equip and train the Red Army for a war of manœuvre. It is recorded that in 1926-27 the Soviet automobile industry produced only 500 vehicles, and that there were only thirty light tanks in the whole of the vast area between the Ural mountains and the Pacific. In these circumstances it is not surprising that Voroshilov and his colleagues threw their weight behind the industrial revolution begun in Stalin's first Five Year Plan, and adopted, indeed expanded, Trotski's early agreements with the German Army for joint Soviet-German military-industrial enterprises and training on Soviet soil; nor was it surprising that Red Army leaders should search the world's press and books for forward-looking military writers and thinkers, and that a number of them (including Captain Liddell Hart) should have been approached to enlist their knowledge, experience and imagination in the service of the new Red Army.

The only hostilities in which the Red Army was engaged between 1922 and 1938 was the brief campaign against the Chinese warlord of Manchuria in 1929, in which Soviet troops crossed the Chinese frontier to break up threatening concentrations of Chinese troops and put a stop to mounting violations of the Soviet Far Eastern frontier. Although the operation was held up by lack of transport and administrative shortcomings, the planning and the political preparation of the troops well reflected both the spirit of the offensive and an attempt to employ manœuvre.

The same ideas prompted Tukhachevski early in the 1930's to experiment with new forms of troop employment which could increase the mobility of the Red Army and its capacity for a rapid offensive. In an essay which he wrote at this time, and which even today reads remarkably up to date, he emphasized the need for the Soviet Union to integrate diplomacy and foreign policy with industrial development and military power. He declared that the war of the future would be on a vast scale and would last longer than the war of 1914-18. The whole life of a country would be involved in such a war, and it was just as important to prepare a country's communications and transport as to have a modern Army, Navy and Air Force. The advent of the bomber had made any country's industry vulnerable, and therefore the Government should disperse industrial plants and factories into less accessible areas. Of the actual war itself, Tukhachevski wrote that only the defeat of the enemy's forces on the battlefield in a series of offensive actions could bring victory, and if the Soviet Union were attacked from east or west, the Red Army should conduct a mobile defence until mobilization was completed and then go over to the strategic offensive. The period of defence should be characterized by tactical counter-attacks, and only rarely should fixed defensive fortifications be relied upon. Although Tukhachevski admitted that in 1930-32 the defensive power of the machine-gun was still greater than the offensive power of the tank, he envisaged the day when the tank would be able to outmanœuvre infantry weapons, and set himself the task of providing the Red Army with the necessary armoured vehicles and supporting equipment. For basically his aim was to make the Red Army as a whole (and here he opposed those who advocated a small compact mobile army with devastating fire power) move at the speed of vehicles and not that of marching men.

In pursuit of this aim, Tukhachevski, in his capacity as Head of Armaments, set up the first 'mechanized brigade' in the Red Army in 1930. It was composed of two tank and two motorized battalions with artillery and reconnaissance support. In 1932 the mechanized brigades were judged sufficiently successful for their organization in mechanized corps, and in the same year an Academy of Mechanization and Motorization came into existence to study armoured warfare and the spread of motor vehicles throughout the Red Army. Exercises held in the years 1933-36 experimented with co-operation between infantry, cavalry, armour and aircraft in encirclement operations, and it is probably no coincidence that the Red Army generals who carried out the great encirclement operations of the second World War, such as Stalingrad, Korsun-Shevchenkovo and Minsk in 1942-45, were middle-grade commanders in cavalry or armoured units in the western military districts of the Soviet Union when these exercises were conducted. Another experiment was the creation of parachute units in 1931, and their employment in the seizure of ground ahead of advancing armour and infantry. Other units were transported by air, and in 1936 a whole rifle division was carried from the Far East to western Russia by transport aircraft of the Red Air Force.

Big organizational changes in the Red Army took place in 1934 which gave the military commander greater authority over his unit and his political commissar, and regulated ranks and discipline along the traditional lines of an orthodox army. By this time, too, the results of the Five Year Plans were making their appearance in the forces: the tank park had reached 7,000 in 1935, and was backed by 100,000 military lorries and 150,000 tractors. As a result of his experiments from 1930-35, Tukhachevski, who was promoted Marshal of the Soviet Union in that year, formulated his military doctrine in new Field Regulations, published in 1936. The Regulations emphasized that victory in war could only be won by an offensive carried out at speed and maintained by full co-operation between all arms. Infantry, supported by tanks, artillery and airpower, would decide the land battle; the artillery, tanks and ground-attack aircraft were to break open the enemy's defensive system, which would then be seized and held by the infantry. The artillery was also to be responsible for assisting the armour by destroying the enemy's anti-tank fire power, so that the armoured forces could be used on a massed scale. Tanks and mechanized troops should be used at corps strength and not distributed in small units in support of infantry formations.

A ground offensive operation should be carried out by forming 'assault groups' composed of infantry, tanks and artillery and launching them at the weakest point in the enemy's line. When one or more of these groups had succeeded, the commander threw in 'support groups' backed by artillery fire. When a decisive break-through was achieved the commander used all the mobile means at his disposal—tanks, lorry-borne and tank-borne infantry and cavalry—to split up the enemy's units and form local encirclements in which the enemy would be pounded by artillery fire and air attack. These operations would be followed by pursuit, in which parachute and air-borne units would join armoured forces and cavalry in driving forward as far as possible into enemy territory. The Regulations also dealt extensively with defensive operations, and emphasized all-round fire protection of defensive positions and the need for constant counter-attacks.

These Field Regulations clearly owed all that was best in them to imaginative thinking by military theorists and planners, but although these types of operations had been practised in exercises, the Red Army's training was not up to the high standards of the Regulations. Western military observers who attended Soviet manœuvres in 1936 noted that the troops being exercised largely ignored the Regulations, carried out frontal attacks with wooden persistence and paid little attention to co-operation between the arms of service. Nevertheless, although the doctrine was slow in penetrating to all levels of a mass Army such as the Soviets had, it did exist in the High Command, and certainly compared favourably with similar theory in France, Japan or Italy.

Before further progress could be made Stalin's purge struck the Red Army, and for two years, from 1937 to 1939, the Soviet officer corps was virtually cut to pieces. Thousands of commanders, staff officers and political advisers were shot or imprisoned; three out of five Marshals were executed (Tukhachevski, Blyukher and Yegorov), and those who succeeded them were in many cases unfit for their high posts and out of tune with the military thought of their predecessors. The new Head of Armaments, later promoted to be Marshal Kulik, drew the erroneous conclusion from the Spanish Civil War that the day of the large armoured formation was over, and ordered the disbandment of the mechanized corps, and the re-subordination of the armoured forces as independent tank brigades and tank battalions attached to rifle divisions. He deprived the infantry of automatic weapons and the ground forces of an effective anti-aircraft gun. It was fortunate for the Red Army that the two 'local' wars against the Japanese during the period of the purge (the battles of Lake Khassan in 1938 and Khalkhin-Gol in 1939) were handled by men who had absorbed the new doctrines: respectively Marshal Blyukher and the future Marshal Zhukov. Indeed, the encirclement of the Japanese Sixth Army on the Outer Mongolian frontier planned and executed by Zhukov was effective and swift, though it was achieved at a heavy cost in Soviet casualties. But when the Red Army attempted to take on an invasion of Finland in the winter of 1939-40 its chronic shortcomings reached disastrous dimensions. Indeed, until Marshal Timoshenko took overall command in February 1940, and thoroughly trained Soviet assault and support troops in the storming of fixed defences with all-round fire support, the new 'post-purge' generation of Soviet commanders abandoned all they had been taught of modern methods, and flung their infantry at the Finnish strong-points with complete disregard for human loss.

Among the many lessons of the Finnish war (and of the successful German campaigns in Poland and France) which the Soviet military leaders digested was, once again, the need for large armoured formations, better handling of troops by senior commanders and an improvement in signals and radio communications. The first led to the re-establishment of twenty-five mechanized corps early in 1941, and the deployment of covering armies along the Soviet Union's western frontier consisting of two rifle and one mechanized corps, a total of five or six rifle divisions, two tank divisions and one motorized division. Some armies also had a cavalry corps under command.

As far as military thought was concerned, this was a period when the Army leaders, impressed by the excellence of much of the equipment which was arriving from the armaments factories— the T.34 tank had begun to reach the new tank divisions in 1941— allowed themselves to slip into the facile optimism of the political leaders on the subject of an enemy attack on the Soviet Union. If such an attack took place, they maintained, it would be halted on the frontier, and the war would immediately be carried on to the aggressor's territory. True, the spirit of the offensive was still there, and morale in the Army was high; but it was a spirit which ignored or suppressed the danger signals contained in Germany's great successes with armour and Army–Air co-operation. Perhaps the most extreme case of this misunderstanding of the realities of warfare was the Directive issued by the Defence Commissariat on 22nd June 1941 after the German attack had been under way for some hours. This called for the halting of the German invaders, but the Red Army was not to pursue them over the frontier until further orders were received.

The shock of the German invasion caught the Red Army unprepared for defence against Blitzkrieg and in the middle of the reorganization of its armoured forces and redeployment of troops in the frontier areas. The powerful German armoured groups of Generals Hoeppner, Hoth, Guderian and von Kleist cut through the Soviet covering armies, encircled two of them west of Minsk, and raced to the rivers Dvina and Dnieper, where second-line Russian formations were concentrating. A bloody and prolonged battle developed round Smolensk which held up the German advance for two months, but which bled the Russian armies in the centre white, and opened the way to a series of military disasters unparalleled in Russian history. In the north, the Germans broke through to the gates of Leningrad and cut the city off from the rest of Russia; in the south, the weakened Russian centre allowed the Germans to advance on Kiev from the north, and a break-through in the Ukraine led to the encirclement of the city and 250,000 Soviet troops. Worse still was to come, for in October almost the whole of the Soviet Western Front was trapped east of Smolensk, including all or part of eight armies, and the German Army began its march on Moscow. Here, however, the invaders were checked; the Soviet mobilization was beginning to affect the man-power balance, and by gathering round Moscow the dozen or so generals who had emerged from the long and bitter retreat with credit, the High Command created the con-ditions for a holding victory in front of the capital. Moreover, the German Army was itself exhausted, and the fierce Russian winter had affected the Germans more adversely than the Red Army, whose morale was also raised by the fact that they were defending their own capital. Moscow was a Russian victory, though, thanks to the tenacity and professionalism of crack units of the German Army, defeat was not turned into a rout.

The Red Army emerged from its six-month-long ordeal severely chastened. Much of its leaders' confidence had gone and, in spite of the Moscow victory, intense pessimism over the possibilities of beating the Germans was widespread among those who had faced the full fury of the invaders' onslaught. Within the General Staff, however, the problems of readjusting not only tactics and fighting methods, but also basic issues of military thought, to the German war were tackled painstakingly and comprehensively. A Directorate for the Evaluation of War Experience was set up in the General Staff in 1942 and, although we have no direct evidence of the type of analytical work carried out by this Directorate, it seems reasonable to assume that part of its task was to assess the errors and shortcomings of Soviet military thought. On the one hand, the Germans had shown the value of the offensive, of massed armoured strikes and of skilled ground–air co-operation; on the other, Soviet military thinkers had provided little answer to the problem of defeating such operations. There is some evidence from the Soviet military press in the period 1959-60 that this debate over pre-1941 Soviet military thought was still in progress, and that the issue was between those who blamed prewar thinkers for having failed to consider defence against an enemy strategic offensive and those who claimed that the basic work on this had been done, but that Stalin's political assessment of the type of war which the Red Army might have to wage ruled out practical training and exercises in the field of strategic defence. It is interesting to note that one very authoritative commentator writing in 1961 came down firmly on the side of the critics of prewar military thought, though, from the limited amount of information available, it would seem that the second view also had much to recommend it.

After the Battle of Moscow both sides prepared furiously to seize the initiative for the summer campaign of 1942, and it was in fact the Russians who struck first in the Ukraine and on the sector south and south-east of Leningrad. Their offensives were, however, ill planned and badly carried out, and played into the hands of the local German Army group commanders. While the Soviet Second Shock Army was destroyed south of Leningrad (and its commander, General Vlasov, went over to the Germans), Marshal Timoshenko lost three armies in the Donets Basin, and was unable to prevent a subsequent strategic break-through by the Germans to the Don and the Volga, and into the Caucasus. The Russians recoiled into the industrial city of Stalingrad, where they dug themselves in, and succeeded in holding on to a small strip of territory on the west bank of the Volga, and in forcing the Germans to throw in more and more men and materials to effect the capture of this city whose very name seemed to have mesmerized Hitler. By October 1942, the Germans had over 300,000 men concentrated in the head of a great salient from the Don to the Volga, but left the flanks along the Don and across the North Caucasian steppes guarded by Rumanian and Italian troops. With this situation in mind, the Soviet Supreme Headquarters, with advice from the local Stalingrad Front Command, planned a strategic encirclement of the German Group by a pincer movement north and south of Stalingrad aimed at the sectors manned by satellite troops. A big concentration of troops was built up in conditions of great secrecy and, on 19th November, the Russians struck. The satellite flanks collapsed, and in spite of mistakes and miscalculations on the Soviet side, the two arms of the pincer met west of Stalingrad on 23rd November. Three months later the frozen and starving remnants of the German Sixth Army capitulated, and the Russians had won their first strategic victory with mobile forces. One feature of the Russian counter-offensive was that the northern arm of the pincer was spearheaded by a Tank Army consisting of two tank corps, a cavalry corps and six rifle divisions, a formation based largely on Tukhachevski's concept of the massed use of tanks and cavalry in his 1936 Field Regulations. Although the Commander of this Tank Army was not a success, the High Command learned many lessons from the Army's operations and, when the next major clash with the Germans came at Kursk in the summer of 1943, the composition of the Tank Army had been altered to exclude the cavalry and the infantry, and to back up the two tank corps with a heavy mechanized corps.

The Battle of Kursk, in which the Russians resisted the temptation to pre-empt or forestall the German attack, marked a landmark in the Soviet-German duel in that for the first time the Russians did what they claimed to have been able to do in 1941: they met and defeated a German offensive where they stood. In exceptionally heavy fighting from 5th July to 5th August, the Russians beat off attacks launched by nearly one million Germans, and then brought up three Tank Armies (the Third, Fourth and Fifth)[1] to break through the German lines and lead a pursuit to the Dnieper river. Part of the Third Tank Army, under General Rybalko, successfully forced the Dnieper near Kiev from the line of march, and then held a bridgehead defensively against fierce German counter-attacks—a good example of the versatility of the new Soviet mobile forces. It should be noted, however, that an attempt to use air-borne troops in a crossing of the Dnieper failed, and these troops were not employed again in this role in the Soviet-German war.

The campaigns of 1944 and 1945 which ended with the capture of Berlin and Vienna and the occupation of eastern and central Europe witnessed the perfection of the battle techniques and strategies which had emerged gradually and painfully since 1941. A further specialization of troops in the assault role developed with the formation of Guards and Shock Armies: there were eleven of the former and five of the latter in 1944-45. These were normally manned formations which were, however, especially well supplied in artillery and mortars, and undertook the initial assaults on prepared positions at the beginning of offensives. Tank and mechanized armies and corps were quickly moved into the breaches made by these armies—sometimes, as on Marshal Konev's sector in the Berlin operation, on the evening of the first day—and launched out in pursuit and encirclement of the enemy (cavalry was brought up to operate in marshy or wooded country), acting in close co-operation with the tactical air armies attached to each Front. Almost every operation contained or ended in one or more encirclements of large German forces, while the mass armies of a predominantly infantry composition followed up, liquidating pockets of resistance and occupying and defending enemy strong-points. In some operations—for example, the invasion of East Prussia and the storm of Königsberg—the infantry armies attacked on secondary sectors simultaneously with the Guards or Shock Armies, and sometimes took over from the assault formations when the latter suffered exceptionally heavy casualties.

In most respects, therefore, the Red Army which reached Berlin and Vienna had indeed developed into the kind of force which Tukhachevski and his associates had recommended and foreseen in the period 1930-36. It had the mass character which, as a Russian dealing with Russia's geography, he demanded as an essential prerequisite for success. Its commanders had learned to use tanks in the mass—in 1945 one Front commander had up to 1,700 tanks at his disposal—and it had kept and improved on the spirit of the offensive and of battlefield manœuvre. True, it still had some crippling shortcomings in 1945: the slow horse-drawn carts for bringing up supplies, the primitive medical and

administrative services on secondary sectors, and the poor standard of intelligence and initiative of some of the recruits of the later
war years. But it must be remembered that to this day there are no
complete figures of total Soviet losses, and the call-up had had
to dig deeply into the very young and elderly age groups. This
writer personally met boys of sixteen in the Red Army in 1945
and one infantryman who had lost an eye in the Russo-Japanese
war of 1904-5.

The year 1945 was not only the end of a victorious war, but the
beginning of the atomic era, in which military thinkers were faced
with the need to re-cast many of their basic principles in an
attempt to determine the real significance of atomic weapons
should war break out again. Yet, while the West embarked on
this task within and outside government circles, the atom bomb
ushered in a period of stagnation in Soviet military thought.
Among the reasons for this was the reluctance of Stalin to
attribute decisive significance to a weapon which the Soviet Union
did not possess: he described it in 1946 as a device 'to terrify the
weak-nerved', and said it was not able to win wars. There is
slight evidence from Soviet military journals in 1945-46 of some
attempt by experienced commanders to develop new ideas on
warfare, but by 1947 all writing had become subject to Stalin's
dead hand. Military doctrine was officially compressed into five
'constant factors' enunciated by Stalin in a speech shortly after
the Battle of Moscow, at a time when an important aspect of the
struggles between Germany and Russia was endurance versus
battlefield experience. Stalin's five factors were: stability of the
home front, morale of the armed forces, quantity and quality of
the Army's divisions, quantity and quality of armaments, and the
abilities of the commanders. Valid though each of these factors
was, to ignore the importance of surprise and of mass destruction
which atomic weapons could cause was condemning military
thinkers to idleness and over-confidence, and the Army as a
whole to ignorance of the realities of war. Moreover, Stalin
continued to envisage a third World War in terms of a ground-
based campaign in Europe, and maintained 175 rifle, tank and
mechanized divisions and forty artillery and anti-aircraft divisions

on active service in the Red Army (renamed the Soviet Army in 1946). There is some evidence that Stalin also viewed his vast Army deployed in eastern Europe and western Russia as a deterrent force which could overrun western Europe if the Americans threatened to use their monopoly of the atomic bomb to launch an aerial attack on the Soviet Union. But the fact remains that, while Stalin lived, Soviet military thinkers were not allowed to go into even classified print on the true significance of atomic and nuclear weapons or to discuss the American strategic air threat to Soviet targets. One after another the distinguished Soviet Marshals repeated the 'Stalinist' formula of the five constant factors and, what is most extraordinary, they were required to do this at a time when Soviet defence scientists, engineers and constructors had been given the go-ahead to develop advanced aircraft, missiles (including the I.C.B.M., which was not thought practicable at that time—1946-49—in the United States) and atomic and nuclear weapons. We can only conclude that Stalin's prudence (and ambition) led him to authorize the acquisition of the latest kinds of weapons, but his native suspicion and conservatism made him reluctant to abandon methods of warfare which he felt he understood and had mastered during the second World War. Moreover, his jealousy and vanity would probably not allow him to permit his military advisers to speculate in the field of war and military doctrine in ways which might give them an advantage over himself in knowledge and understanding of new techniques; knowledge which, to his excessively suspicious nature, could conceivably provide the military men, who had force at their disposal, with the kind of lever of power which Stalin had feared in 1937-39, when he weakened the defence potential of the country to secure his own personal position of power.

In these circumstances it is not surprising that within months of Stalin's death in March 1953 a comprehensive debate on military thought began among members of the Soviet High Command on the problems of war in the nuclear age. Among the most prominent contributors were Major-General N. A. Talenski, a long-service General Staff officer; Army-General P. A. Kurochkin,

Head of the Frunze Military Academy; and Marshal of Armoured Forces P. A. Rotmistrov, Head of the Armoured Forces Academy. For two years the Soviet Marshals and Generals argued among themselves, enjoying the unaccustomed freedom of debate, and in 1955 emerged with a military doctrine which they believed corresponded to the potential American threat and to Soviet military capabilities. Briefly, the consensus of opinion was that the American Strategic Air Command was capable of penetrating Soviet air defences and attacking almost any targets on Soviet territory with nuclear weapons, and that this ought to be the main factor in considering Soviet military policies. Secondly, the Soviet forces ought to be in a position to blunt any American air attack by improving the country's own air defences and by the ability to destroy at least a part of the American strike force at its air and naval bases *before* it was launched—if completely accurate information reached Moscow of an imminent American attack. This was the so-called 'pre-emptive strike' policy, which was, in fact, rejected by Mr Khrushchev as being too risky and unreliable. Thirdly, the debaters recommended ground and air forces reduced in size, made more mobile and with greater fire-power, including tactical nuclear weapons. One aspect of this recommendation which was implied but not spelt out in the argument was that, in view of the high levels of radiation which would be inflicted on Soviet territory by an American nuclear attack, a highly mobile army and air force would have a better chance of breaking out of eastern Europe and the Soviet Union in a rapid campaign against the N.A.T.O. powers (and perhaps also in the Middle East) and thus escaping from heavily irradiated Soviet territory than would the more cumbersome army of Stalin's day.

With the exception of the doctrine of pre-emption, this military doctrine was accepted by the Party leadership, and organizational changes based upon it began in the Soviet forces in 1955. The Air Defence Command was raised to the status of a fourth 'Branch' of the Armed Forces (along with the Army, Navy and Air Force) and the new headquarters combined fighter, missile and anti-aircraft artillery under the command of a Marshal of the Soviet

Union. Progressive reductions in the ground and air forces produced by 1959 a more mobile conventional force which, however, increased its fire power by the introduction of tactical missiles carrying nuclear warheads. Overall Soviet fire power against N.A.T.O. Europe was maintained and increased by a steady build-up of medium-range ballistic missiles in western Russia able to hit targets in Britain, West Germany, France and Italy with nuclear weapons. At the same time the General Staff and the Military Academies produced a tactical doctrine for waging ground and air warfare in a nuclear setting. According to this doctrine, nuclear fire power on the battlefield should be used to destroy the enemy's nuclear weapons and to break up his defences: dependent on the degree and type of destruction achieved, the ground and air forces should then, and only then, be given their tasks in exploitation of the nuclear strike, which might include occupation of territory, destruction of isolated pockets of resistance, or pursuit of a weakened or fleeing enemy. Troops should advance at great speed along widely separated axes, and field commanders would be expected to operate with considerable initiative, seizing what opportunities they could to further their advance.

This tactical doctrine, evolved on the basis of the work of Soviet military thinkers in the General Staff and the Military Academies, has remained valid until today, and is not likely to undergo major alteration in the years immediately ahead. The ability of ground troops to pass through zones contaminated by radiation by means of sealed armoured vehicles, underwater river-crossings, and the use of personal protective clothing is constantly being exercised and no doubt will improve. On the other hand, the Soviet Union faces the same doubts and uncertainties as do we in the West in assessing the actual effect of the use of nuclear weapons in combat on the troops involved and on the civilian population. So far, the Soviets have assumed that well-trained troops will be able to overcome the shock of the use of these weapons and carry out their allotted tasks at all levels, although this must surely remain the biggest question-mark in contemporary warfare.

The field in which Soviet military thought has changed in emphasis since 1955 is in the broader field of politico-military strategy. Some time in 1959, helped by his visit to President Eisenhower at Camp David, and by his knowledge of the progress of Soviet intercontinental ballistic missile development which was approaching operational status two years after the first successful firing of August 1957, Mr Khrushchev came to the conclusion that the United States, under responsible leadership, no longer felt the temptation to use its strategic power to launch a surprise nuclear attack on the Soviet Union—and said so in public. He believed that the deterrent power of both strategic weapons systems was roughly equally effective, and in this he was helped by the growing legend that the Soviet Union had overtaken the United States in strategic power by means of a short cut through the I.C.B.M. Mr Khrushchev established the Strategic Rocket Forces as a fifth 'Branch' of the Armed Forces in January 1960, announcing that they were to be the main type of armed force and that priority would be given to their growth in numbers and perfection in quality. This would also allow the Soviet Government to cut defence expenditure on other arms of service, and cut the man-power of the surface Navy, the Tactical Air Force and the Army by one-third. There was therefore a significant swing away from the traditional Soviet reliance on the superiority of ground forces towards an entirely new concept for the Russians: deterrence through strategic power.

The only trouble with this change of emphasis, as the Soviet leaders found out after the *détente* atmosphere of Camp David had disappeared on the collapse of the Summit Meeting in Paris in May 1960, was that the Soviet Strategic Rocket Forces, although the first in the field experimentally, were not able to keep up with the American production capabilities, once reliable systems such as Polaris and Minuteman began to be deployed. The programme of strategic force development announced by President Kennedy in March 1961 foreshadowed a target of 800 Minutemen I.C.B.M.s (later raised to 1,500) and forty-five Polaris submarines, while the Soviet programme was probably running in the region of 75-100 I.C.B.M.s with twenty missile-firing submarines for the same period.² In these circumstances it is not surprising that Mr Khrushchev should have made an attempt to solve the Berlin problem by intimidation in 1961 before these American strategic forces—and similar increases in American Army and Air Force strengths—became effective. Nor is it surprising that the Soviet government should have unilaterally resumed testing nuclear weapons in 1961, with a strong emphasis on very-high-yield weapons—up to fifty-eight megatons in one case. In fact, it is probably true to say that the Cuban missile crisis which dominated 1962 had, along with many political and psychological aims, the goal of reducing the gap between American and Soviet strategic power by establishing an expendable strategic strike force base within 100 miles of U.S. territory which geographically outflanked the American early-warning network.

The Cuban adventure, however, failed, and since mid-1963 the Soviet Government has encouraged the growth of a *détente* in East–West relations, and has returned to an up-to-date version of its 1960 defence policy, including renewed emphasis on the primacy of its strategic missile forçes and small reductions in man-power in the other branches of the Armed Forces and in the defence budget. It is impossible to assess the duration of the present *détente*, but it is likely that there now exist sound military reasons, which both military thinkers and responsible commanders would support, for continued decrease in tension for the foreseeable future. Clearly the Soviet economy cannot overtake the production capability of the United States in numbers of strategic delivery vehicles. While the use of very large warheads by the Russians may in certain circumstances offset the unfavourable balance to a limited degree, generally speaking the Soviet Union is likely to have settled down to living with the concept of strategic inferiority. This involves the adoption of a foreign policy of low risks where the United States or N.A.T.O. is directly concerned, and the steady growth of the Strategic Rocket Forces, the Long Range Air Force and the nuclear-powered and ballistic-firing submarine elements of the Navy. It also involves extensive research into air defence techniques, particularly anti-ballistic missile weapons systems, in which the Soviet Union and the United

States were in 1963 at about the same stage. Finally, Soviet military doctrine and planning will continue to lay great stress on the role of the ground forces in any hostilities in the European theatre, and will aim at increasing the fire power (nuclear and conventional), mobility and standard of training of its forces in central and eastern Europe.

To sum up, military thought in the Soviet Union has had a chequered career. At one time, in the early 1920's, the revolutionary upheaval in Russia was so great that military thinkers after the civil war had very nearly a clear field to work in, and the restrictive nature of tradition was reduced to almost nothing. Out of these early debates two concepts emerged: that the essential requirements were the offensive and mobility; and there can be little doubt that at this point the writings of forward-looking military thinkers abroad had considerable influence on practical organizers in the Red Army such as Marshal Tukhachevski. With the Army purge and the emergence of an inexperienced generation of commanders, the doctrine of the offensive became distorted into a grossly over-confident political tenet, which played a large part in the disasters of the early part of the Soviet-German war.

After the war, in which a practical doctrine of the employment of mobile shock groups was welded on to the traditional advantages provided by Soviet man-power strength, military thought went into a period of decline under Stalin. It was not until 1955 that full consideration was given to the vulnerability of Soviet targets to air and missile attack, and since then official military thinkers have grappled—in the main along similar lines to their Western counterparts—with the problems of the use of nuclear weapons, both strategically and on the tactical battlefield. Two points really underlie this analysis of Soviet military thought: first, that there are no unofficial free-lance military thinkers in the Soviet Union, no genuine defence correspondents attached to Soviet newspapers, and no non-governmental institutes where problems of defence and warfare can be thrashed out in public. Therefore, we in the West only discover a tiny proportion of the argument which must go on behind the closed doors of the General Staff and in the Military Academies. Secondly, the Soviet

Union has been ruled since 1945 (with one brief interval from 1953-55) until recently by two men, Stalin and Khrushchev, each of whom regarded himself as an expert on military matters, and was prepared to use the full weight of his political power to have his views on military thought accepted by the Armed Forces. What is, perhaps, most intriguing is the possibility that the strictly professional military thinkers within the defence establishment will now exercise more influence on the defence thinking of the new political leaders than under Mr Khrushchev. If so, the body of military thinkers and theoreticians may be nearer to the seat of power in the Soviet Union than in any other major power in the second half of the twentieth century.

NOTES

1. The First and Second Tank Armies had been operating in the second echelon of the Kursk defensive deployment, and part of the First Tank Army dug its tanks into the ground and used them as static firing points.
2. Figures based on the *Military Balance* for 1961-63 (pub. Institute for Strategic Studies, London).

§12§
American Strategic Doctrine and Diplomacy

HENRY A. KISSINGER

The Nature of Modern Power

The technical characteristics of modern weapons are well known. We are aware that humanity has the power to destroy itself in a matter of hours. Any place on the earth can be demolished from any other in minutes. Offensive power has far outstripped defensive power. Even a defence that is ninety per cent effective may not be able to prevent catastrophic damage.

But the conclusion to be drawn from this state of affairs is not so obvious. Some believe that if the risks have become incomparably greater, the essential principles of strategy have stayed the same. For others war has become unthinkable; they ask that diplomacy settle all conflicts through the exercise of negotiating skill.

Each view has its difficulty. If massive quantitative changes can bring about qualitative ones, then the increase in destructiveness threatened by nuclear weapons must be considered crucial. A basic discontinuity is established when a statesman is compelled to risk tens of millions of lives instead of thousands, when his decision no longer involves the loss of a province but the survival of society itself. Even if the classical principles of strategy are not entirely outmoded, the statesman will inevitably be reluctant to put them to the test.

However, to say that the unqualified reign of diplomacy has begun is an equal over-simplification. If war has now become the last resort of desperate men, this has not made diplomacy any easier. On the contrary, it has made it more intractable. In the past, unsuccessful negotiations never returned matters to their starting-point; they called other pressures into play. But many of these pressures are no longer available, and thus diplomacy, too, has become less flexible. Where no penalty for non-compliance exists, there is no incentive to reach agreement. As statesmen have become increasingly reluctant to resort to war, negotiations have become more and more ritualistic.

Therefore, any assessment of the impact of power on diplomacy must begin with a discussion of the characteristics of power in the nuclear age. A few definitions may be useful:

1. *Offensive power* is the ability of a political unit to impose its will on another.

2. *Defensive power* is the ability of a state to avoid coercion by another.

Defensive power may be further subdivided into purely defensive policy and precautionary policy. Power has a purely defensive use when a country waits for a threat to materialize before dealing with it. It is used in a precautionary manner when policy is directed towards preventing potential and not actual challenges. The policy of the United States before the second World War was purely defensive, its tendency being to allow threats to become unambiguous and then to muster every effort to overcome them. This could be afforded because the wide margin of survival guaranteed that no conceivable early reverse could menace the national interest.

Britain's policy in the eighteenth and nineteenth centuries illustrates the precautionary mode of action. Britain acted on the principle that Antwerp must not fall into the hands of the major powers. This was not because of any certainty that such an event would have hostile implications, but rather because Britain would no longer be strong enough to resist if the worst occurred.

3. *Deterrent power* is the ability to prevent certain threats or actions from being carried out by posing an equivalent or greater threat.

There is no inevitable symmetry between offensive and defensive power. Some states have had little of the first but much of the second. Switzerland, for example, has managed to combine inaccessibility of terrain with the ability to mobilize a considerable proportion of the national resources. States in this position have been able to prevent other countries from imposing their will. On the other hand, they have not played a very active role in international affairs.

Power has no absolute measurement; it is always relative. In the seventeenth century it would have been futile to try to compare the power of Japan with that of Great Britain, since they possessed no means of bringing their strength to bear on each other. This geographical separation of power remained a fact until the middle of the nineteenth century. And after that, one small continent, Europe, was physically far superior to the rest and could dictate international affairs.

Power also depends on psychological as well as objective factors. Until it is actually used, it is what people think it is.

These characteristics of power have been further complicated in the modern period. For one thing, the impact of modern power is now world-wide. The major nuclear countries are able to devastate any part of the globe from their own territories. Moreover, they have become the chief opponents of one another. At the moment when the risks of power have never been greater, foreign policy has become truly global.

These risks are especially heightened because offensive power is now far superior to defensive power. No defensive system in existence or being envisaged seems capable of preventing damage incomparably more devastating than any society has ever experienced. This has caused the distinction between precautionary and defensive foreign policy to erode. In view of the perils, foreign policy would seem to have to be precautionary. Its aim would be to keep potential enemies from acquiring a potentially disastrous offensive power. But the actual policy of the major powers has become a defensive one, designed not to prevent the accumulation of hostile capability but to retaliate against attack—when for many reasons it may already prove too late.

Deterrent power has become the most significant aspect of contemporary strategy. However, deterrence is above all a psychological problem. The assessment of risks on which it depends becomes less and less precise in the face of weapons of unprecedented novelty and destructiveness. A bluff taken seriously is more useful than a serious threat interpreted as a bluff. Strategy henceforth cannot confine itself to expertise in designing weapons systems, but must involve a close understanding of the opponent's calculations.

Moreover, deterrence proves its mettle negatively, for just as long as things do *not* happen. Unfortunately it is never easy to show why something has not occurred. Success may seem to have been won by the best strategic theories or by barely tolerable ones. It is also possible to maintain that the country against which defensive preparations are taken never had any intention of attacking in the first place. Thus successful deterrence can furnish arguments to sustain obsolescent theories and designs, or it can encourage neutralism. It provides little incentive for the kind of innovation, political and strategic, consistent with a rapidly changing technology.

In short, power has grown disproportionate to most of the objectives in dispute. No matter what spectrum of power the major contenders may dispose of, the fear of escalation is inescapable. Thus the major nuclear powers recoil from the direct use of force against each other. They have the capacity to destroy each other, but this fact works to reduce their ability to threaten because the threat is not credible and the risks are too great. This poses an unprecedented challenge to those formulating strategic doctrine.

Strategic Doctrine and the Domestic Consensus

In devising its strategy, every advanced country has more technical choices than it can afford. Whether it chooses missiles with large or small warheads, whether it emphasizes nuclear or conventional power, will depend more on its strategic doctrine than on the technology available to it. But strategic doctrine must not become something theoretical or dogmatic. Its role is to define the likely dangers and how to deal with them, to project feasible goals and methods of attaining them. It must furnish a mode of action for the circumstances it defines as 'ordinary'. Its adequacy will be tested according to whether these ordinary events do in fact occur and whether the forces developed in their anticipation are adequate to deal with the real challenges.

In the inter-war period French strategic doctrine exalted the value of the defensive and built its plans around the Maginot Line. However, the likely German attempts to overthrow the Treaty of Versailles could be prevented only by French offensive action. In other words, by the time the Maginot Line might prove useful, the Versailles settlement would already have been overturned. Thus the French strategic doctrine contributed to the paralysis of French policy. When German armies reoccupied the Rhineland and attacked France's allies in eastern Europe, French power remained passive and French diplomacy stood impotent. Even when the long-awaited attack in the West finally came, it turned the flank of the French fortifications.

A wrong strategic doctrine can lead to disaster. An excessively rigid strategic doctrine can absorb great energy in the attempt to reconcile what happens with what is expected. If it is too complicated, it can break down under the stress of decision-making. The Schlieffen Plan, Germany's military design for the first World War, provided for every contingency except the psychological strain on the commander. It failed largely because the German leaders lost their nerve. In the face of Russian advances into eastern Germany—foreseen by the Schlieffen Plan—they rushed reinforcements from the west, weakening their offensive power at the crucial moment. It adds to the irony of the situation that these reinforcements were in transit when the decisive battles in both the east *and* the west were being fought.

But if there is no doctrine at all and a society operates pragmatically, solving problems 'on their merits' as the saying goes, every event becomes a special case. More energy is spent deciding where one is than where one is going. Each event is compartmentalized and dealt with by experts in the special difficulties it involves without an adequate understanding of its relation to other occurrences. This is the risk United States policy has been running since it undertook the stewardship of the Free World.

To be effective, a strategy must fulfil several requirements. It must be able to win a domestic consensus, among both the technical and the political leadership. It must be understood by the opponents to the extent needed for effective deterrence. It must receive allied endorsement if alliances are to remain cohesive. It must be relevant to the problems in the uncommitted areas so as to discourage international anarchy. Unfortunately, the reconciliation of these various tasks is far from easy and perhaps impossible.

The nature of power has never been easy to assess; but in the nuclear age this problem is complicated by the immense destructiveness of weapons and the rapid change of technology. Though risks are enormous, power has become ever more intangible. The weapons are novel and abstract—and everything depends on them. The debate over the Nuclear Test Ban Treaty focused attention on the question of the adequacy of nuclear warheads. But in fact other weapons-systems components contain many more uncertainties. We know only by theory the estimated hardness of Minutemen silos, and relatively few missiles of each category have been proof-tested. There is little experience with salvo firing, and air defence systems must be designed without knowledge of the specifics of the offence. Each series of nuclear tests always produced a considerable number of unexpected phenomena.

Difficult as it is to be certain about the technical characteristics of weapons systems, the uses of modern arms are even more debatable. What threats, for example, can one make with solid-fuel missiles? If weapons are in an extreme state of natural readiness, how can one demonstrate the increased preparedness that historically has served as a warning? It is probable that missiles can perform most of the technical functions heretofore assigned to aeroplanes and that the gradual phasing out of bombers therefore makes good technical sense. But has adequate thought been given to the kind of diplomacy which results from a retaliatory threat depending largely on solid-fuel missiles in underground silos? During the Cuban crisis of October 1962, an effective warning was conveyed by dispersing bombers to civilian airports. What equivalent tactic can we employ when strategic forces are composed entirely of missiles?

By questions like these the contemporary strategic debate is given a theoretical, almost metaphysical character. An ever-widening gap has appeared between the sophistication of technical studies and the capacity of an already over-worked leadership group to absorb their intricacy. It is unlikely that even the most conscientious President can devote as many hours to a given problem as the analyst has had years to study it. He will have to work with approximations, and his decisions will have to be made under stress. Even if he perfectly comprehends the logical symmetry of a strategic theory, he must also weigh the consequences of its failure. In other words, there is a danger that doctrines of too great a complexity could bring about the kind of psychological failure which we noted in connection with the Schlieffen Plan in 1914.

Inevitable problems of confidence and competence between the technical and political levels of domestic decision-making may make it difficult to implement a strategic doctrine. Architects of strategy need a continual awareness that their audience is not a group of colleagues of similar technical competence but of hard-pressed individuals for whom strategy can be but one of a number of concerns. Thus excessive complexity may lead to paralysis. The strategists must at every stage ask of the decision-maker: Does he understand the doctrine? Does he believe in it? Will the doctrine meet emergencies or provide an excuse for inaction? Does it instil a sense of mastery or produce a feeling of impotence? What does the decision-maker really mean when he accepts a strategy? Does he accept it with the notion: In prescribed circumstances this is what I will do, I will do nothing? A wise student of strategy will not fail to understand that technique can never be an end in itself, and that policy ultimately depends on the intangibles of motivation and purpose and will.

U.S. Strategic Thought

Considerations such as these are especially relevant to the strategic debate as it has developed in the United States since the second World War. The United States emerged from the war in a position of unchallenged military superiority. The war seemed to have confirmed all traditional American strategic axioms. The United States despite its late mobilization had, together with its allies, crushed the aggressor. Victory had been achieved by a massive outpouring of material. Strategic bombing, in which the United States could engage without fear of retaliation, was seen by many as a key to victory and victory was conceived in terms of unconditional surrender.

Inevitably this caused American strategic thought in the post-war period to start as an adaptation of the second World War maxims. Nuclear weapons were incorporated into existing practices as a more efficient explosive. 'Plans for national security', said General Omar N. Bradley in 1948, 'must consider the possibility that the United States will be subject to air and airborne attack at the outset. The likelihood and the practicability of this kind of attack increases daily. . . . We would [therefore] have to immediately secure bases from which an enemy might attack us by air. Next we will have to launch an immediate counter-attack . . . predominantly through the air. . . . To make our counter-blows we will need bases which we do not have now. The seizing and holding of [these] bases . . . will require Army combat elements. . . . Lastly comes the phase of total mobilization and maximum offensive efforts. In conjunction with the air and naval arms, the Army will engage in joint operations designed to carry the war to the enemy with ever-increasing intensity. The closer we get to the enemy, the more determined will be his resistance. . . .'[1] The theory of massive retaliation was far from new when Secretary Dulles proclaimed it.

During the 1950's it became evident that the growth of Soviet long-range nuclear power presented new problems. For the first time an aggressor could mount a threat to the United States not only from outlying bases but from its homeland. The subtle studies of Albert Wohlstetter demonstrated the vulnerability of the U.S. Strategic Air Command.[2] Wohlstetter insisted that the strategic balance was 'delicate' depending on such factors as the vulnerability of the bases of the retaliatory force, the relative state of active and passive defence and the ability to read enemy targets.

Though Wohlstetter's intention was to call attention to the vulnerability of U.S. strategic forces, a consequence of his theory was to give a new lease of life to traditional notions of total victory. For, by reversing the focus of his concern, it was possible to demonstrate that victory in a general nuclear war was still a significant concept.

This led to the notion of 'flexible response' first publicly enunciated by the U.S. Secretary of Defence, Mr Robert McNamara, at Ann Arbor on 16th June 1962: 'to the extent feasible, basic military strategy in a possible general nuclear war should be approached in much the same way that more conventional military operations have been conducted in the past. That is to say, principal military objectives . . . should be the destruction of the enemy's military forces, not of his civilian population.'

In the early enunciations of the 'flexible response' theory, Administration spokesmen emphasized the counter-force feature and implied that a general nuclear war could be fought to its conclusion on the basis of purely military considerations. This impression was strengthened by statements, particularly Mr McNamara's presentations to the Armed Services Committees, which described only one basic 'scenario' for general nuclear war: a full-scale nuclear attack on the United States.

The logical attractiveness of this theory obscured many difficulties. For one thing, the reliability of a counter-force strategy is certain to decline in the years ahead. As the retaliatory forces multiply and become more dispersed, it will grow increasingly difficult to pin-point the targets precisely or to give the President enough confidence that their exact location is known, which amounts to the same thing.

Moreover, as missile systems become more diversified and sophisticated, some will be hardened as underground installations, some will be mobile on land, others at sea. This will enormously complicate the problem of co-ordinating an attack.

Thus, even if the proportion of the Soviet retaliatory force the United States is able to destroy were to remain constant—an unwarrantedly optimistic assumption—the absolute number remaining is bound to increase. Whatever its technical feasibility, there are bound to be increasing political and psychological obstacles to a strategy that is based on fragmentary intelligence and that depends on large numbers of weapons for which there is no operational experience in wartime.

At the same time, the basic assumption that a general war is likely to start with a Soviet nuclear attack on the United States is open to serious question. Given the disparity in the size of strategic forces between the Soviet Union and the United States, it is hard to see what would induce even a rash Soviet planner into so reckless a course. According to Mr McNamara's testimony of 30th January 1963, the United States' capability after absorbing a first blow should be sufficient 'to strike back first at the Soviet bomber bases, missile sites, and other military installations associated with their long-range nuclear forces to reduce the power of any follow-on attack—and then if necessary, strike back at the Soviet urban and industrial complex in a controlled and deliberate way.'

A U.S. strategic force that can absorb a Soviet surprise attack, strike back at Soviet military targets, and still be sufficiently strong to attack urban centres in a deliberate way, must be enormously superior to the Soviets'. Moreover, most United States I.C.B.M.s will be in hardened sites and the Polaris will be mobile at sea. It is almost impossible to imagine circumstances in which the Soviets would launch an all-out attack on such a force.

Moreover, this theory implied that because the United States was numerically superior and therefore in a position to spare Soviet cities, the Soviets will have what Mr McNamara calls an 'incentive' to spare those of the United States. Of course, Soviet military theorists have consistently denied the possibility of this kind of war. This would not be decisive were it not in accord with the realities of the strategic equation. For a war of attrition, even if it were technically feasible, cannot be in the interest of the weaker side. Against a numerically superior opponent, the sensible strategy would be to begin attacking cities, perhaps 'controlling' the response by destroying some smaller towns first. To be sure, the United States could retaliate in kind. But whatever the significance of the notion of superiority in a war confined to military targets, there can be little doubt that a saturation point is soon reached when civilian populations become the objective.

Above all, whatever the technical merit of the first formulation of 'flexible response', it was almost certainly out of tune with psychological realities. It is not easy to see how a President could ever gain sufficient confidence to stake everything on weapons for which there is no operational experience in wartime, on the basis of tenuous intelligence and with the certainty of tens of millions of casualties.

This is why United States doctrine has grown more modest and has begun to set much more limited aims for the strategy of 'flexible response'. 'Fully hard I.C.B.M. sites can be destroyed but only at great cost in terms of the numbers of offensive weapons required to dig them out', said Secretary McNamara in 1964. 'Furthermore, in a second-strike situation we would be attacking, for the most part, empty sites from which the missiles had already been fired. The value of trying to provide a capability to destroy a very high proportion of Soviet hard I.C.B.M. sites becomes even more questionable in view of the expected increase in the Soviet missile launching submarine force. . . .'[3]

The purpose was primarily to limit the damage to the United States in follow-up attacks: 'Thus, a "damage-limiting" strategy appears to be the most practical and effective course for us to follow. . . . While there are still some differences of judgement on just how large such a force should be, there is general agreement that it should be large enough to ensure the destruction, singly or in combination, of the Soviet Union, Communist China, and the Communist satellites as national societies, under the worst possible circumstances of war-outbreak that can reasonably be postulated, and, in addition, to destroy their war-making capability so as to limit, to the extent practicable, damage to this country and to our allies.'[4]

In these terms 'flexible response' emerges as a sophisticated adaptation to the realities of the nuclear age. American strategic doctrine has had to face this root fact. Heretofore the chief problem of strategy was to assemble power adequate to the objective. In the age of thermonuclear weapons, the problem of an excess of power in relation to objectives has become dominant. Superiority has lost its traditional meaning and the relation of force to diplomacy has grown more tenuous.

Power and Alliances

As the United States attitude towards general war has changed new problems have arisen in relation to alliance policy. In the past, a nation would come to the assistance of another because defeat of the ally either was considered a prelude to its own defeat or involved a relative decline in its world position. The consequences of resistance seemed preferable to the risks of inaction. With modern weapons it is not self-evident that the ultimate consequences of passivity will be worse than the immediate results of conflict. If allied strategic doctrine relies on the threat of general nuclear war, the outbreak of a war involves risks which in the past were associated with total defeat. But if an attempt is made to create a more flexible response, fuel is added to the suspicions which are always ripe in a coalition of sovereign states. Colour is lent to the argument that the senior partner takes the interests of his allies less seriously than his own. The problem of N.A.T.O. then is that the pressures of the new technology run counter to traditional notions of sovereignty. The challenge is either to find a more embracing political structure or to see a gradual erosion of allied cohesion. This is true because in an alliance of sovereign states the uncertainties inherent in strategic analysis are compounded by the fact that sovereignty implies the unilateral right to alter one's strategic views. If an alliance contains a dominant partner this problem is accentuated. Then survival is likely to seem to depend not only on the actions of the opponent but also on the constancy of the senior partner. As a result, the weaker allies have a tendency to cling to the *status quo*, which has the advantage of familiarity and is also a guarantee of the senior partner's consistency. In postwar European-American relations, the Europeans have at times seemed more eager to extract American reassurances than to develop a responsible policy of their own. Moreover, in every effort to develop autonomous political and strategic views, they have run up against perplexities of a nuclear age.

A case in point is the debate about nuclear control within N.A.T.O. In strictly technical terms it is desirable that all nuclear weapons in an alliance should be under central control. But unitary control of these weapons is in some ways incompatible with an alliance of sovereign states, for it makes the survival of all allies seem to depend on the decision of one. The clash of the

American notion of nuclear requirements with the desire of some of the partners of the United States to keep maximum control over their destiny has accounted for some of the tension in the Atlantic Alliance.

Concentration of nuclear power in the hands of one country raises one set of problems; the range of modern weapons poses another. In the past, a threatened country could either resist or surrender. If it chose to resist, it had to be prepared to accept the consequence of a certain amount of physical damage and loss of life. No distant ally could be of help unless it was able to bring its strength to bear in the area of conflict.

Modern weapons, however, have given rise to a new situation. What each member country wants from an alliance is the assurance that an attack on it will be considered a *casus belli*. Deterrence is achieved by adding the threat of a distant ally to its own power. But each state has no less of an incentive to minimize its jeopardy should deterrence fail. In this respect the range of modern weapons may provide unprecedented opportunities. In 1914 Belgium could not base its defence on a strategy which made Britain the primary target; but in the age of inter-continental rockets this technical possibility exists.

Thus it is not difficult to see why part of the strategic dispute within the N.A.T.O. alliance involves jockeying to determine the sector of war if deterrence fails, though this obviously cannot be made explicit. Though the interests of the alliance may be ultimately indivisible, this does not guarantee the absence of dispute on how objectives should be implemented.

One remedial suggestion has been to place greater reliance on the process of consultation. No doubt formal consultative processes can and should be improved. But it is well to remember that even within any given government, consultation does not guarantee an identity of views. Whatever the field of consultation, a decision is finally required, and it is bound to be more difficult where sovereign states are involved. Some (leaders of the British Labour Party) have suggested that Britain might give up its nuclear weapons in return for a greater voice in American policy. Allies should, of course, always receive a respectful hearing. But what exactly does a 'greater voice' entail? A veto over all our foreign policy? A veto over S.A.C. plans? What happens when views differ or if interests do not coincide? These questions involve both a technical and a political component.

On the technical level, the effectiveness of consultation depends on the competence of the participating parties. Though in our own bureaucracy, many departments have the right to offer their views, a much smaller number carry actual weight. Since the weight given to advice is proportionate to the competence it reflects, we may well ask whether in the long run our allies could consult effectively while the United States possesses virtually all the technical knowledge and physical control of nuclear weapons. One suspects that if the alliance is to remain politically vital, its requirements will be much broader than a technical consideration of strategy.

As for the political aspect, it is likely that the concerns expressed about the absence of joint strategic planning are the symptom and not the cause of many allied tensions. If the alliance cannot develop procedures for a common diplomacy or at least agree upon a prescribed range of divergence, it would seem contradictory to insist on unitary strategic control. (It should not shock us to see countries reluctant to entrust their survival to an ally, when N.A.T.O. has not even managed to develop a common trade policy towards Communist-bloc countries.) Harsh disagreements over such issues as Suez, the Congo, negotiating tactics over Berlin, or the defence of South Arabia demonstrate that differences in the alliance are neither strange nor new. At present we see the United States in the curious position of staking great prestige on the N.A.T.O. Multilateral Force and a system of unitary strategic control, while matters so critical as East–West negotiations or the war in South-East Asia are dealt with more or less unilaterally. In short, the real problem posed by the new military technology is the imperative of a merging of sovereignty. Nothing short of this is likely to answer the problem. Indeed, if it is not achieved, some growth of neutralism seems inevitable.

Power and Neutralism

Neutrality is not a new concept, of course. However, its forms have changed in the modern period. Traditionally, states have been able to gain formal or legal recognition of their decision to remain non-belligerent in war. Often this decision has been taken *ad hoc*. Thus, despite her formal alliance with a belligerent, Italy remained neutral at the beginning of each of the world wars. Neutrality can also be a deliberate act of national policy. Some states have announced in advance that they would not join a conflict regardless of the issues or the nature of the opposing forces unless their own territory was attacked. Sweden and Switzerland have made unilateral declarations of neutrality. Or else, as in the case of Belgium, neutrality may be given international status through a formal agreement of the major powers.

Whether a neutral country will be able to maintain its position depends both on the temptation it presents to an attacker and on the assistance other countries are willing to supply. The temptations in turn reflect the advantage to be gained by violating the neutrality. Since Belgium lies athwart the invasion routes into France, she has been less fortunate in escaping war than Sweden.

Countries aspiring to neutrality can rely for their defence on their own strength or on the implied assistance that other countries may furnish. If they aspire to self-sufficiency, they are likely to develop military forces far in excess of those required by a member of an alliance system. Even taking into account the difference in resources, Sweden's military power is much greater than Norway's.

On the other hand, when a neutral, either because of insufficient resources or deliberate policy, has made itself dependent on the assistance of other countries, it has in the past often combined the disadvantages of alliance policy with those of neutrality. By itself the neutral was rarely strong enough to deter aggression, while at the same time its neutrality prevented it from making joint defensive preparations with a would-be protector. Belgium's position in the two world wars illustrates this point. But no matter what military policy is pursued, neutrality has in the past implied the desire to abstain from close involvement in international diplomacy.

Though these traditional patterns of neutrality still exist, they have been significantly modified by two contradictory tendencies. On the one hand, the advent of nuclear power has cast in doubt the ability of any non-nuclear country to defend itself against a nuclear opponent. In other words, the neutral is deprived of the capacity to impose military risks out of proportion to the aggressor's objective, if the latter is prepared to use nuclear weapons and if the neutral cannot count on foreign nuclear protection.

At the same time, the bi-polar nature of the international political structure makes the probability of protection far greater than it was in the past. In contemporary international affairs, a country suffers fewer disadvantages from being neutral and may even gain some international stature through the competition of the major powers for its allegiance. The nuclear age has unmistakably eroded the distinction between allies and neutrals. Though neutral, India was assured of much the same protection in the face of the Chinese attack as would have been extended in comparable circumstances to Pakistan, a member of two alliances.

This modification accounts for the emergence of a new type of neutral: countries which deliberately exploit the great-power confrontation in order not so much to enhance their territorial security as to magnify their diplomatic role. Far from standing apart in international conflicts, they actively embroil themselves by attempting to manipulate the great powers and to advance their own purposes in the process.

This type of diplomacy is demoralizing for the stability of the international system, and has adverse effects on both the great powers and the uncommitted themselves. By setting up a contest which, by its own ground rules, can be won by neither of the two nuclear giants, the new type of uncommitted neutral tempts destabilizing adventures and encourages political chaos. In the long run, the new nations will find it difficult to combine neutrality with incessant intervention. To the degree that the uncommitted nations can convince the major powers that their support is consequential, they are either courted or pressured. Neutrality then becomes an invitation to be wooed.

Thus a new element of volatility has been added to international affairs. Though many of the neutrals have a stake in the avoidance of war, they also discover advantages in perpetuating the competition of the super-powers. For they see this conflict bestowing on them an enhanced bargaining position and prospects of economic development to which they could not otherwise aspire.

In their turn, the major powers are handicapped by a paradox. Though their relative superiority over other nations has never been greater, it has also never been less relevant. The use of nuclear weapons against the uncommitted is for all practical purposes excluded. The other military forces have in the meantime become less and less suitable for the low-threshold warfare that is waged in the uncommitted areas.

A diplomacy of weakness has been the result. When the uncommitted nations threaten the West: 'If I go Communist it will be worse for you than for me', this creates a pattern for blackmail. It encourages many local conflicts into which the major powers are drawn, often against their own wishes. As a corollary it means that any major country determined to upset the equilibrium can do so at little cost. The sale of obsolescent Soviet military equipment to the United Arab Republic or to Indonesia can undermine the West's position in a way that would have been unachievable by direct action.

If the uncommitted nations today have unprecedented scope for pursuing their self-interest, they are also subject to novel pressures. In the past, neutrality was usually the posture of very cohesive nations certain of their identity and determined to defend it. But many of the newly independent nations are still in search of an identity. Often the sole link for their peoples is the common experience of colonial rule. Domestic cohesion is only precariously assured.

Thus while the Governments of many uncommitted nations are relatively safe from the traditional military pressures that have weighed on neutrality, they are extraordinarily susceptible to domestic subversion. Those countries with a high capacity for fomenting domestic instability can achieve international influence because of it. The lack of traditional forms of power, including nuclear power, may be more than counter-balanced by the possession of guerrilla training centres and capacities for subversion will be taken very seriously by neighbouring governments.

The most frequent and likely kind of war is the one for which the West is least prepared militarily, politically and psychologically. In guerrilla war superior fire power loses its old relevance. Guerrillas need only join battle where they enjoy local superiority, but the defenders must be strong everywhere in anticipation of the unexpected. No longer is the ability to occupy territory decisive, for the real target has become the morale of the population and the system of the Civil Administration. If these can be undermined through protracted struggle, the insurgents will prevail no matter how many battles the defending forces have won.

What makes the situation particularly complex is that there is no purely military solution to guerrilla war. Pacification requires a government capable of enlisting the loyalty of the population. But such a government is difficult to establish because of the very nature of guerrilla war, whose chief targets are often civil administrators. Moreover, for a Western government aiding an Asian or African ally, the criteria of what constitutes stable government may prove elusive. Government can be stable by being oppressive. By contrast, a developing society inevitably creates dislocations. How to achieve both development and stability, both progress and security?

Too often, there is a tendency to fragment the problem. Some argue that the problem of guerrilla war is essentially political. Others maintain that military success must precede political institution building. But in truth the problems are inseparable. Political construction must be carried out while the guerrilla war is being fought. And in many countries it is essential if civil war is to be avoided. There is no more urgent task for analysis than an inquiry into the nature of stable enlightened government in developing nations.

Conclusion

It is no accident that a survey of the United States' strategic problem should pose more questions than answers. The traditional mode of military analysis which saw in war a continuation of politics but with its own appropriate means is no longer applicable. Policy and strategy merge at every point. No statesman, no matter how seemingly quiet the period in which he lives, can overlook the cataclysmic alternatives before him. No problem can be left solely to the arbitrament of arms. Communication in the nuclear age is particularly important among adversaries. Arms control requires the same sense of urgency as does the study of strategy and of diplomacy.

We thus return to our original problem: the impact of strategic analysis on decision-making. Some years ago, when strategy first attracted the attention of academic analysts, the inconsistency between traditional modes of thought and the nature of modern weapons was obvious. As long as an analysis was systematic, it was likely to uncover discrepancies and weaknesses that needed correction.

Today the situation is more complicated. A great degree of sophistication in technical studies has been achieved—so much, in fact, that the danger today is precisely the opposite of what it was a decade ago. Skill in quantitative analysis may down-grade those factors which cannot be quantified. A complex strategic theory may be so intellectually satisfying that the difficulties of its employment by human beings in moments of great tension and confusion may be overlooked. It may be tempting to treat allies as factors of a security arrangement and to forget that their ultimate contribution depends on many intangibles of political will. In the day-to-day press of events we may lose sight of the fact that we need sound general criteria for measuring political progress in the developing countries.

In all these areas the student of strategy can be useful if he defines his role modestly. He must not pretend that he has panaceas which the short-sighted men in office have failed to discover, for the easy solutions have all been found. Our remaining problems are obdurate because they are complex. The intellectual can forewarn against the fragmentation of policy by calling attention to the inner relationship of events. He can supply perspective to government leaders who are overwhelmed by day-to-day details and are unable to give their full attention to the deeper pattern. Above all, he can insist constantly that no answer will be better than the question which invites it. In a time which is obsessed with answers, this alone is a major challenge.

NOTES

1. U.S. House, Military Functions, *National Military Establishment Appropriation for 1949*, Hearings before the Subcommittee of the Committee on Appropriations, 80th Cong., 2nd Sess. (Washington: G.P.O. 1948), pp. 3-4.
2. Albert Wohlstetter, 'The Delicate Balance of Terror', *Foreign Affairs* (January 1959), Vol. 37, No. 2, pp. 211-234.
3. Senate Armed Services Committee, *Hearings, Military Procurement Authorization Fiscal Year 1964*, 88th Cong., 1st Sess., pp. 40-41.
4. House Appropriations Subcommittee, *Hearings, Department of Defense Appropriations for 1965*, 88th Cong., Part 4, pp. 25-28.

§13§

Problems of an Alliance Policy:
An Essay in Hindsight

THE HON. ALASTAIR BUCHAN

SOVEREIGN states enter into alliances in order to further common political objectives which they are convinced they could not achieve individually. Almost by definition alliances have a limited life-cycle, unless they become transformed into federations or some organic political relationship. National objectives change, the threat which made it worth while to subordinate some national interests to the evolution of a collaborate policy changes also, and the strains of alliance may become too great to bear. For though alliance has been an essential device of international politics for nearly three thousand years, it is bound to develop internal strains once the period of clear and present danger is past, since it must involve a relationship between strong and less strong powers, restricting the freedom of both without giving either a decisive influence upon the policy of the other. 'Cohesion itself cannot be the supreme value for individual allies, as long as an alliance is a limited one and is served by a permanent organization rather than serving as a short passageway to a higher form of community. And it cannot always be such for the alliance as a whole, when too much unity would decrease the political efficacy of an association, notably with regard to countries other than the adversary in peacetime.'[1]

The inherent problems of those postwar alliances which have been fashioned around a core of evident strategic common interest have been sharpened by the nuclear age. The existence of nuclear weapons has given priority to a strategy of deterrence on which it is even more difficult to obtain a common perspective among a number of allies than a strategy of defence. The fact that the United States and the Soviet Union are nuclear powers of a different order of magnitude from any others, present or future, heightens other disparities in the power of the great and the less great in the two major alliance groups. The gravity of any resort to nuclear forces and the speed of decision-making which hypersonic means of delivery may necessitate, create quite new problems of collective control and decision-making. And the dangers of a nuclear confrontation may impose such immobility and restraint on political ambitions as to make some smaller members of alliances restless and to give the major guarantor powers, however theoretically hostile, a degree of common interest that they may not share with all their nominal friends. (The United States has over the past decade, for instance, had as high a degree of interest in preventing Chiang Kai-shek from a rash attack on the Chinese mainland as the Soviet Union had in preventing a rash Communist Chinese response.) In other words, the degree of committed military force which a particular combination of dangers has elicited may be a factor working towards the weakening of the alliance through which this force was contributed.

Nevertheless, a great many treaties of alliance have been signed in the past twenty years and few of them seem likely to be abrogated in the immediate future. I have chosen to centre this contribution around the problems of the North Atlantic Treaty Organization; not because it is the only one, but because it is the most interesting. It comprises an awkward squad of proud and ancient countries with strong military traditions of their own who conduct a much more open debate about each other's shortcomings than, even today, is possible among the countries of the Warsaw Pact. N.A.T.O. is confronted with more difficult choices of military strategy, in a search for the correct relationship of military force to diplomacy, than any other alliance. And although it embraces only fourteen of the forty-two allies of the United States, the problems of collective control and decision-making that have come to dominate N.A.T.O. will, in my view at least, become steadily more significant in the Asian and Pacific alliances.

There are at least three different ways in which one could study the problems of the North Atlantic Treaty Organization. One is to examine the history of N.A.T.O.'s policy and decisions in order to trace the evolution of today's complex political and military relationships, and the ways in which the alliance has reacted to changes in its external environment and to shifts in strength among its own membership.[2] A second is to isolate the four or five problems that have from the beginning proved hardest to solve and trace their fortunes in the various stages of N.A.T.O.'s development: the correct relationship between deterrence and defence in Europe; the complementary status and relative influence of the allies; the German question, as a test of the identity of interest among the allies; the institutional means of collective planning and decision-making; and the role of the alliance in confronting threats to the interests or security of its members outside Europe.

The third method would be to write the history of the alliance in terms of the influence of ideas, of both officials and non-officials: those of Acheson and Bradley, Liddell Hart, Slessor and Juin in the early years; of Dulles and Sandys, Brodie and Wohl-stetter in the middle years; of Nitze or Kissinger, Gallois or Strauss in the attempt to adapt alliance strategy to the missile age; of McNamara, Bowie or Aron in the struggle to bring the alliance to terms with the problems and promise of European unity.[3]

The combination of these methods, which the future Ranke or Gibbon will have to undertake, will be a massive task that will only be possible when the archives of several different countries are open to the scholar. All that I have attempted in this modest tribute is to select one central problem of the Atlantic alliance, the control of strategic planning and policy, and to inquire how it came to be as difficult to solve as it now appears to be, using what President Eisenhower once engagingly described as 'twenty-twenty hindsight'.

There is fairly general agreement today, fifteen years after the signing of the North Atlantic Treaty, about the elements of which the problem of collective decision-making is compounded. One is the difficulty of creating any control group of a manageable size within N.A.T.O., for purposes of strategic planning and for the handling of crises, to which the non-participating members of the alliance would be content to delegate issues of peace and war. The impossibility of having fifteen fingers on the trigger is recognized by all the member countries: the British or French solution of creating a dual or tripartite system of control with the United States is, however, distrusted in the smaller capitals as much as in Washington. The idea of leaving the management of great crises in the hands of the President of the United States may be acceptable in Oslo or in The Hague or Lisbon, but not in Paris or London. Yet any attempt to devise an intermediary solution, a directorate of five or seven rather than three, encounters insoluble problems of prestige as between Ottawa and Rome, Istanbul or Brussels. And so the argument has gone round and round in circles, until it has been replaced by a new argument about the desirability of creating an alliance within an alliance, based on a multilateral nuclear force to which some allies subscribe and others do not. In vain many Americans, particularly since the Kennedy Administration took office, have tried to point out that the real crises which the alliance may face probably will not involve nuclear weapons, that their planning and targeting comprises only one aspect of contemporary strategy: the European allies remain preoccupied with the nuclear weapon, mesmerized by its potentialities and prestige to the exclusion of other forms of strategic power. Britain and France have attempted to find their own solution in the development of national strategic forces: although their actions are basically consistent with the original military structure of N.A.T.O. which, by creating the Standing Group, recognized Britain and France as military powers of a different order of significance than Canada or the other European countries, their assertion of a nuclear role has created new problems without solving the old ones.

If we are inquiring, therefore, how this situation arose, the first question is why N.A.T.O. came to comprise so large and diverse a group of nations and whether anyone foresaw the consequences. Would not the diplomatists of an earlier age, the architects of the Vienna system for instance, have sought to counter Russian power in the Europe of the late 1940's by constructing a strong central system, based on the most effective military states, the United States, Britain and France, for example, and then extending its protection to less viable but like-minded nations: Britain, for instance, giving security guarantees to the Scandinavian countries, France to her continental neighbours, the United States with its existing nuclear power underpinning the whole system as well as guaranteeing outlying countries like Portugal? Such a system, conservative though it would have been, would have permitted a method of collective action to be developed within a small group of countries until such time as others, Germany for instance, could demonstrate that they had a right to be admitted to the central process of decision-making, rather than merely enjoying the protection of the *entente*.

To pose the question is almost to answer it. In the first place, it was considered almost immoral in the late 1940's, especially in Washington, to think in such traditional terms. The world of transitory combinations of interest had gone for ever: although Soviet policy now made the United Nations system unworkable, as well as posing a direct threat to Western Europe, the only legitimate option that was open to a group of threatened states was to organize a regional security pact under Article 51 of the U.N. Charter. (Senator Vandenberg explicitly promoted and defended his famous resolution of 11th June 1948, in terms of the necessity to reinforce the U.N. Charter by creating an Atlantic regional security pact under its authority. In his book, *War or Peace*, published in 1950, Mr Dulles treated N.A.T.O. simply as a regional association similar to the Rio Pact that had been signed in 1947.) And a regional security pact, it was argued, must embrace a region, irrespective of the differing assumptions or weight of the nations within it. The concept of collective security still dominated American official thought, while many Americans harboured the belief, which was not expressed openly until later, that if the European component could be made broad and large enough it could eventually hive off with an autonomous political and defence system.

Neither the British nor the French Government had much real faith in collective security after the experience of the inter-war years. Their central interest was in the full commitment of American power to the defence of Europe, by treaty and, as soon as possible, by physical presence there. 'The real purpose of this pact is to act as a deterrent', said Ernest Bevin. 'We know', said Henri Queuille, the French Prime Minister, 'that once Western Europe was occupied America would again come to our aid. . . . But the next time you would probably be liberating a corpse.' (French official statements of that date, with their note of pleading for speedy American commitment on almost any terms, read a little oddly today.) The bilateral Franco-British Treaty of Dunkirk (1947) might have provided the basis for a triangular relationship. But in the process of waiting for the American commitment, Britain and France had founded their own collective military system, the Brussels Treaty of March 1948, which embraced Belgium, France, the Netherlands, Luxembourg and the United Kingdom. If the United States were to join in a collective system for the defence of Europe, the three additional countries could not now be excluded.

Under the savage pressure of the Berlin blockade and of Soviet policy in Europe in the winter of 1948-49, the number of countries who wished to share in this process of commitment began rapidly to multiply. Even since the war Canada had envisaged some form of American commitment to Europe as the basis of her own policy there: she therefore was eager to see the new system as broad-based as possible. In February 1949 Soviet pressure on Norway for a Scandinavian non-aggression pact brought Norway to the negotiating table in Washington and after Norway came Denmark. As enthusiasm for the idea of collective Atlantic security grew, in the winter preceding the signing of the Atlantic Treaty, polite pressure was even exerted on Ireland and Sweden to join N.A.T.O.; it was as politely resisted.

Portugal and Iceland were acquired, like the British Empire, in a fit of absence of mind, because they both happened to control important strategic air bases. But Spain was too deeply hated in European left-wing parties to be a candidate for membership, and three years later the United States made a utilitarian agreement with Spain, of a kind which could have been made earlier with Portugal and Iceland, in order to acquire bases. The Americans and the British seemed to have wanted Italy in N.A.T.O., largely for fear that Tito's defection from the Soviet system, the year before the North Atlantic Treaty was signed, might lead to Soviet pressure in south-west Europe or in the Danube valley without adequate bases to oppose it. Moreover, it seemed that the strength of the Italian Communist Party could only be contained within a wide economic and political association with other Western countries.

In the late summer of 1950 the United States Army made up its mind that a German military contribution to the alliance was essential if the system of collective security to which the United States was now fully committed was to become the system of collective defence which the continuing vigour of Communist policy in Asia as well as in Europe seemed to necessitate. The autumn of 1950 brought the American and European conflicts of view into collision. It became clear at last to European Governments that the price of the American guarantee was the development of a system of collective defence in Europe. It was this realization as much as the knowledge that it was the ex-enemy power which was to be the largest source of conventional man-power which caused so much heart-searching in Paris and many other capitals in the early 1950's. But in the atmosphere of the Korean War European governments found it near impossible to resist the American argument that N.A.T.O. would continue to receive Congressional and public support only to the extent that it provided the strongest possible military defence of Europe. Yet had the U.S. planners had any inkling of the strategic stalemate that was to develop in less than a decade, of the penumbra of fear and doubt that would come to surround nuclear weapons, and therefore of their strong guarantor value, would they have been so insistent on linking a guarantee to a collective defence system? These are the kind of unfair questions that historians will one day ask.

Thus N.A.T.O. mushroomed into its unwieldy size by reason of a central misunderstanding about the differing requirements of a guarantee pact and a collective security organization. For over ten years successive American Administrations failed to understand the European preoccupation with the nature of the American guarantee. For fifteen years European governments have found it difficult to accept the American insistence that they should convert their collective security obligations into a stronger system of conventional defence and reduce the burdens which the United States finally shouldered in 1952 in order to make its guarantee more credible.

The first real sign of doubt about the heterogeneous membership

301

of the alliance did not become apparent until the United States began to exert pressure, in the autumn of 1950, to bring Greece and Turkey into N.A.T.O., a proposal which was reluctantly accepted at the Ottawa meeting of the N.A.T.O. Council in October 1951. Reporting that meeting as a journalist, I can remember the doubts of the Scandinavians, the French, the Benelux countries and Canada about the wisdom of extending an Atlantic collective security pact to countries so far from the Atlantic, and the openly expressed fear that Greek and Turkish membership would involve countries with no interests in the area in Balkan politics. At a time when N.A.T.O. has failed to make any impression on the Cyprus dispute and when Canadian and Scandinavian troops, under the aegis of the U.N. not of the regional security pact, are desperately trying to prevent the Cypriots from presenting Greece or Turkey with *casus belli*, these fears of thirteen years ago seem justified.

But the size of the alliance has not been N.A.T.O.'s only source of difficulty in trying to evolve a common strategy or in reacting speedily to external developments. Two other developments can be isolated which have had a major effect on the complex situation of today. One was the attempt of first Britain and then France to create, within this large system of nominally equal states, the reality of an *entente* and the developing American resistance to it. The other was the destruction of the principle of American-European reciprocity by the nuclearization of the defence of N.A.T.O. Europe.

The political and military links between London and Washington which had been forged in the second World War had remained unbroken in the period before the North Atlantic Treaty was signed, even though Britain had been denied access to all information about American nuclear weapon design and production. British officials played a leading part in the evolution of the central N.A.T.O. machinery and command structure, most particularly in the setting up of the one organization which accepted that though all were equal some were more equal than others, the Standing Group of representatives of the American,

British and French Chiefs of Staff with its headquarters in Washington. Moreover, although there was no direct communication on nuclear matters, the British, who had embarked on their own nuclear programme in 1946, were not inhibited from offering their views. It is often said, I think correctly, that the British Chiefs of Staff paper of 1952, which drew attention to the strain on certain key sections of the economy which would be created by an attempt to maintain large conventional defence establishments on the Continent and a strategic nuclear air arm, had an important influence on the revision of American strategy in 1953 with its greater emphasis on nuclear deterrence and less on conventional defence forces.

But as American strategy began to grow more complex, first with the development of the hydrogen bomb, and then with the beginnings of a direct Soviet threat to North America and the introduction of new considerations about credibility, vulnerability and different postures of deterrence, so the general discussions in the Standing Group came to satisfy Britain less and less. Although there were other considerations involved, Britain's desire to give increased emphasis to its own nuclear weapons programme in 1956-57 was directly connected with the desire to gain access to the full range of American strategic planning, a policy that bore fruit with the amendment of the U.S. Atomic Energy Act in Britain's favour in 1958. Thus the British method, the development of an effective nuclear strike force, was held, both in London and elsewhere, to be the most effective way of converting mere alliance into *entente*.

France had had this British tactic under close scrutiny even before the Government of M. Mollet decided in 1956, eight years after Britain, to lay down a French national nuclear weapon programme. She also had found over the years that the nominal status of a great power within the alliance is not very meaningful without access to American strategic nuclear planning. President de Gaulle tried and failed to find a shorter route than that employed by Britain in his direct proposal of October 1958 for a tripartite system of consultation and crisis management both inside and outside the N.A.T.O. area.

France, with her nuclear armed bomber force becoming operational, is arriving at the position which Britain achieved in 1958. But in the meantime there has been a decisive American, and indeed allied, determination to resist any attempt to develop an inner *entente* around the ownership of national nuclear forces. The reasons are complex (though one of them is simple enough: the lack of finesse and the patent sense of distrust with which the General has handled the United States). They are compounded partly of technical military considerations, fear that small national nuclear forces will have inadequate precautions and protection for a secure posture of deterrence; in part of fear that if France uses a national nuclear programme to follow Britain into full *entente* with the United States, so eventually will Germany and every other power with the economic capability, thus putting the American guarantee to Europe in question; in part of a sense that has been growing gradually since President Eisenhower's second term, that it is time for the United States to begin the process of reducing the danger of nuclear war by gradually extending the area of understanding and agreement with the Soviet Union rather than building up the military strength or the political cohesion of her major allies. The evolution of this attitude has been clouded and complicated by the desire of many influential Americans to see the Western *entente* develop, not between the United States and her most powerful allies, but with a new united European entity—to substitute partnership for *entente*.

The consequence is that, for good or bad reasons, the policies of the Fifth Republic have had the effect of undermining the objective of great-power *entente* within N.A.T.O.; or rather of diverting it to an American decision to build a closer relationship with Germany based on the novel and artificial concept of a multilaterally armed and controlled nuclear force. This may have short-term political benefits, particularly during a period when the United States is anxious to obtain German acquiescence in a policy of diplomatic exploration with the Soviet Union and the countries of Eastern Europe. Moreover, Germany, as the strongest land power in central Europe, has a full right to a seat in the inner group where N.A.T.O. strategy is decided and where decisions might have to be taken in a crisis. But a system that lacks France cannot really be considered an effective one for a Western defence organization.

One reason why the idea of entering a military pact with the European states overcame the traditional American opposition to entangling alliances, and indeed aroused great enthusiasm among responsible Americans, was that it appeared to embody a satisfactory principle of reciprocity. The United States would concentrate on those aspects of Western defence to which she was best adapted: the development of air, sea and nuclear power; the Europeans would concentrate on strengthening the landward defences of Europe against the Soviet Union; each would be dependent on the other's efforts and could therefore exercise a healthy influence upon the other's policies. Had it been possible to develop this formula many of today's inter-allied tensions would not exist.

The general reasons why this formula has broken down are well advertised. On the one hand they concern the rising technological and industrial ambitions of the major European states: on the other the constant American irritation with the failure of Europe to honour its half of the bargain in terms of conventional forces, an irritation that became more marked after 1961, as the delicacy of the overall strategic balance made it desirable to develop as flexible a European defence system as possible.

But perhaps the single action that did most to destroy the original political basis of N.A.T.O., and thus to make all the problems of collective policy-making harder to solve, was the introduction of nuclear weapons into Europe. Probably this was inevitable; certainly it is hard to see how in the 1960's a satisfactory local balance of forces could have been maintained without some nuclear armed interdiction aircraft and missiles to offset an equivalent Soviet capability. But what no one realized at the time was that by introducing the battlefield nuclear weapon into Europe, on what proved to be a largely fallacious theory that it favoured the defence and would compensate for Europe's shortcomings in the mobilization of ready divisions, the entire operational control of the alliance was being delivered into

American hands. Leaving aside the confusion that arose in professional military thinking about the practicability of limited nuclear war, or whether tactical atomic weapons were part of the deterrent or the defence forces of the alliance, the effect of the double key system was to make the reaction of an individual divisional or brigade commander of any nationality to an attack on his front dependent on a decision of the White House. European governments had, in fact, lost the control over the issues of peace and war which the structure of N.A.T.O., with its Council and committee system, in theory gave them. It is for this reason that students of the alliance have argued for some years now that either a new system of collective decision-making must be devised, perhaps in Washington rather than Paris, to act closer to the heart of N.A.T.O.'s military power, or else that it will split into separate European and American systems.

There is one aspect of the tightening American control over decision-making in N.A.T.O., since the introduction of tactical weapons in 1957, that is worth noting. Since 1951, when it was decided to concert a collective security agreement into a collective defence system, the Supreme Commander Europe has been an American. It was not difficult for General Eisenhower (1951-52) or even General Gruenther (1953-56) to gain the confidence both of Washington and of the major European governments, since the latter retained a significant degree of autonomy and S.A.C.E.U.R.'s role was more that of a co-ordinator than commander. But the position of General Norstad (1956-63) was much more difficult for he was also commander, and his position, as an international leader and as an American, became increasingly ambiguous as differences of opinion about nuclear strategy began to develop between Washington and the European capitals: he often found himself fighting for the European point of view with the government whose uniform he wore. General Lemnitzer who took the post in 1963 has found himself in much the same position.

The history of the office of S.A.C.E.U.R. bears some resemblance to that of the Viceroy of India. In the earlier days of British rule, when the Viceroy was a remote figure dealing mostly with the heads of princely states, there was little conflict of loyalty.

As the British grip on the administration of India strengthened and Indian nationalism began to develop, successive Viceroys found themselves adopting the Indian side of the argument against Whitehall, whose servant and representative they were supposed to be. In the Valhalla to which all misunderstood public servants deserve to go, General Norstad and his successors may find much common ground with Lords Halifax, Linlithgow and Wavell.

Of the original fifteen signatories of the N.A.T.O. treaty, only five are active political figures today. Mr Dirk Stikker of the Netherlands has recently retired to private life after a valiant but only partially successful attempt to breathe vitality into the complex international machinery which was set up under the Treaty. M. Spaak, now Foreign Minister of Belgium again, is one of the leading figures in the fight to prevent European dissatisfaction with the Atlantic system from degenerating into a desire for a Little *Entente* in Western Europe. Mr Lester Pearson, now Prime Minister of Canada, has transferred the main focus of his international interests into an attempt to build an informal association of small states which can strengthen the ability of the United Nations to keep the peace. Mr Halvard Lange of Norway is concerned with much the same objective. Mr Dean Acheson, from his position of private eminence in Washington, is principally concerned, in his public speeches, with the value of the alliance as a means of promoting a settlement of the German question. The altered preoccupation of these five architects of the N.A.T.O. treaty are instructive, for they embrace the questions which any student of the alliance must ask himself today. The successes of the N.A.T.O. system are obvious. The United States is as deeply committed as she was fifteen years ago to the integrity of Europe and, after the period of confusion caused by the revolutionary impact of the missile upon strategic thinking, it is clear that she has in her Minuteman and Polaris programme the means of enforcing her guarantee. The febrile estimates of Soviet strength in Europe that prevailed until a few years ago have given place to more considered judgement and it is clear that there is now a better balance of ready force there, even though the

N.A.T.O. local defence system is not as strong or as flexible as many could wish. At any rate the prospect of a sudden Soviet *promenade militaire* against Western Europe does not cause much loss of sleep these days. It is doubtful whether, after the experience of the Cuba crisis in October 1962, the Soviet Union is prepared to contemplate a trial of nerves or strength even over Berlin. Though the financial cost is heavy (some $50,000 million a year on the direct defence of the N.A.T.O. area or the deterrence of attack on it) it is bearable for a group of expanding societies.

The central political problems which the alliance faces in the second half of the 1960's, during the four or five years before the member states acquire, after twenty years, the option of withdrawing from the alliance system, are three.

The first question is whether N.A.T.O. can serve the ends of the Western strategy by exploiting the present centrifugal tendencies in eastern Europe. What this means in military terms is adjusting the extremely complex system of defence and deterrence that has been created in Europe, if not to rather crude ideas such as the original Rapacki plans, at least to more carefully considered arms control proposals that would diminish the dangers of a highly nuclearized confrontation in central Europe and somewhat diminish the level of armaments there. Without such initiatives the attempts to normalize relations between the two halves of Europe, by trade or other exchanges, may prove inadequate.

The second question is closely related to this, namely whether the leaders of the alliance will have the wit and the patience to see that a slackening of tension in Europe will involve greater rather than less American engagement in the affairs of Europe, even though the United States may also be deeply committed in the Far East; or whether the facile analogy between economic and strategic developments which is implicit in talk of a separate European force and strategy, or of a strategic 'partnership', will take hold of the popular imagination. A decision in Washington to increase American freedom of action outside Europe, even if it meant losing the political support of the European powers, or an indefinite extension of President de Gaulle's attempt to develop a wholly separate French policy toward the Soviet Union, could bring the alliance to an end, for the institutions it has developed, inter-governmental and not supranational, have no inherent momentum of their own.

The third question is related to the second. One reason why N.A.T.O. seems to be an inadequate instrument of Western strategy is that the problems of confronting the Communist bloc have become so much more complex. Any form of direct threat to Europe and the United States now poses unacceptable risks for the Soviet Union. This, combined with the Sino-Soviet split which is creating competitive Chinese and Russian diplomacies in many countries, is leading Moscow back to an 'indirect strategy', of which the principles were so lucidly expanded by B. H. Liddell Hart twenty-five years ago.[4] In confronting this kind of threat in Indo-China, in Africa, in Latin America, in the Middle East, there is confusion of thought in most Western governments, most particularly in Washington, about whether N.A.T.O. is merely a regional pact or the master system of the West. The bipolarity that now necessarily governs most aspects of direct strategy does not necessarily apply to subtler forms of indirect struggle, and individual Western countries can pursue divergent policies with impunity to themselves yet at great damage to the interests of the West as a whole. Divergent French and American postures over South-East Asia, divergent British and American policies over Cuba, divergent British and German policies in eastern Europe, may do no immediate harm to the countries concerned, yet lead to a swifter decay of *entente* than clashes over weapons and military policy in Europe.

In an era in which international relations are becoming more fluid than was conceivable during the glacial periods of the cold war, yet when the dangers of escalation to strategic war are inherent in any flare-up anywhere in the world, it may well be that impetus to devise better means of collective policy-making between the United States and her major European allies will be provided by the diversification rather than the centralization of the Communist threat.

NOTES

1. George Liska, *Nations in Alliance* (Baltimore 1962).
2. Mr Robert Osgood has written the nearest thing to a definitive history of N.A.T.O. that is possible, with the documents that are at present available, in *N.A.T.O.: The Entangling Alliance* (Chicago 1962). However, it brings the story only to September 1961.
3. Although the alliance awaits, and may await for ever, its philosophical historian, Mr Robert Levine, has made an enterprising beginning in *The Arms Debate* (Cambridge, Mass. 1963).
4. B. H. Liddell Hart, *Strategy: The Indirect Approach* (London 1941).

§14§

Training and Doctrine in the British Army since 1945

ALUN GWYNNE JONES
(LORD CHALFONT)

WHEN from time to time the function of armed force in international politics undergoes fundamental change, it is not surprising that there should be confusion in the training and tactical doctrine of armies. It is characteristic of the older military establishments that their methods are rooted in the past, addicted to usage and tradition, and influenced by organizational patterns that often owe more to administrative convenience and instinctive conservatism than to the requirements of efficiency in battle.

Since 1945 the British Army has been faced with two major developments, one political and one technical, that have combined to demand an entirely new approach to training and doctrine. The first, a peculiarly British concern, is the liquidation of imperial responsibilities and the decline of Britain from the standing of a great military power; the second closely inter-related and universal development is that caused by the impact of atomic and nuclear weapons on strategy and tactics.

When the second World War ended, the real significance of nuclear weapons had not been fully grasped. The sheer destructive power of the explosion was obvious enough at Hiroshima and Nagasaki, but its ultimate effect upon the 'usability' of military power was not yet clear. The concepts of total war and unconditional surrender had apparently been vindicated by the defeat of Germany. Victory had been achieved by the application of massive force, relentlessly applied in a fight to the finish; great armies, universal conscription and elaborately organized reserves had become accepted ingredients of the military establishment; and the British Army set out as soon as the war was over to analyse and disseminate what it believed were its lessons.

The basic lesson was the need for large armies, both active and in reserve. One of the reasons commonly advanced for the humiliating defeats of 1940—when the propagandists at last stopped representing them as a glorious victory—was unpreparedness. Britain, it was suggested, had not introduced conscription in time to train forces capable of withstanding the

313

German assault. The pattern of training and theory between 1945 and 1950 was therefore the indoctrination of a large national service Army with the concepts of total war on land. The principles upon which this teaching was based were contained in the first series of postwar training pamphlets, issued between 1950 and 1952, and especially of three basic documents—*The Conduct of War*, *The Infantry Division* and *The Armoured Division*. The approach of the military establishment to the role of force was crystallized into a single sentence in the Chief of the Imperial General Staff's introduction to *The Conduct of War*: 'Weapons and methods of waging war are changing constantly. The basic principles, however, remain the same.' The doctrine was one of complete destruction of the enemy's will to resist; its application in training involved the inculcation of offensive spirit, the will to destroy, a carefully contrived crusading zeal in which the enemy forces were to be looked upon as something evil. This emotional attitude to war was, even before the introduction of nuclear weapons into the equation, the subject of attack by military theorists, and especially by Liddell Hart.

Although Liddell Hart pointed out as early as 1945 some of the implications of nuclear weapons as an instrument of policy; and although he enlarged upon his warnings in *The Defence of the West* in 1950, his objections to the doctrine of unlimited war were not based entirely upon considerations of mass destruction. He believed, quite simply, that complete victory was an illusion. In his remarkable little book *The Revolution in Warfare*, published in 1946 but written before the atomic bombs were dropped in Japan, Liddell Hart referred to one of the most striking premises in the writing of Clausewitz: 'To introduce into the philosophy of war a principle of moderation would be absurd. War is an act of violence pursued to the utmost.' Liddell Hart argued that generals and politicians had consistently misunderstood the metaphysical elements in the Clausewitz doctrine—the basic philosophical assumption that when the human mind reasons in the abstract, it cannot stop short of an extreme, but that when it passes from abstractions to reality the circumstances are fundamentally changed. These misconceptions of the profound truths of Clausewitzian doctrine, wrote Liddell Hart, carried into warfare the primitive drives of an impassioned mob, brushing statesmanship aside. He suggested that the combination in the second World War of an unlimited aim with an unlimited method—the adoption of a demand for unconditional surrender with a strategy of total blockade and bombing devastation—had involved the paradox of seeking to preserve European civilization through practising the most uncivilizing means of warfare since the Mongol devastations.

Liddell Hart, in fact, advanced a theory of military power that seemed perverse to generals and statesmen still in a state of euphoria at the end of an apparently victorious war. He wrote: 'The problem, like a coin, has two sides—the "head" is the prevention of war, but the "tail" is the limitation of war. If experience has taught us anything we should now be capable of realizing the danger of concentrating on the perfectionist policy of preventing war, while neglecting the practical necessity, if that policy fails, of limiting war—so that it does not destroy the prospects of subsequent peace.' Nearly twenty years later, this was to become the painfully achieved consensus of strategic thought wherever the power of reason was applied to the problems of war. For the moment, as might have been expected, there was no room for it in the training and doctrine of the British Army. In the five years that followed the end of the war the methods and concepts of 1939-45 provided the foundation of official military thought, pragmatic and complacent as always, mistrustful of the theories of 'military bolshies' and long-haired armchair strategists.

In the next five years, between 1950 and 1955, the natural inertia that followed the war had come to an end. New and significant developments began to affect the military policies of the West and especially of Britain. In 1949 the Western countries became collectively aware of the threat to Europe from the East and the North Atlantic Treaty Organization was born, with a formal military command organization under the first Supreme Allied Commander for Europe, General Eisenhower. Instead of being able to contemplate the possibility of an occupation force becoming progressively smaller, the allies now faced the formidable 'Lisbon Goals': a plan to raise ninety divisions for the defence of Europe against Russian attack. The connoisseur of these matters will note with some pleasure that even as the Lisbon goals were being formulated, Liddell Hart was writing, in *Defence of the West*, published in 1950: 'If Western Union had available even 20 high-quality divisions, modernly equipped and ready for action on the spot like a fire brigade, the whole situation would be changed for the better.' In the same period the Korean War reinforced the arguments for large armies, certainly so far as the Americans were concerned. It was Britain's colonial empire, however, that provided the decisive arguments for the conscript army in peacetime. In the early 1950's the war in the Malayan jungle kept thousands of British troops occupied in containing the Communist terrorist campaign and no sooner were there signs that it had been defeated when it was followed by the Mau-Mau rebellion in Kenya and the E.O.K.A. crisis in Cyprus. Initially these developments, apart from posing an apparent requirement for more troops in the standing army, had no radical effect on training and doctrine. So far as the British Army of the Rhine was concerned, the professional soldiers turned with every appearance of relish from the enervating and demoralizing chores of an occupation army to the more stimulating business of training for an operational role. There was, however, no evidence of fresh thinking about organization and tactical doctrine. Armoured and infantry divisions reappeared complete with their ponderous impedimenta and their reassuringly familiar tables of organization. Mobile laundry and bath units, divisional postal units, workshops and provost companies proliferated; and the hallowed battle drills of the Twenty-first Army Group were brought out, polished lovingly and put to work again. Even the first shadow of 'tactical' nuclear weapons across the battlefield did not, at first, have much effect. It had become an article of faith in the intelligence staffs of the West that the Soviet Union had a great superiority in land forces in central Europe, in Poland and in the west of the U.S.S.R., and that there was little prospect that the European powers, even with American help, would ever be prepared to make the sacrifices that would be necessary to redress the balance in terms of the sheer weight of defensive force then considered necessary. The solution seemed to be nuclear weapons on the battlefield.

It is worth noting that many strategic theoreticians were sceptical of the belief that nuclear weapons could ever take the place of men or that they necessarily operated in favour of the defence. Many believed that they represented unusable military power, that their use on the battlefield would create conditions of chaos in which control would become impossible and in which no organized battle could last for more than a few hours. These doubts did not, apparently, assail the guardians of official doctrine. British planners declined for some time to accept the need for any radical changes in tactics, training or organization. The battlefield nuclear weapons were regarded quite simply as a bigger and better form of artillery. An eminent British general, addressing the students at the Army Staff College at Camberley at the time, impatiently dismissed a question about training for nuclear war. 'An atomic bomb, my boy, is just like any other bomb. If it falls on your head, it kills you—if it doesn't you've got nothing to worry about.' It was hard to tell whether the young officers who walked out of the lecture hall that day were pensive, or just stunned.

Even in Germany, among the forces on the ground, the tactical implications of nuclear weapons were slow to percolate into the training of officers and troops. There were a few perfunctory genuflexions in the general direction of ground zero. Troops were exhorted to hurl themselves face down to the ground on seeing the mushroom-shaped cloud—a piece of advice that on reflection seemed of doubtful value since, by that time, if they were in any condition to see the cloud at all, they would presumably be flat on their backs. The first organized reaction to the nuclear threat was to go as far underground as possible: an unexceptionable instinct in terms of self-preservation, but often irrelevant to the need to conduct an effective defence. At one memorable demonstration of a defensive position under the nuclear threat, given before the assembled students of the august Imperial Defence College, a company of infantry dug itself into the Westphalian plain with remarkable skill. It used in the operation, however, the engineer resources of an entire division and took three days in the process. Even allowing for the perfectionism of a Rhine Army demonstration it was clear that this sort of excavation had no place in a fluid defensive battle.

The new demands of guerrilla warfare seemed equally hard to absorb. At first the need was quite simply for more troops, as in the Palestine operation, to act as reinforcements for the police; or, as in the desultory anti-bandit operations in Eritrea, to engage in punitive expeditions and 'flag marches' conducted with the stylized ritual of the North-West Frontier. In Malaya, however, the British troops met for the first time an enemy trained in the classic guerrilla tactics of Mao Tse-tung. Small, tough bands of men, moving in the jungle like fish in water, were a very different problem from the gesticulating, half-comic figures of the traditional mob familiar from generations of Staff College 'playlets' on 'duties in aid of the civil power'. Buglers and men with banners inscribed 'Disperse or I fire' in English and Urdu were of marginal use in these vicious little wars. Soon the men on the spot were learning the trade; in Malaya for example, the Far East Land Forces training centre quickly became one of the best tactical schools of the postwar Army. It evolved a coherent philosophy of counter-guerrilla warfare; devised effective battle drills for the jungle; and trained every officer and soldier arriving in Malaya before he began his jungle operations. In Kenya remarkable operations were carried out by British officers and soldiers disguised as Africans and operating in the forests for long periods, meeting an unconventional enemy with unconventional tactics. Back at home units destined for the Far East and the Middle East were still being trained in obsolete 'cordon and search' operations and barrack square anti-riot manœuvres left over from the days of imperial policy.

By 1955, therefore, the nature of military operations had been transformed by the introduction of the nuclear weapon to the battlefield, and by the development of guerrilla warfare as an element in the tactics of subversion. Neither had produced any real change in the training of the British Army. Ten years after the end of the war an article by an eminent soldier in the Journal of the Royal United Service Institution expounded the theories of area defence in jungle warfare as practised against the Japanese in the Arakan, suggesting that 'there are surely pointers to the future in these campaigns'.

The views of the military theorists had no more effect than the developments in weapons and techniques. In his *Defence of the West* (1950), Liddell Hart had written of the defence of Western Europe: 'From my own reflection on the problem it seems to me that the primary need under present conditions is to develop a highly mobile land force of the minimum scale necessary to check the Russian spearheads that could infiltrate in face of air attack. . . .' While the infantry of the Rhine Army were contemplating the prospect of troglodytic immobility along the German river lines he was writing: '. . . the foot fighting element ought to be carried in tracked vehicles so that they have a cross-country mobility and manœuvrability equal to the armoured fighting units.' So far as the irregular wars in the colonies were concerned, the theorists had not yet come to close grips with the impact on revolutionary warfare of the doctrines of Mao Tse-tung. Guerrilla warfare still meant the resistance movements of Poland, France and Yugoslavia, or the unconventional heroics of Lawrence and those who inherited his cloak and dagger in the Western Desert and the Burma jungle.

The training and doctrine of the British Army in 1955 was still essentially that of a nation in arms, dedicated to the principle of unlimited war fought by massive forces and only reluctantly discarding the organization and tactics of El Alamein and the Normandy beaches. In 1956 these outworn concepts were reflected in an operation that began, in an atmosphere of failure and humiliation, a new era in British military policy. The Suez campaign, quite apart from its resounding implications for British foreign policy, demonstrated quite simply that whether one supported or deplored the political decision to attack Egypt, the military machine was incapable of producing the right force in the right place at the right time. As Captain Cyril Falls commented with disarming mildness in *The Art of War* (1961): 'it revealed deficiencies in equipment which might prove serious in an affair similar in character, but in which resistance was stouter and better organized.' It is true that the political conception was extraordinary; in the words of Guy Wint and Peter Calvocoressi, in their book *Middle East Crisis* (1957), 'all in all, the expedition was about as successful as the classic Walcheren expedition of 1809 which is commonly cited as the supreme example of a government's lack of determination, foresight and competence'. The fact remains, however, that the military establishment had proved incapable of meeting the demands of foreign policy, however eccentric those demands might have been. The revelation came at a time when other factors were beginning to cast doubt upon the policy of maintaining a large standing army. The most decisive of these was financial. The enormous stocks of ammunition and equipment built up during the war were either being used or becoming out of date. To replace them and at the same time to go on paying, clothing, feeding and housing a conscript army was beyond the resources of the defence budget.

Although in October 1955 Field-Marshal Lord Montgomery had said, with characteristically Olympian brevity, 'National Service is an essential feature of modern defence', the makers of official policy now became convinced that it was nothing of the kind. Belatedly embracing a strategic concept that was already losing its validity—the doctrine of massive nuclear retaliation—they decided to rely upon small regular forces, acting upon the double fallacy that nuclear weapons could take the place of men in the military arrangements of the country and save the Government a lot of money while doing so. In 1957 a famous Statement on Defence was published, one which still bears the name of the Minister of Defence who presented it to Parliament. The 'Sandys White Paper' has become as specific a designation as the Gladstone bag, although it has proved to be a shade less durable. It enshrined the concept of a small force in Europe designed to act as a 'trip wire' which, if stumbled against by an attacker, would bring down the whole might of the strategic nuclear striking force, and of a centrally held strategic reserve to deal with overseas problems, enabling garrisons abroad to be reduced. As any major war was now considered certain to develop rapidly into a global nuclear exchange, large reserves—one of the secondary reasons for National Service—were held to be superfluous. Britain was to develop ballistic missiles to supplement and eventually replace the V-bomber force. Faced with a defence policy described by Mr Sandys as the 'biggest change in military policy ever made in normal times' and by *The Times* as 'both courageous and clear thinking', the Army sensed the beginning of a new order, and set about formalizing its training and tactical doctrines. It chose to do so under the general headings of global, cold and limited war; and although the lines that divide these categories are frequently blurred, at any rate in the case of cold and limited war, this remains the framework upon which Army training and doctrine is still being evolved.

The literature of strategic and tactical theory in this period has been prolific. In the United States, in particular, strategists and analysts have evolved the most subtle and often over-sophisticated concepts of the role of nuclear weapons. Before examining the development of Army methods since 1955, it is necessary to select some of the main threads from this crowded and often somewhat abstract tapestry of military theory.

The decisive factor has been the change in the balance of nuclear power, and with it the rapid evolution of new ideas about when nuclear weapons might be used—and, more important, when it would be clearly suicidal to use them. So long as the United States had a monopoly of atomic, and subsequently thermo-nuclear, weapons, the doctrine of massive retaliation was valid. The Soviet Union could be threatened with annihilation as a reaction to *any* military expansion, anywhere in the world, however limited in aim or method. The threat was, in strategic terms, credible: the Russians had to believe it because they had no means of defence against the nuclear striking force of the United States and they possessed no power of retaliation that would deter the United States through fear of reprisal. It was this doctrine that provided the basic strategic assumption for the Sandys White Paper, which dismantled the nation in arms, and replaced it with a concept of unlimited nuclear war which made the *levée en masse* look like a back-street brawl.

Even as the new atomic age doctrine was being promulgated by the Stationery Office, it was losing its effectiveness; it was, in effect, no longer 'credible'. At first the Soviet Union had countered it by posing a nuclear threat to Western Europe, by means of medium-range missiles stationed close to the frontiers. It was to this threat, early in the 1950's, that the West had reacted under American prompting, by introducing nuclear weapons into the battlefield of central Europe; but now the entire balance was to change. As soon as the Soviet Union achieved the means to strike not only at Europe, but also at the United States, with nuclear weapons, the doctrine of massive retaliation began to lose its force; it died completely when the Russians achieved a 'second strike capability': that is, the ability to absorb an American nuclear attack and still inflict great damage on the United States. The trip-wire concept was no longer credible. It was necessary now to provide a combination of deterrence and defence at all levels of possible military action. Revolution or guerrilla war would have to be met on the ground, with tactical doctrines carefully evolved and troops specially trained for the task. In Europe there would have to be enough troops to react in a limited way to aggression for long enough to identify it—to distinguish between a border incident and a full-scale attack; they would have to be able to fight with or without their battlefield nuclear weapons and their tactical nuclear bombers, depending upon the development of the battle. Even if all the non-nuclear means of deterrence and defence failed, it would still be necessary to control the use of nuclear weapons, either by attempting to limit their use to the battlefield, or by rigid control of delivery systems and targets in a limited strategic exchange designed to enable diplomatic activity to continue. The consensus of most responsible military theory, with its emphasis on damage limitation and graduated action, had reached by the early 1960's a conclusion that might reasonably be summed up in a phrase written by Liddell Hart fifteen years earlier: '. . . the best chance may lie in trying to revive a code for limiting rules for warfare—based on a realistic view that wars are likely to occur again and that the limitation of destructiveness is to everybody's interest.'

The theoretical impact of this doctrine of flexible or controlled military response on the organization and training of armed forces is profound. It requires highly trained ground troops in large numbers with a wide range of light, air-transportable equipment, and a high degree of strategic and tactical mobility. Nuclear delivery systems must be varied, susceptible to the most delicate control and virtually invulnerable to surprise attack. The relevance of Britain's nuclear striking forces to these concepts is examined by Alastair Buchan elsewhere in this book. The training and doctrine of the British Army, in the formal categories of general, limited and global war, have tended to follow the main axis of theoretical advance, but, understandably, at a slower pace. Less understandably, they have sometimes been led into diversions that have been wasteful, frustrating and often dangerous.

Early ideas about the nature of general war with nuclear weapons had been based on the belief that they would always be difficult to manufacture and prohibitively expensive. Just as the commanders of ground troops regarded battlefield nuclear weapons as a more powerful form of artillery, so the strategic planners looked upon longer-range delivery systems as no more than an extension of the bombers of the second World War. This gave rise to the concept of the 'broken-backed war' in which, after an exchange of nuclear weapons, conventional armies and navies were engaged in seizing the enemy heartland and destroying his capacity to fight. This doctrine was used to justify the retention of traditional tactics and training methods as well as the maintenance of large reserves, which could be mobilized during the 'broken-back' phase. The concept was extended to the battlefield, where it was assumed that nuclear weapons would be distributed carefully to corps and army commanders like chocolates in a nursery; not because too many at once might be bad for them, but because they were very expensive and hard to come by. The result was that battlefield targeting became a ponderous ritual and the criterion was that battlefield nuclear weapons would be used only on substantial targets of the size or equivalent importance of an infantry battalion.

It soon became evident that there would, in fact, be no shortage of nuclear weapons, either strategic or tactical, and military theorists realized long before official planners that, after an exchange of large numbers of megaton weapons, the possibility of controlling a broken-back war was remote; as were the chances of conducting an organized land battle with both sides throwing nuclear weapons about like tennis balls. In his *Deterrence or Defence* (1960) Liddell Hart returned to his *leitmotiv* of the limitation of the aim and methods of conducting war: proposing the reorganization of the continental army into armoured striking forces and light infantry divisions, he wrote: 'Such a reorganization would provide the N.A.T.O. countries with a chance of effective defence without the extreme peril of resorting to nuclear weapons—and thus strengthen the deterrent. For the prime need today is to reinforce the H-bomb deterrent, which has turned into a two-edged threat, by developing a non-nuclear fireguard and fire-extinguisher—on the ground, and ready for use without hesitation or delay.' While Liddell Hart was distilling the essence of the flexible response, those responsible for the training of the British Army were evolving elaborate plans for a nuclear battle in Europe. Successive commanders of the British forces in Germany were convinced that not only would any war in central Europe be nuclear from the day it started, but that such a war could be conducted according to the normal principles of tactical manœuvre. Dispersion and mobility became the twin gods and many commanders believed firmly that tactical nuclear weapons operated in favour of the defence. Even after command post exercises, war games and other manœuvres had demonstrated conclusively that a nuclear battlefield after forty-eight hours was a wasteland, with headquarters, communications and supply lines shattered, the myth of the 'Corps in the Nuclear Battle' persisted, and the plum-coloured pamphlet that enshrined it remained the bible of the Army of the Rhine. It is only in the last few years that possibilities of conventional defence in Europe have been taken at all seriously.

One of the valuable by-products of the Army's preoccupation with the nuclear land battle was the final death of the fallacy that nuclear weapons can replace men in the defensive battle. Like the

Americans before them they discovered that the fluidity of the battle and the high rate of casualties meant not fewer soldiers, but many more. This lesson in man-power requirements was to be underlined by experience in the category of operations which the planners called cold war. The implicit basis of the 1957 White Paper was that British commitments overseas would gradually fade away, leaving the new professional Army to be concentrated into a Strategic Reserve in England: a small, mobile, hard-hitting force, as the half-satirical jargon of the soldier is accustomed to describe it. This belief, based upon a mistaken reading of the strategic effects of constitutional advance in the colonies, remained an article of official faith for about five years. What was happening, meanwhile, was that as each emergent nation of the new Commonwealth came to independence, more British troops were needed to prop them up than had been needed to keep them in order. So far from dwindling, the overseas commitment grew.

So far as tactics and training were concerned, the Army by now was absorbing the valuable lessons of its wide experience in anti-guerrilla war. A team of officers from the Commonwealth Brigade Group in Malaya, working in close co-operation with the American forces in South-East Asia, began to analyse not only the lessons of Malaya, Kenya and Cyprus, but those of the French in Indo-China as well. The doctrines of Mao Tse-tung and Che Guevara were closely studied. The result of this searching re-appraisal was a new training doctrine which rejected both the old doctrines of imperial policing and the radical views of the dedicated advocates of special forces. The lessons of the past were that success against guerrilla forces depends upon first-class intelligence—political and military, on effective machinery for co-ordinating political and military resources, and on training of local forces. It was clear that no new state could make good its claim to independence if its existence depended on the continued presence of large numbers of foreign troops.

In its so-called 'cold war' role the Army achieved an enviable expertise, partly because of its imaginative use of the lessons of the past, and partly because operations of this type were quite its favourite occupation. Attractive foreign stations, travel and excitement with a judicious admixture of danger exercised a powerful appeal upon the military mind. It was, said one euphoric young officer in Cyprus, like big game shooting with the added interest that the game could occasionally shoot back. In Malaya one of the most distinguished commanding officers said that his jungle operations made him feel like a Master of Fox Hounds, with the Adjutant as his whipper-in, the company commanders as huntsmen and the troops as a first-class pack of hounds. Possibly unaware of deeper implications of this gruesome analogy, soldiers enjoyed the cold war better in the Middle East and Far East than the eternal round of exercises in Westphalia and on Salisbury Plain. 'Join the Army and see the World' had come back to the recruiting posters.

If the Army had evolved an eccentric training doctrine for its general war and an admirable one for its cold war, it seemed to have run out of ideas about limited war. Or possibly there were so many ideas that no one could decide which to choose. It was, after all, very hard to define limited war. There can, of course, it was said almost in passing, be no limited war in Europe. The possibilities were therefore restricted to Africa, the Middle East and the Far East. Nasser in Africa, Russia or the satellites in the Persian Gulf, the Chinese hordes in South-East Asia or Hong Kong were all considered as potential threats. Proposals for dealing with them shifted erratically between the possibilities of a Korean-type war with large conventional forces and the use of low-yield nuclear weapons on lines of communication or interdiction targets. Sky cavalry, fleet task forces and opposed amphibious landings all had a run for their money, but no coherent doctrine could possibly be evolved because no one could imagine what limited war would be like. Throwing up their hands in despair the planners sought refuge in the pages of their pamphlets on the Infantry and Armoured Divisions. These, they said, were to be the guides, much as a man lost in London might try to find his way to Trafalgar Square with a map of Nottingham. The pamphlets, it will be remembered, were written in the early 1950's and they enshrined the dogma of Normandy and the

Western Desert. In the event, the hard facts of money and man-power cut through the doubts and hesitations. It soon became obvious that with the strategic reserves available and the limitations of mobility imposed by shortages of air transport and naval forces, a brigade group was the most that could be lifted and committed to battle quickly and efficiently. This limitation of force, together with the political inhibitions that arose from Britain's new and secondary role as a world military power, made it impossible to contemplate limited war by British forces alone, in the sense of opposed landings or air-borne assaults against hostile territory. It now became clearer than ever before that Suez had been the last, rather sad essay in British gunboat diplomacy. From now on limited war for the British Army was to mean operations of the sort conducted in Kuwait in 1961: the deployment of small forces at the request of a friendly government, on territory that offered a secure base for operations; and if the lessons of Kuwait meant anything, the operation would have to be conducted in deterrent terms, designed to prevent aggression or subversion rather than to defeat it. If Kassem's forces had attacked Kuwait before the British troops arrived, the operation could probably never have taken place at all. If they had attacked *after*, there would have been a crucial, possibly decisive, test of British military power overseas. The unacclimatized troops were suffering badly from the severe heat; anti-tank defences were suspect; there was a dangerous shortage of artillery; and the efficiency of some of the equipment was seriously affected by the climate—the radiators of vehicles boiled dry and the crews of tanks became exhausted even when they were not closed down for action. From the Kuwait experience much should have been learned. At first there was a depressing reluctance in official circles to accept the obvious weaknesses in the operation. It was held up as an example of the remarkable speed and efficiency of British planning and deployment. The argument that it had forestalled an attack was allowed—indeed inflated—to obscure the much more important possibility that if the attack had come it might have ended in a British humiliation. A medical officer who saw and reported on the danger of committing unacclimatized men and unprepared equipment to severe extremes of climate was furiously denounced by senior officers as a 'military bolshie' who had failed to see the wood for the trees. There were signs that the military authorities would have dearly liked, on the Oriental principle, to decapitate all convicted critics of the Kuwait operation as bringers of bad news. Behind the scenes, however, calmer counsels began to influence the preparation and training of troops for limited war operations, and when the Government of the Federation of South Arabia asked for help in the Yemen border area in 1964 the operations, mounted from Aden, were, in their early stages at any rate, rapid and effective.

The omens for the future are reasonably encouraging. There are signs of a realistic approach to the tactical problems of a European land battle; the lessons of Malaya and Kenya seem to have been absorbed into the new training manuals; a lively appreciation of the importance of strategic and tactical mobility in 'brush-fire' wars has begun to shape the training and doctrine of the strategic reserve. Two major obstacles, closely inter-related, remain in the way of those in the Army whose aim is still further enlightenment: the man-power problem and the organization of the basic fighting arm, the infantry.

When the Sandys White Paper proposed a regular Army of 165,000 officers and men, the figure was very largely reached by an actuarial estimate of the numbers that could be provided and maintained by voluntary recruiting. Based as it was on the doctrine of massive nuclear deterrence, it had no relevance to the tasks that the Army was, and still is, being asked to perform. In 1956 a committee under the D.C.I.G.S. (General Hull, now Field-Marshal and Chief of the Defence Staff) had carried out an examination based on operational requirements and had recommended 200,000 as the minimum figure. A compromise of 182,000 was eventually accepted by the Army Council as a planning figure, but it has always been clear in the minds of Army planners that many commitments would have to be reduced. In the event the tasks of the Army have increased. The simple arithmetic is inescapable—the Army is not big enough to do what it is being asked to do. One of the possible solutions to the problem is the introduction of a measure of partial conscription: selective service or conscription by ballot. Unfortunately, the shadow of universal service hangs over political and military attitudes; politicians believe that compulsory service is poison at the polling stations; the military establishment rightly rejects the appalling inefficiency of universal conscription with its ponderous training machine and its demoralizing and indiscriminate waste of time and man-power. Besides, soldiers enjoy the closed-circle atmosphere of an all-regular force, with its powerful associations of club, family and other exclusive social groups. Finally, there is the curious doctrine, a reflection of the indomitable belief of the British people in their own unique qualities of character, that while compulsory military service may be acceptable on the Continent or in remote foreign parts like the United States, it is in some way alien to the British way of life.

Although some of the difficulties experienced by the Army in arriving at workable tactical doctrines and training methods are demonstrably attributable to their shortage of man-power, others spring from their own handling of the resources that are actually available. The principal fault is that the present organization has a disproportionate balance of arms. This springs partly from an old-fashioned insistence upon the comparative priorities of 'teeth and tail'—the ratio of fighting troops to administrative service— and partly from certain rigid organizational characteristics in the teeth arms. The 'teeth to tail' ratio is a totem symbol left over from the days of simple weapons. This is not to say that its validity has entirely disappeared; it is still important to ensure that men are not wasted on inessential administration when they could be more gainfully employed; but in an army which is comparatively small, and has such weapons and equipment as surface-to-air guided missiles, air-portable anti-tank weapons and armoured personnel carriers, the old concept of the 'big battalion' is dead. The requirement is for a small, highly mobile force, equipped with a complex system of weapons and equipment. Whether this force is to be deployed in global or limited war, or employed in the internal security duties of cold war, it requires, by definition, a highly organized communications system, and a degree of intelligence effort and technical support far greater than the Army has contemplated in the past. The cavalry, the artillery and the infantry are useless if the higher commander is blind from lack of intelligence; if he cannot control a swiftly changing situation by means of smooth, efficient communications; and if the intricate weapons, vehicles and electronic equipment are not maintained by teams of highly trained technicians. It follows that the number of tanks, guns and bayonets which can be deployed in a modern army is limited, not by the number of men who can be recruited into the 'teeth arms', but by the number of trained electronic technicians, signals operators and vehicle fitters who can be provided to keep them in the field. This ratio is changing, and the organization of the Army must change with it.

Such a change of balance, once the necessity for it were accepted, should be a comparatively simple matter of man-power planning; but the way is barred by a formidable obstacle: the existence of a number of units of the teeth arms, the total of which can only be changed by amalgamations or disbandments. In the Royal Artillery and the Royal Engineers the problem is almost entirely one of Lieutenant-Colonels' commands and the danger of damaging the officer career structure. In the Royal Armoured Corps it is more difficult, and in the infantry, that most conservative and jealously guarded of 'Establishments', it seems almost insuperable. At present the infantry consists of sixty battalions, and it is planned that this number should exist in the all-regular Army. Of these, three are parachute battalions and eight are battalions of footguards partly employed in carrying out public duties in London. The remaining forty-nine battalions are infantry of the line and they are organized, for purposes of recruiting and training, into Infantry Brigades.

The whole infantry organization takes up over a quarter of the total man-power of the Army as at present planned: of about 160,000 other ranks in the all-regular Army, about 45,000 are allotted to infantry. Of these, about 35,000 are taken up in manning the sixty battalions, the remainder being employed in the training machine and on special duties away from their units.

The deployment of this considerable slice of the Army's planned man-power is governed by certain limiting factors inherent in the existing infantry organization. The sixty battalions, most of which, in spite of recent amalgamations, have powerful traditional and territorial associations, represent a fixed number of units which are kept in existence with scant regard for operational requirements or the limitations of man-power shortage. This means that at times when fewer than sixty battalions are operationally justifiable, a number of surplus units have to be kept in existence because to disband them or place them in suspended animation is not possible without giving grave offence to the traditional susceptibilities of the infantry. If man-power ever becomes plentiful this could possibly be justified on grounds of stability and good morale, but in times of man-power shortage the Army is faced with the frustrating alternatives of spreading its men evenly throughout the sixty battalions and thus keeping them all below strength, or of applying the man-power according to a system of priorities. In the first case the capability of units in the more important operational stations is lowered, and in the second case those battalions not engaged in immediately important operational tasks are reduced to a very low strength. But they still exist in some form and although operationally ineffective they use up man-power which could profitably be used elsewhere.

Superimposed on this is an uneconomic system of training, posting and drafting. Leaving aside the Brigade of Guards and the Parachute Brigade, which have special roles and peculiar problems, Infantry Brigade Depots are involved in these training and administrative tasks. Finally the whole problem is bedevilled by the system of recruiting to territorial regiments and brigades. This produces a completely unbalanced structure in which brigades like the Highland Brigade can recruit more men than they need, while the Home Counties and East Anglian Brigades, for example, are desperately short of men. There is no way of directing recruits into the brigades where they are needed, nor of transferring them after enlistment. The picture which emerges is one in which the major fighting arm of the Army is made up of arbitrary and immutable number of units, with an uneconomic training organization and an unbalanced recruiting system, using up too much of the Army's most precious commodity—man-power.

One possible remedy for this would be a formally constituted Corps of Infantry, organized on the same lines as the Royal Regiment of Artillery, with complete freedom to direct recruits or trained soldiers into the units in which they are needed; with the ability to vary the number of battalions in existence at any time to fit the operational requirement; and with a centralized training organization serving the whole corps. Eventually this must come, but it can only come in a climate of military and political opinion gradually conditioned to it. It would, however, be unwise to wait for another generation of soldiers to grow up before beginning the process which will lead eventually to the rational and logical establishment of the Corps of Infantry. This could be done in three phases. Phase one should be designed to correct the present uneconomic dispersion of training effort. It could be done, without damage to the existing regimental structure, by concentrating the training and administration of recruits into three or four Training Establishments, instead of the fourteen Depots which exist at present. Phase two, which should be simultaneous with phase one, would be the gradual transformation of the existing brigades into regiments, a process which has already, very reluctantly, been embarked upon. For example, the Welsh Brigade would cease to consist of the Royal Welch Fusiliers, the South Wales Borderers and the Welch Regiment, each providing one of the sixty battalions of infantry; it would become the Regiment of Wales with three battalions. Each could have distinctive dress, for the present, and maintain its distinctive traditions, but eventually we should aim at a stage when they become the First, Second and Third Battalions of the Regiment of Wales; any one of these battalions could be temporarily removed from the order of battle if the operational situation ceased to justify the existence of sixty battalions.

The third phase must be the gradual coalescence of these larger regiments into brigades corresponding with and based upon the three or four training depots. With each stage of this development the direction of recruits and the transfer of soldiers becomes possible through a wider area, until, in the final phase, a Corps of Infantry emerges. This would consist of the number of battalions operationally essential. Recruits would be enlisted into the infantry and posted to the battalion which needed them most; and the training and administrative overheads would be significantly reduced. It is not irrelevant to point out that such an organization is essential if the 'battle group' concept, a force of all arms commanded by a Lieutenant-Colonel or a Colonel, is ever to see the light of day.

It was in an attempt to cure some of the more obvious anomalies of this sort in single-service organization and planning that, in 1963, the service ministries were unified into an enlarged Ministry of Defence. It is too early yet to assess fully the effects of the reorganization, although there are already signs that it is bedevilled by delaying tactics inside the services. It is possible to argue that it was painfully overdue. Military theorists since the late nineteenth century had been advocating it with no effect; and it seems appropriate that in these pages the last words should be those of Liddell Hart. In 1946 he wrote on the planned allocation of military resources: 'The best corrective is to plan defence as a whole, with due regard both to natural limits and changing conditions. True economy of force can achieve a much sounder insurance policy, through integrated planning inspired by foresight.' In 1950, in *Defence of the West*, he went farther: 'The obvious forward step, and the natural one, is the combination of the three services in one.'

Thirteen years later the military establishment took its first step along the road to integration. The rearguard positions of the forces of reaction have still to be overcome.

§15§

The Making of Israel's Army:

The Development of Military Conceptions of Liberation and Defence

> The Jewish state is in its essence neutral. It needs an army only for defence (though equipped with every modern weapon) to keep order at home and resist attack from outside.
>
> Theodor Herzl,
> *The Jewish State* (1896)

YIGAL ALLON

THE Israel Defence Army was officially established on 27th June 1948. At this date, the Jewish Haganah forces[1] had for six months been engaged in a war of self-defence against local Arab guerrillas reinforced by volunteers from neighbouring countries. It was just six weeks since the British Mandate of Palestine had been terminated, the State of Israel proclaimed, and the newly formed state invaded by the regular armies of six neighbouring states—Egypt, Transjordan, Iraq, Syria, Lebanon and contingents of Saudi Arabia incorporated into the Egyptian Army—which had joined forces with local Arab units. To proclaim the State of Israel in the face of open threats by joint Arab forces of a seemingly overwhelming superiority appears to have been on the part of the Zionist leadership an act of extraordinary audacity, not to say foolhardiness. To understand it, it is necessary to outline the historical background of the making of the Jewish military force which had started, some seventy years earlier, as a collection of small groups of watchmen, and which culminated in the regular forces of present-day Israel.

As early as the 1880's, when the country was still under Ottoman rule and the Jewish population numbered hardly more than a few tens of thousands, local 'cells' had begun to be formed for self-defence against robbery, theft, marauding, murder and rape. These were for the most part non-political in character; yet they had, indirectly, political implications and consequences. The Jews felt they could not safely depend on the Ottoman authorities, and accordingly became more and more accustomed to self-dependence for the protection of their lives, the honour of their women, their property, and indeed of their very right to live in the Holy Land.

By the beginning of the present century, various embryonic military organizations with political leanings had made their appearance and had begun to think, for the first time, in terms of nation-wide service. They were ready to volunteer for any security service in any Jewish settlement, however remote—indeed, the remoter the better; and they joined up with local farmers and youth groups in the defence of these isolated villages with their fields and plantations.

During the first World War, especially after the Balfour Declaration and the entry of the United States into the war, the Palestinian Jews were (rightly) suspected by the Turks of disloyalty to the Ottoman Empire and co-operation with the British. When the Turks discovered that intelligence work was being carried out behind the German-Ottoman lines by a Jewish group of early settlers, mainly young people, they clamped down on all Jewish military or semi-military organizations, and expelled to the north (the Galilee) all the Jewish communities settled in the south close to Egypt, whence the British forces were approaching Palestine.

During this period, the first Jewish battalions were created within the framework of the British Army fighting in the Middle Eastern theatre. These were composed of volunteers and conscripts from Palestine, Britain and America; and they provided the Jewish youth with their first opportunity to acquire better military training and organization, and also to accumulate a certain amount of light military equipment which proved subsequently to be of great use.

The establishment of the British Mandate over Palestine immediately after the war signalled the beginning of the fulfilment of the Balfour Declaration promises concerning the right of Jewish immigration and settlement in Palestine, with the avowed object of creating a Jewish national home. It was from this time that the tension between Arabs and Jews assumed a more political character. At the start, it was confined to a very small section of the Arab community; but as a consequence of certain events— principally, the expulsion from Damascus of King Feisal I, and the indecision and hesitant policy of certain circles in the Mandatory Government—Arab hostility began to spread. It never included the whole Arab population, but political tension between Jews and Arabs became from this time a permanent feature of life in Palestine; and the new situation significantly affected the development of the Jewish military organization.

There followed a series of military conflicts between Arabs and Jews, known as riots. They came in cycles, each being on a larger scale, better equipped, and more properly military than its predecessor. The Jews, finding they could not rely on the authorities alone, had no alternative but to develop their own military organizations, and had to persist in developing them even though they were regarded and treated by the authorities as illegal.

The planning and development of pioneering Zionist settlement were from the start motivated, at least partly, by political-strategic needs. The location of the settlements, for instance, was determined by various considerations: economic viability; the needs of local defence; overall settlement strategy, which aimed at ensuring Jewish political presence in all parts of the country, with a view to ultimate solutions of the political problems of the country; and, finally, the role such blocks of settlements could play in an all-out clash which might be decisive for the future of Zionist aspirations. Accordingly, land was purchased, or (more often) reclaimed, in remote parts deep in Arab-populated areas and, as far as possible, close to the political borders of the country. Individual or small groups of settlements—ordinary villages, *kibbutzim*[2] and *moshavim*[3]—were thus isolated from one another by geographic distances, topographic barriers, and demographic differences, as well as by political obstacles created by the Mandatory régime; and every Jewish settlement had to be also a Haganah fortress. Consequently, economic and agricultural planning alone were not enough: they had to be accompanied by military planning and arrangements and the budget had to take care of both swords and ploughshares.

These needs introduced into the military thinking and execution of the Haganah various new elements. Among these were a more coherent nation-wide strategy, which took into account local conditions; comprehensive planning; greater mobility; and a more extensive use of automatic light machine-guns. Above all, they hastened the establishment of an illegal civil High Command fully authorized by the legal political institutions, and of a military

General Staff (likewise illegal) composed of all the usual branches with a Chief of Staff at the head.

The riots of 1936 and 1939, initiated by the Grand Mufti of Jerusalem, Haj Amin El Husseini (who later found refuge in Nazi Berlin), inflicted heavy casualties and damage on the Jewish community. At the same time, and indeed for this reason, they stimulated and accelerated the further expansion of the Haganah. During the riots, the Arab guerrilla forces grew to an unprecedented size and strength, and the British forces generally (there were honourable exceptions) either showed themselves thoroughly unwilling to suppress this wave of violence, as was their duty in accordance with the Government's undertakings; or, when they did attempt to do something, proved their inefficiency by breaking butterflies on wheels. The Haganah authorities recognized the new situation and its dangers. It seemed clear that if the riots did not come to an end immediately they might grow more serious; and in that case they would inevitably provoke a confrontation between the two sides at a time when the Arab side enjoyed the advantage of superiority in numbers, territorial continuity with neighbouring brotherly states, and British neutrality, if not actual indirect support. A confrontation in these circumstances was bound to result either in an undermining of the Jewish hold on certain areas of the country or in the enforcement of a policy in London contrary to the Balfour Declaration and the Mandatory undertaking. The need for effective defence accordingly became more than a need for protection of lives and property: it was now reinforced by the need for political survival.

Two encouraging phenomena on the British side contributed a great deal to the growth of these new trends in the Haganah. The first, which was official, was the establishment of a legal Jewish Settlement Police. This was composed of three main elements: (*a*) a small number of fully mobilized units, paid and equipped with small arms by the Mandatory Government to carry out all local guard duties; (*b*) a larger number of special police (reservists), who were allowed to use the weapons of the mobilized units for training and in emergencies; and (*c*) mobile units, confined to limited areas, also maintained by the Government, and responsible in their areas for patrolling roads and crops, reinforcing settlements under attack, and ambushing Arab guerrillas on their approach to or retreat from Jewish zones.

The other phenomenon was unofficial, but also of great significance. I refer to Captain Orde Wingate (later General Wingate). Thanks to the interests of the Iraqi Petroleum Company, which had suffered heavy damage to its oil pipe-line to the Haifa refineries at the hands of Arab guerrillas, a mixed Jewish-English unit, known as Special Night Squads (S.N.S.), was formed under Wingate's command to protect this vital pipe-line. The unit, however, was too small and its weapons too poor to accomplish its appointed task. Wingate therefore co-operated with similar Haganah units already in operation, often borrowing weapons from the Haganah arsenal, carrying out raids and ambushes, mostly at night, over wide areas in the Galilee on both sides of the pipe-line. In the morning the illegal units generally disappeared, and the legal unit returned to its base.

These two police forces, one legal, one semi-legal, were manned by the Haganah and used as a cover for training and operation. The appearance of Wingate, with his extraordinary Zionist ardour inspired by the Bible, his unconventional military gifts and his outstanding courage, was an event of historic importance for the Haganah. He identified himself so closely with the Haganah that he came to be regarded as a member of it. His Jewish counterpart and comrade in the illegal branch of the Haganah was Yitzhak Sadeh, a military genius of international calibre, one of the greatest commanders in Jewish history, the father of modern Jewish fighting, the teacher of most young Israeli commanders. He and Wingate together significantly modified the tactics of the Haganah. By patrolling remote fields, plantations and roads, ambushing enemy paths, and carrying out raids against enemy bases which helped to check the enemy's initiative, they contrived to pull out Haganah tactics from trenches and barbed wire into the open field of a more active defence.

By the end of 1936 it had become evident that this guerrilla war was not going to be brought to an end by an ultimate clash of either side's concentration of forces. Since both sides were regarded as illegal by the British authorities, neither side could for any length of time achieve such a concentration in the presence of the British forces. This had, moreover, the effect of putting a limit to the development of the size of the units in combat. It therefore forced the Haganah to concentrate on guerrilla tactics, making the most of its few legal units and resorting to its more numerous illegal units when the need was most pressing. The Haganah, and especially its field unit 'Fosh' (the initials of the Hebrew words for 'field companies'), learned to fight in the field, by night and by day, mostly in sections and platoons, sometimes as a company, and very occasionally, in co-operation with Wingate, within the framework of a battalion subdivided into smaller units. These units learned how to search for an enemy in hilly country and cultivated areas; to place an ambush; to carry out a raid; to outflank an enemy; and to disengage rapidly whenever necessary for military or political reasons.

The immediate aims of the Arabs were to annihilate as many existing settlements as possible, either by isolating them or by direct attack; to prevent the creation of new settlements; to break down Jewish resistance, and deter the Jews from claiming statehood. Their ultimate aim was to force the British to repudiate their commitment to the Zionist movement and to secure a permanent Arab majority in Palestine. The aims of the Zionist movement were directly opposed to these. It sought to protect all Jewish settlements, rural and urban, however remote or difficult to defend; to maintain normal life as far as possible, in production, business, transportation; to prevent economic breakdown, and thereby disprove the Arab claim that they were in control; and, finally, to expand Jewish rural settlements in still remoter areas of specifically strategic importance.

The years 1937-39 in fact turned out to be a peak period of pioneering settlement, accompanied by military penetration into vulnerable areas based on the newly formed *kibbutzim*. The combatant units were, in this period, supplemented by engineering units, which undertook to design prefabricated settlements equipped for defence. It is worth mentioning the method generally employed. In a given place, they would erect a whole settlement-outpost prefabricated out of wood, composed of a number of huts, a communal dining hall, kitchens and so on, the whole surrounded by a wooden double-wall filled with bullet-proof rubble and punctuated by firing-slits. In the middle of the campus there was a watch tower with a projector at the top; and the entire settlement was encircled by barbed wire and mine strips. The erection of the settlement, on nationally owned Jewish land, was generally accomplished in the space of a single day, starting early in the morning and ending late at night. The settlers were usually young people who were members of the Zionist pioneering movement and of the Haganah; they put themselves at the disposal of the national institutions, which decided—generally in consultation with the candidates—where and when they were to settle for good. By day, the Jewish Settlement Police provided the immediate defence, while the illegal units undertook the ambushes and patrols farther off, guarding the approaches to the new settlements. The settlers themselves, carrying light arms while at work, and taking it in turn to guard their new settlement, were a modern version of the labourers in *Nehemiah* who 'worked with one hand and held a weapon in the other'.[4]

Under the protection of this settlement-fortress not only was the land cultivated but, in due course, a new and better campus built near by. The completion of the new campus was, in the circumstances, regarded as something of a triumph, which was marked by bringing the mothers and children from the rear-base to their new home. It all sounds very unmilitary; but in the conditions prevailing in Palestine in the 1930's, it was a remarkably effective method of achieving political and military goals.

Under the pressure of militant Arab nationalism, the Haganah itself grew in size and strength. It included at that time almost every Jew and Jewess in an appropriate unit. It trained a large number of young N.C.O.s and officers. It acquired more and better weapons. Above all, it extended its nation-wide character and strengthened its command; it even made a successful beginning in establishing a permanently mobilized unit in reserve. All this was accomplished, moreover, without minimizing the importance of regional and local commands, and never at the expense of the tactical initiative of lower commanders. Without overlooking setbacks and defeats, it can be said that from the military point of view this period as a whole ended in victory. Not a single settlement was abandoned, and new settlements, forming new Jewish blocks in important areas, were added. As the Arabs found their attacks to be ever more costly, their initiative gradually diminished, until a relative peace—though an uneasy one—was achieved towards the spring of 1939.

While the Zionists won the war of the 1930's, the Arab Supreme Committee won the political struggle. They successfully opposed the recommendations of Lord Peel's Commission (1937) to partition Palestine into two states, one Jewish, one Arab, and extracted from the British Government the infamous White Paper (1939). This undertook to fix the relative numbers of Arabs and Jews in Palestine to the permanent disadvantage of the Jewish community by drastically limiting Jewish immigration, even from Nazi Germany. It prohibited Jews from settling in extensive areas of tiny Palestine, even where the land was owned by Jews, thus creating a new ghetto in the promised land itself. It ordered the disbanding of the Haganah; and it promised self-government in the near future, which in the circumstances would simply put the Jews at the mercy of the Arab majority. It was clear that this policy, if carried out, would mean the end of the Jewish dream of statehood, and perhaps also the physical extinction of the Jewish community in Palestine. This was more than any Jewish leader— even the most moderate, such as Chaim Weizmann—could accept. It seemed that after years of a working relationship between the Jews and the British in Palestine (which had not been an unmixed success, but also not a total failure) an open clash was, after all, unavoidable.

And, indeed, preparations began almost immediately to fight the White Paper policy: the White Paper policy exclusively, and not the United Kingdom as such. A number of ships with illegal immigrants from Europe reached the Palestinian coast (others were sunk on the open seas). New settlements were established in prohibited areas by the old familiar methods. The difference was that these were to be used as a means of war against the British of the White Paper policy, not against the Arabs; and that they had now to be erected between evening and morning in order to avoid British patrols.

The preparations had gone as far as the creation of a special group of volunteers, who were being trained in sabotage and commando operations with a view to extending the struggle to the purely military sphere, when the second World War broke out. This put the Jews in a dilemma. The British were fighting, gallantly and—at the start—alone, the greatest enemy of the Jews in history. In the circumstances, could the Jews continue to fight the British in one of their vital bases in the Middle East, thus weakening their military effort against the common enemy? The answer was, of course they could not; and the main problem, on this horn of the dilemma, became that of finding a way of being accepted as allies, declared or otherwise, in the actual fighting against the Germans and Italians. On the other hand, could the Jews adopt a position which might be interpreted by London as implying their reconciliation to the White Paper policy? Again the answer was, of course they could not: the idea of resistance to the White Paper had to be kept alive, and military preparations for such resistance actively maintained. David Ben-Gurion memorably defined this paradoxical position when he said: 'We will fight the Germans as if there were no White Paper, and we will fight the White Paper as if there were no Germans.' This was admirably said; but in practice the second part of Ben-Gurion's proposition proved to be less easy to carry out than the first. What in fact happened was that the Jewish community in Palestine devoted itself to the general war effort against the Axis powers but, alas, unwisely neglected its own independent illegal units. This was perhaps inevitable; and the more so, since along with the genuine anxiety to participate in the defeat of Germany, there lurked in many Jewish minds the illusion that history might repeat itself, and this war yield a new Balfour Declaration with a clearer and firmer British commitment to Jewish statehood.

Events on the Western Front in the first years of the war created a new situation in the Middle East. France was overrun, and the French forces in Syria and Lebanon declared their loyalty to Vichy. Turkey was still uncommitted, but suspected of a readiness to join the Axis powers if their successes continued. Egypt was threatened from the Axis bases in the Western Desert; Arab circles leaned towards Berlin and Rome; and in Baghdad, Rashid Ali's pro-German *coup* irritated the entire Middle East. It seemed that the whole area was threatened by a potential gigantic pincer movement. Observant leaders of the Jewish community in Palestine suddenly realized that Palestine could become a battleground of major campaigns, and that it might even, like other territories, be evacuated by the allies. If this happened, the Jewish community would face two enemies, the Germans and the Arabs; and it was this realization that marked a fresh turning-point in the history of the Jewish military organization in Palestine.

It operated as an immediate spur to action. In May 1941, the High Command of the Haganah, with the approval of the World Zionist Eexcutive, responded to the suggestion that an independent illegal striking-force, consisting of nine companies regularly mobilized for action, at any time and in any place, should be established as soon as possible. This unit, known as the 'Palmach' (the initials of the Hebrew words for 'striking companies'), was designed to act either independently or in co-operation with the allies according to changing circumstances. The formation of the Palmach coincided with the allies' decision to invade Syria and Lebanon in August 1941; and because the allies, it appears, were pressed for time to prepare for this invasion, the first two companies were invited, through the mediation of the Political Department of the Zionist Eexcutive, to participate in the campaign in autonomous operations, as guides and saboteurs, as advanced units, and on intelligence assignments behind the enemy's lines. All these operations were successfully carried out, to the great satisfaction of the Allied Command in the area. From that time until the allied victory at Alamein, an official co-operation was continued, but without the incorporation of the members of the Palmach into the British Army—in contrast to the tens of thousands of Jewish youth who had joined the British Army and been incorporated into it. This amounted to a *de facto*, though indeed provisional, recognition of the illegal Palmach by the British authorities. Both parties refused to go any farther. The Palmach insisted on remaining independent of the British, and the British stressed the strictly temporary character of this co-operation. It seems that both sides realized that they might before long find themselves on opposite sides of the barricades; accordingly (to adapt Aristotle's saying about old men) they were bound to love as if they would one day hate.

The necessity to prepare for a campaign against a modern military machine such as the German gave the Palmach commanders an opportunity to think, to plan, and to prepare their men on the most modern lines. The inequality of strength was obvious. A general frontal engagement would mean the end of the Jewish forces. A very specific plan therefore had to be drawn up which would suit the specific conditions of the country. The motive power behind it was the determination to save as many lives as possible of the civil population; to hamper the advance of the German Army, in order to help other fronts; and, if death was the issue, to die fighting the enemy rather than in the crematorium. The scheme that was devised was a highly imaginative one. It was decided to turn the area consisting of the whole of Mt Carmel, the valley of Zebulun (between Haifa and Acre), the mountain chains of the Western Galilee based on Haifa Bay on the Mediterranean, and an airfield strip on the coast into a huge, escape fortress for all the Jews in Palestine, then just over half a million. It was a kind of modern Massada, with greater force and better chances. The combination of a hilly country with some access to the sea and air, fully supported by the allied forces in the matter of supplies, defended in depth and assisted by guerrilla raids against enemy lines of communication, bases and installations, was thought to carry a fair chance of survival. The subsequent successes of the Allies at Tobruk, Leningrad and other surrounded bridgeheads were a proof that the scheme was not unrealistic. It was even hoped that, if and when the tide turned, this Carmel fortress might become a bridgehead for invasion, making it possible to meet the advancing enemy armies half-way.

Happily, there was never any need to carry this plan into effect. But the very formation of such a grand strategy—the military training and organizational preparations, the study of the enemy's structure, strategy and tactics which it involved—provided the Haganah and its striking-force, the Palmach, with a new dimension of military imagination and experience. It distinctly advanced Jewish military thinking to a more mature stage.

As a whole, it would be safe to say that the second World War strengthened the Jewish community in Palestine. Tens of thousands of volunteers served in British uniform in various branches of the services and acquired valuable training and knowledge which they brought back to the Haganah, to its great benefit at later stages.

Once the paths of the Palmach and the British authorities had parted, the former went on growing in numbers and constantly improving its standards of training. Lack of funds, however, soon threatened its existence. The difference between British and Zionist budgets made itself felt, and the Palmach was faced with a grave decision. It could disband itself and either join the British Army or go home; and this in either case would mean the disappearance of the backbone of the Haganah. Alternatively, it could attempt to become economically self-supporting, and thereby ensure its existence as a permanent mobilized unit. The second alternative was not an easy one to adopt. It meant that people serving full-time in an army would be required also to earn their own livings—an unusual demand, to say the least. Nor did the improvement in the situation on the front after Alamein help to keep alive the sense of urgency which reconciles men to sacrifice. Nevertheless, the knowledge that the allied victory, with all its historic importance, was not yet the final victory of Zionism, and that the Zionist struggle for independence was likely to begin when the world war was over, gave a fresh impetus to the acceptance of hardship. The argument itself was, of course, very simple. If the White Paper remained in force, the Jews would fight the British. If it were abrogated, the Arabs might initiate large-scale riots. In either case, the Haganah men, and especially the Palmach fighters, had to prepare for military clashes when the allies celebrated V-Day and began demobilizing.

For the Palmach, an original plan was finally adopted. The Palmach platoons were to be stationed in *kibbutzim* all over the country. Adjoining platoons would form companies, and adjoining companies would form battalions. All members of the force would spend half of each month working on their *kibbutz* and the other half in training. Their earnings from the half-month's work would be enough to maintain them for the whole month. The plan succeeded completely in solving the financial problem of the Palmach's continued military existence. But it was a success also in other, unexpected ways. Besides giving the young people of the Palmach the experience of working for a living, it proved also to be invaluable as an ideological and social force, and as such helped to create the high morale and spirit which the unit sustained to the end.

The introduction of battalions as tactical units and the beginning of the formation of a brigade were not allowed to undermine the flexibility of the Palmach as a guerrilla force. The individual soldier and the various units continued to be trained to think and act in the smallest possible units (it used to be said that the smallest unit in the Palmach was the soldier and his weapon). Consequently, they retained their individual quality even within the larger framework. Though greater importance was now attached to the stabilizing of well-defined units, from the section through the platoon and company to the battalion and brigade, in actual operations the use of the task-force—composed of various elements of warfare, sometimes drawn from different units—remained the common practice according to the nature of the military objective.

Successful co-operation and co-ordination of junior commanders and smaller units require in a marked degree the qualities of intelligence and insight; in the Palmach the intensive training in guerrilla tactics helped to develop these faculties. Experience shows that it is easier and safer to turn guerrilla units into a regular force than the other way about. It seems to me now that the multi-purpose training of the Palmach was one of its greatest assets. Its members received a physical training of a distinctly Spartan kind. They learned to use different types of weapons, from knives and hand-grenades to machine-guns and mortars, as well as explosives. They received very intensive courses in field-training, by day and night, in small and big groups. Their sense of orientation was sharpened. They learned, on foot, the topography of the length and breadth of the country. They became acquainted with specific terrains in which they might be expected to fight. They even devoted a great part of their studies to learning the national habits and military structure of possible future enemies, namely, the British and the Arabs. In addition to their infantry training at commando level, they all received elementary amphibious training, to prepare them for the landing of illegal immigrants. After a hot debate between the Palmach commanders and the British-trained Jewish officers, the British conception of battle-drill was dismissed as an over-schematic and artificial way of acquiring fighting habits in the field. Finally, in order to be able to expand the force if and when general mobilization took place, the Palmach trained any capable member in a commander's course, even when there was no immediate prospect of providing him with a unit of his own and he had to go on serving as a private for a while. In the event, this method did enable the Palmach to expand rapidly in an emergency.

The Palmach became the laboratory of the Haganah, where new systems of training and organization could be tested. Its achievements belonged, of course, to the whole Haganah, and its high standards served as a model to other units of the Haganah. It was in fact the first fully mobilized Jewish army to act completely under an independent Jewish political authority since Bar-Kochba's some eighteen centuries earlier. Accordingly, the Palmach was rather more than just one of the military units of the Haganah. It was an inspiring element within the Jewish community for resistance against foreign oppression, and a reliable instrument in the hands of the political leadership for achieving national goals.

In any military undertaking, decisions about strategy, tactics, training and organization can only be taken in the light of all the relevant factors. To understand these aspects of the Haganah's military undertaking against the British in Palestine, it is necessary to indicate the specific factors which influenced, if not determined, its subsequent conduct of the struggle. The Jews were still a minority in Palestine: they numbered about half a million (about one-third of the population); they were concentrated in cities and villages mainly along the coastal plains but also in certain blocks in the Galilee, and scattered in isolated villages—mostly *kibbutzim*—in the Arab interior, in the Judaean hills and the northern Negev. Even the most thickly populated Jewish areas were interspersed with Arab settlements; and in some cities the population was mixed. British military bases and police stations were spread throughout the country, occupying strategic positions; the Mandatory administration was in full control; and the British Navy was conspicuously present in the Mediterranean. The British troops were well trained and equipped, and seasoned by their participation in the recent world war. They, too, however, were suffering from postwar fatigue; and both the British economy and British public opinion were impatient for the speediest and most complete demobilization. As far as the Arabs were concerned, it was recognized that, if a struggle took place between the Jews and the British in Palestine, the most that could be expected of them was an unfriendly neutrality towards the Jews; while in the country itself co-operation between the Arabs and the British was exceedingly likely.

What strategy was to be chosen? A fully fledged, openly declared war would have furnished the British with an excuse to take severe action against the Jewish community, with the best chances of success. The British forces suffered none of the disabilities of illegality; consequently, they had the advantage in mobility, as well as an overwhelming superiority in the means of waging war. As the country had no jungles or big forests, and as most of the hills and mountains were populated by Arabs, the strategy of classic guerrilla warfare was ruled out. The choice, in the end, reduced itself to one of three alternative strategies: at one extreme, terrorist tactics, directed without discrimination against all British targets and personnel; at the other extreme, a 'limited' struggle which renounced military action and confined itself exclusively to bringing in illegal immigrants, establishing new settlements in prohibited areas, and holding mass demonstrations; and the 'middle way' in fact adopted, which rejected personal terrorism, both on moral and on practical grounds (it was considered immoral because non-Jewish, and impractical because it could provoke counter-terrorism), and accepted the second alternative—illegal immigration, new settlements in prohibited areas, and mass demonstration—combined with direct military action based on guerrilla tactics.[5]

The term 'struggle' has been used deliberately (and, I believe, accurately) rather than the term 'war', even though it included military action. For, first, though the actions were based on guerrilla tactics, it was not an overall guerrilla war; and, second, it was a definite part of the Haganah's strategy and tactics to avoid casualties, or at least reduce them to a minimum, on the British side as well as the Jewish, in all attacks including those on military objectives. Accordingly, a great deal of care was exercised, and a great many risks taken, in the planning and execution of the military operations to achieve this aim.

The outline of the strategy that follows attempts to deal briefly with each of the elements mentioned. The illegal immigration was effected mainly by vessels across the Mediterranean, but some of it also on foot across the land borders, and some even by illegal air-flights. By the end of the period 1945-48 some sixty-five ships had crossed the Mediterranean, and the number of immigrants, most of them survivors of the Nazi destruction of European Jewry, had reached a total of nearly 100,000. It had three main purposes: to increase the actual number of Jews in Palestine; to expose the pitiful inadequacy of the White Paper immigration quotas; and to win world sympathy, including British public opinion, for the Zionist cause, thus forcing Whitehall into the tightest of corners against a background of broken promises and the tragedy of the Jewish people. The illegal settlements were aimed at two objectives: first, to achieve footholds in strategically vital areas against anticipated events; and, second, to expose (again) the

White Paper policy, which in effect declared the greater part of Palestine to be out of bounds to the Jews. The object of the military actions was not to destroy the British forces in Palestine; this would have been beyond the scope of the Jewish forces though, indeed, they were capable of annihilating substantial units and bases. It was, rather, to undermine their position, their sense of security and their prestige; above all, it was to convince Whitehall once and for all that, without the consent of the Jews, Britain could not keep Palestine as a safe and workable base in this vital region. By the renunciation of killing, on the one hand, and, on the other, the high military accomplishment of the Palmach raids and actions, with the heroic participation of the people as a whole, it was hoped at once to arouse sympathy, and even admiration, for the Jews of Palestine, and to prove to the world—including the Jews themselves—that they were a force to be reckoned with. The unusual combined operation sketched above—illegal immigration, illegal settlement and illegal military action—was therefore aimed at forcing the problem on all parties concerned, and forcing them to seek a positive solution. It was hoped, in short, to prove to Britain and the rest of the world that an unjust and unworkable policy may cease to be a policy at all; and thereby to induce Britain to change it for a better—or, alternatively, for a worse, in which case the Jews would receive a fresh impetus to the struggle directed towards forcing her to abandon the Mandate.

In the military struggle itself, the preparations made during the second World War (to a great extent, with British help) to resist a possible German-Italian invasion proved to be of great value to the units which now had to carry out their modified operations against the British.

The immigration ships were manned mostly by Jews, and whenever one succeeded in penetrating the naval blockade and reached its appointed destination on the Palestinian coast, generally at night, the bridgehead was defended by infantry ambushes, supplemented occasionally by boats. The immigrants were unloaded on to small boats, some carried on the ship itself, some brought from the coast. Those who could not help themselves were carried to the shore on the shoulders of their rescuers, and were taken on the same night, by guides and armed escorts, equipped with false Palestinian identity cards, to selected towns and villages where they were safely deposited among the civil population. This rescue work had been preceded, of course, by intensive preparations in Europe. These included the transportation of the refugees from eastern and central Europe to the Mediterranean coast of Europe; the organizing of an underground of the refugees in the D.P. camps; the purchasing and equipping of the ships; and, finally, the loading and despatching of the ships across the Mediterranean. All this was arranged by the illegal Haganah command in Europe, consisting mainly of Palmach men, Palestinian Jewish ex-servicemen of the British forces (who deliberately remained in Europe), reinforced by fighting elements of the refugees themselves—ghetto-fighters, partisans, and other combatants. It was a huge enterprise, which cut across international borders, and defied effective British intelligence (in Europe as well as in Palestine), British naval control of the Mediterranean, British air-reconnaissance, and the strong mobile forces of the British in Palestine itself. It compelled the Haganah to develop itself into an effective military organization capable of planning, directing and executing this complex operation; and the units engaged in the actual landings gained valuable experience in combined coastal operations, including their tactics and their logistics and other organizational aspects. The strengthening of the Haganah, moreover, was matched by that of the people as a whole. The Jewish community in Palestine gained experience of the price of nationhood. Whenever a ship was successfully landed, the news was publicly announced the following day, to ensure that none of its political meaning was lost to the community. When a landing had to be carried out by day, the fighters were instructed to hide their arms, and the people were summoned to the beaches to mingle with the refugees in order to prevent their arrest by the British. Some of them lost their lives while marching against machine-gun fire. This kind of episode had the effect of strengthening the solidarity of the population with the fighters, and did a great deal towards uniting the people into a nation in the making.

The illegal settlements were a simpler undertaking than the illegal immigrations but they, too, greatly extended the military experience of the Haganah. As already explained, the necessary planning involved the choosing of the site, the engineering of a whole prefabricated village, the handling of transportation, defence arrangements, and co-operation between soldiers and civilians. Though some of this was quasi-military, it yet helped to advance the Haganah as a military force conscious of a national responsibility.

The most valuable experience, however, was provided by the strictly military operations, both big and small. The chosen targets were railways, bridges, armoured vehicles, police stations, military bases, refugee prison camps, radar stations, armed patrol boats and ships in Palestine and Cyprus. All these targets were defended by stationed guards or mobile patrols, or by both. Some were near the Jewish areas, and some in remoter parts along the borders of Palestine. Except for the Transjordan Frontier Force, which was manned by Arabs and commanded by British officers, the Arabs did not participate in the actual fighting against the Jews. But they willingly supplied British intelligence with information about the movements of Jewish units;[6] and most of the Haganah's operations had therefore to be carried out at night. Because of the need to avoid Arab observers as well as British patrols, the retreat from a target sometimes took hours. When the target happened to be especially far from Jewish bases, it might have to be extended over two days, the men marching by night and hiding by day. Such an operation required, besides an intensive physical training, a high degree of tactical skill and administrative competence. It involved the ability to act as small units or as co-ordinated small units over wide areas; to operate as a company and more, up to a battalion as a tactical unit, against one target or adjoining targets; and, above all, to employ big and small units in one operation under a brigade command. This experience was gained not only on the battlefield but also in exercises of movement and fire in the empty desert south of the Dead Sea. The fact that practically every man of the Palmach, along with a good number of people from other field-units of the

Haganah, was deliberately given the opportunity for Commander's combat experience in all ranks served to temper the fighting ability and spirit of the Haganah for the greater engagements of the future.

Not least important to the military development, at this stage as at all other stages, was the non-military phenomenon already touched upon: the close relationship between the civil and military branches of the community, the full control of the military organization by the elected civil bodies, and the conscious loyalty of the troops to their undeclared and as yet unrecognized national Jewish government. The maturity this indicated may count as perhaps one of the greatest achievements of the Haganah as, pre-eminently, a national army of liberation and defence.

Tension between Jews and Arabs began to mount throughout 1947, during the prolonged deliberations of the United Nations. Both camps began to speed up their military preparations by expanding their man-power, intensifying their training and accumulating more arms. It soon became evident not only that the British would evacuate Palestine but that they would leave behind chaos, and that an all-out clash between Arabs and Jews was therefore inevitable. When, on 29th November 1947, the General Assembly of the United Nations resolved by a two-thirds majority (including the United States and the Soviet Union) to partition the country into two sovereign states with a common economic framework and an international enclave in the Jerusalem area, the Arabs immediately rejected this decision. Arab riots began, and Arab guerrillas made their first appearance in the remoter areas of the country.

The Mandatory Government proclaimed its neutrality, and the British forces in Palestine were ordered only to guard the remaining provisional bases and the remaining routes to Haifa harbour, the gate for evacuation. A United Nations proposal to set up an international 'caretaker' agency for Palestine, to supervise the carrying out of the United Nations resolution, was rejected by London.

The strategy of the Haganah in this first period of Israel's War of Liberation may be summarized as follows:

1. Remote settlements were on no account to be abandoned.[7] This, it was recognized, would impose a considerable military burden on the High Command, by forcing it to maintain long lines of communication and supplies. On the other hand, the settlements could be expected to divert to themselves at least part of the Arab pressure on the Jewish centres in the plains; they could be used as bases for guerrilla operations behind the enemy's lines; and they would serve as ultimate objectives to be reached when the time came for a liberating offensive in the whole area.

2. Direct clashes with the British were as far as possible to be avoided, in order not to impede their plans for evacuation. Major offensives against the Arabs were likewise to be avoided for these might lead to British intervention, and thus (again) delay their evacuation.

3. Jewish territorial continuity was to be established in each predominantly Jewish zone and, as far as possible, between the zones themselves. Territorial continuity meant greater safety for internal roads of communication, the saving of man-power and the possibility of establishing a reasonable military posture to meet the openly threatened official invasion by the armies of the several neighbouring states.

These aims were for the most part achieved, and helped greatly to prepare the ground for the larger aims of the immediate future. This preliminary phase also helped to shape further the military organization itself, in the following ways:

1. The Palmach, the striking force of the Haganah, entered the war with four fully mobilized battalions organized within a brigade, and expanded rapidly into ten battalions divided into three brigades, under a central command quartered close to the High Command of the Haganah to facilitate hour-by-hour communication about its special tasks within the country or across the borders. It was assigned special operations of its own within the framework of the overall strategy; or was used as the spearhead of major operations on difficult fronts under the front

commander. In these latter operations, the Palmach acted in conjunction with other units.

2. In this phase of the war, the embryonic Navy and Air Force were separated from the Palmach, and gradually developed into distinct forces with their own commands. They remained, however, to the end, subordinated to the General Staff of the Army.

3. A substantial number of battalions, drawn from the field-corps of the Haganah, and gradually formed into brigades, were permanently mobilized. At the start they were confined to given territories but soon became mobile on a nation-wide scale, thus enabling the High Command to concentrate forces in any theatre.

4. The Home Guard, composed of older people, women and young people under the age of eighteen in the villages and towns, was partly mobilized within the framework of the Haganah's Home Guard. They generally undertook the passive defence of Jewish quarters in mixed cities, on farms and in settlements; but sometimes they were mobilized and sent from the cities to rural areas as reinforcement, acting as watchmen and workers. In addition to the importance of the direct service which the Home Guard gave, it helped to relieve field-units of defensive duties, thus freeing them for active combat.

5. Various services, such as transport, medical aid, civil defence and engineering, were established without undue difficulty. As most of the civilian population was in one way or another organized by or connected with the Haganah, it was relatively easy to find the man-power and civil equipment required for these services.

The advances outlined above were all accomplished by voluntary methods; for there was as yet no Jewish State with the power to enforce service. It seems that the combination of idealism and a common danger made possible the mobilization of an army in the making for the defence of a state in the making.

The second phase of the war was very brief but decisive. It covered the interval, sometimes only a matter of days, never more than a few weeks, between the British evacuation of particular areas and its final evacuation of the country as a whole on 14th

May 1948, the date of the expiry of the Mandate. In this brief period, the Jews and Arabs confronted each other in the physical absence but political presence, so to speak, of the British. This curious situation gave the Haganah the opportunity to initiate main efforts in crucial areas, directed towards establishing territorial continuity within and between Jewish areas, extending Jewish control of areas previously held by Arab forces, and consolidating defence arrangements in preparation for the threatened invasion of the Arab regular armies from across the borders. In this period, not only were most of the Arab attacks on the settlements repulsed, but the Jewish forces liberated such vital areas as Upper and Lower Galilee, including Arab centres like Saimach and Beisan, and mixed towns like Safad and Tiberias; Western Galilee, including the mixed city of Haifa;[8] the large Arab centre of Jaffa; important parts of New Jerusalem; and many strategically important villages in many parts of the country from north to south. Hardly less important were a number of successful field campaigns undertaken to relieve besieged places in the Jerusalem Corridor and at the entrance to the northern Negev. Although the Haganah suffered some painful setbacks during this period—such as heavy casualties, the destruction of Jewish convoys and transport vehicles on their way to isolated areas, and the loss of a number of Jewish settlements around Jerusalem—the balance sheet on the whole was extremely favourable. These achievements proved to be crucial in establishing a sounder geo-strategic posture for defence against the imminent invasion of forces of superior strength.

The third phase of the war, which lasted from 15th May to 10th June 1948, brought at last the long-threatened simultaneous offensive of all the neighbouring Arab armies on all fronts. It was a very difficult period. The Arabs' superiority in numbers and equipment was all too obvious; and the psychological impact of the invasion was as full of danger as the military strength of the enemy. In these circumstances, it was fortunate indeed that the Haganah, though not ready to embark at once on a full-scale counter-offensive, yet rejected a purely defensive strategy. If it had concentrated solely on defence, the war would have been lost, for in that case the initiative would have remained with the enemy, which was in a position to choose, almost freely, its time and place for attack, and to concentrate sufficient strength to break the Jewish lines of defence almost everywhere. The Haganah accordingly adopted a combination of defensive methods and offensive action, which came to be known as 'active defence'. There was, of course, no continuous line of defence. Every settlement or group of adjoining settlements was defended for the most part by the settlers themselves. In some places, strategic hills and strongholds were held by regular troops; and a series of night raids, carried out by the Israelis on the enemy's soil, sometimes deep into its territory, forced the enemy to exercise great vigilance in the defence of bases, bridges and other military objects. This was the time when the first pieces of artillery—very few in number and very old-fashioned—were used by the Israelis. A small number of light aeroplanes, such as Piper Cubs and Austers, which were bravely used for reconnaissance, light transport and even primitive bombing and strafing, were now supplemented by a few better aeroplanes, mainly Messerschmitts. It has to be added that the psychological value of the artillery and the aeroplanes was at least as great as their military value.

The number of Israeli raids and local counter-attacks, most of them made by night, gradually increased. Most of the enemy's direct attacks on the fortified settlements failed, and the very few— some two or three—that succeeded proved to be very costly. Yet the enemy did achieve, at least on two fronts, substantial gains. The Egyptians managed to advance as far as within twelve kilometres of Rehovot; the Syrians established a bridgehead across the Jordan in the Upper Galilee; the Transjordanians were stationed in the two Arab towns of Ramla and Lydda, the latter including the international airport, a half-hour's drive from Tel-Aviv. They also succeeded in repulsing Israeli attacks around Genin.

Gradually a stalemate was reached. The Arab armies lost their offensive momentum, and the Israelis, though becoming increasingly more active in defence, were not yet prepared for large-scale offensives. It seems that both sides were seeking a breathing-space; accordingly, both agreed to respond to a United Nations call for a one-month cease-fire, beginning on 11th June.

The Israelis, encouraged by their successes and drawing lessons from their defeats, used this month of the cease-fire to consolidate as far as possible every aspect of their military organization. During this period the first legal ceremonies were held. The Haganah was formally declared the official army of the new state, to be known as Israel's Defence Army.[9] All the troops took an oath of allegiance to the state. An official uniform was introduced. Ranks were created for officers and N.C.O.s, the highest of which was that of *rav-aluf* (Major-General), held by only one person, Ya'acov Dori, the new Chief of Staff, formerly Chief of Staff of the Haganah. The Commanding Officers of the various fronts and of the Palmach, the Air Force, the Navy and the armoured brigade, and a few key-officers of the General Staff, held the rank of *aluf* (Brigadier-General). These ranks have been retained to the present day. The remaining small, semi-autonomous, underground organizations were ordered by the Government to disband, and their members were absorbed as individuals by the Army.

This transformation of the Haganah into the regular army of an independent state was, in one sense, nominal rather than substantial. The overall organization, the chain of command, the personalities, the loyalties remained as before. But, in another sense, the change was real indeed. For it symbolized the historic change of Palestine into a sovereign Jewish state, and of the Jewish community into a nation; and as such it had great spiritual significance.

The entire field army now consisted of seven regular brigades, three Palmach brigades and one armoured brigade. The last was still very poorly equipped, but the rest were now better equipped with Czechoslovakian and French arms, including better (though still insufficient) artillery. The Air Force acquired a number of Czech-made Messerschmitts and English-made Spitfires bought on the Continent, and a number of Dakotas for transport and bombing. The Navy improved its equipment and training, for naval guerrilla warfare and small landings as well as coastal patrolling. Each unit now had its own direct command, but remained a part of a single army under the supreme command of the Chief of the General Staff, who in his turn was responsible to the Minister of Defence, Mr David Ben-Gurion, and his Deputy, Mr Israel Galili, former Commander-in-Chief of the Haganah. A War Cabinet was formed, which was authorized by the Cabinet to make certain decisions on behalf of the Government; and another important new body, the Defence Affairs Foreign Committee of the Knesset (Parliament), was authorized by the House to act on its behalf. The Israeli forces as a whole were still inferior to those of the enemy in numbers, equipment and geostrategic conditions, but they were superior in organization, discipline, fighting-spirit, unity, and the sense of 'no alternative'. Either you win the war, or you will be driven into the Mediterranean—you individually and the whole nation: this was the meaning of 'no alternative', a phrase widely used at this time by troops and civilians alike, to express the nation's consciousness that it was fighting for its survival. It was obvious that, once the cease-fire was over, both sides would try to take the initiative in a resumption of hostilities.

The fourth and final stage of Israel's War of Liberation, which started on 11th June 1948, saw a radical change both in the fighting ability and the logistics of Israel's Defence Army. Because the enemy was so strong and so close to the most populated Jewish areas, the Israelis dared not adopt a purely defensive strategy. It was clear that if the invading armies were allowed to enjoy the advantage of offensive action, they might break through Israel's sparse lines, crush its forces and gain possession of all Jewish-held territory, which, being narrow, would be all too easy to subdue. The strategy decided upon was therefore the only correct one: to take the initiative as soon as the United Nations' imposed cease-fire had ended. Not wishing to violate the U.N.'s decision by anticipating the enemy's offensive even by one day, and knowing that the enemy was accustomed to attack in daylight, the Israelis decided to anticipate the enemy by just a few hours, and launch their own offensive at midnight, when the cease-fire officially ended.

The war could not have been won without crushing the enemy's forces. The accomplishment of this ultimate goal required a greater concentration of Israel's forces on specific fronts than any previously attempted, with the object of achieving a local superiority to offset the overall inferiority of its forces. This could not, of course, be done on all fronts simultaneously, and an order of priorities had to be set up. The most urgent tasks seemed to be the following: to eliminate the danger to Tel-Aviv and its immediate surroundings by liberating Lydda and Ramla and penetrating the hilly country east of the coastal plain; to lift the siege of Jerusalem; and, if possible, to out-flank the Transjordanian-held Old City from the north. The next task was to secure the Haifa region by liberating Nazareth and the remaining parts of Lower Galilee. At the same time, the Egyptians in the south, the Iraqis in the east, and the Syrians in the north, had to be checked by tactics of active defence, based on settlements and mobile forces, until offensive action could be undertaken against them.

These operations—which included, in the liberation of Lydda and Ramla, a daring raid of a mechanized battalion into Lydda itself—were wholly successful. Engaging four brigades under a single command (the Palmach command) on the Central Front, and two brigades under a single command (the Northern command) on the Northern Front, they gave the Israeli Army new experience, new dimensions and greatly increased confidence. Although much larger forces were now engaged against a single target, guerrilla tactics were not abandoned. Day and night fighting in large bodies supported by artillery was combined with guerrilla actions, which were fused into the general planning in a way that proved to be highly successful throughout the War of Liberation and its aftermath. Generally speaking, all the goals were achieved; and had a second cease-fire not been imposed by the United Nations, on 19th July 1948, the Israeli offensive might have continued, with short intervals, shifting the main effort from one front to another, until a complete destruction of the enemy, or at least its withdrawal from the entire territory of Mandatory Palestine, had been achieved.

The second cease-fire lasted until 10th October 1948; and from this time the Israeli command was obliged to take into account not only the usual factors but also the possibility of further United Nations intervention in the form of cease-fires. These, it seemed, were again likely to be imposed when the Israelis had the upper hand, and the exploitation of their success could yield substantial gains in territory, as well as further destruction of the enemy's units. The immediate military consequence of this situation was that every operation, besides being part of an over-all plan, had also to be complete in itself.

The period of the second cease-fire, 19th July to 10th October 1948, was successfully used by the Israelis to rest their forces; to reinforce their units with fresh man-power drawn from the growing local youth and from the new immigrants flocking in—now legally—from the concentration camps in Cyprus as well as from Europe, and by more and better equipment supplied by Czechoslovakia and France; and to reorganize the Army's chain of command. The reorganization took the following form. The entire country was divided into four territorial commands, always referred to at this time as 'fronts'. These were the Northern Front, which included the entire Galilee and thus confronted the Lebanese, Syrian, Iraqi and Kaukgie's Central Galilee forces; the Eastern Front, covering the Samaria and Sharon areas, and confronting Iraqi and Transjordanian forces in the Triangle;[10] the Central Front covering the Tel-Aviv–Jerusalem axis, and confronting the main body of the Transjordanian forces flanked by Iraqis in the north and Egyptians in the south; and the Southern Front, which covered the southern half of Palestine from Rehovot in the north down to the Red Sea, most of this area being held by the Egyptian forces reinforced by a Saudi Arabian contingent. A further act of reorganization during this period was one directly affecting the Palmach. Although its three brigades remained intact to the end of the war, the separate headquarters of the Palmach were disbanded. A new unit called 'Nahal' (the initials of the Hebrew words for 'pioneer fighting youth'), designed in part to replace the Palmach, was created, which organized both collectively and on an individual basis all the embryonic pioneering youth movements, each platoon comprising simultaneously a military unit and a group of prospective settlers.

The Israeli Army during this war avoided the divisional level, and instead (as explained) was divided into frontal commands. While the commands themselves were confined to specific areas, the brigades did not belong permanently to given fronts, but could be placed at the disposal of any frontal commander according to the changing needs of the war, and thus concentrated for major efforts on different fronts. This best suited the prevailing conditions of the Palestinian theatre, when the Israeli forces were small in size and inferior in strength, and therefore could only achieve superiority in particular battles by mobility, concentration, manœvrability and the use of surprise. A reinforced Home Guard was relied upon to fill the gaps in the depleted fronts. The Commanding Officer of each front was entirely responsible for all aspects of the defence of his area, including the operational planning and execution of the offensives. He also had special liaison with the civil organization, local and regional.

The Israeli offensives that followed the end of the cease-fire on 10th October 1948, especially those in the Negev and the Central Galilee, not only helped to achieve and consolidate territorial gains and to weaken the enemy, but also further improved the shape of Israel's strategy and military organization. The troops became more accustomed to operate in larger units, with better and smoother co-ordination, by night or day, yet without losing their guerrilla flexibility and power of improvisation. They learned to make better use of their limited air and artillery support, acquired greater skill in field engineering, and, above all, developed greater mobility and manœuvrability. During this period, too, the tactics of 'indirect approach', so admirably expounded in Captain Liddell Hart's teachings,[11] were most extensively and successfully used, especially in the campaigns in the Negev and the northern Sinai Peninsula in January 1949.

As a result of these campaigns, the entire Galilee was cleared and restored to Israel; Israeli troops reached the Litani River on Lebanese territory; and the Egyptian siege of the Negev (stretching from Ashdod and Ashkelon on the Mediterranean through Faluja and Beit Jubrin to Hebron in the hills in the east, based on long lines of communication between El-Arish, Rafah and Gaza along the coast and between Kantara on the Suez Canal and Abu Agaila, Auja El Hafir, Bir-Asluj and Beersheba in the Central Negev) was lifted, the Egyptian forces crushed, and the entire northern Negev, including Beersheba, liberated. One gallant Egyptian brigade, however, surrounded and isolated in the Faluja pocket, remained there until the armistice.

The final clearing of the Gaza Strip and of the Southern Negev down to the Red Sea had been left for separate operations. These were undertaken towards the end of December 1948. On 22nd December a large-scale operation, spread over a wide area and highly mobile, was begun, with two objects in view: first, to clear finally the main road south of Beersheba down to the Sinai border, in order to eliminate the immediate danger to Beersheba and open the way to the final destruction of the Egyptian Army in the Gaza Strip; second, to prepare the ground for liberating the entire southern half of the Negev held by Transjordan. Omitting details, it is enough to say that a combination of guerrilla actions and quick moves by large bodies completely broke the Egyptian hold south of Beersheba, and, in a very fast move, the border of Sinai was crossed on 28th December. The main crossroad of Sinai, Abu Agaila, was taken after a brief and sharp battle; one small mobile task-force penetrated as deep as forty miles from the Suez Canal (then still in British hands); and the main body moved rapidly north-westwards, with the object of taking El-Arish, the capital of Sinai, and approaching the Gaza Strip from the rear—that is, from the most unexpected and therefore least-defended direction.[12] The entire Egyptian Army had in fact been cut off from Egypt, and it seemed that it was about to be finally defeated. The main Israeli task-force was standing ready for the last blow at the gates of El-Arish when the Government, acting under American political pressure, ordered the advance to be stopped and all troops to be withdrawn from Sinai. The order was resented by the troops, but accepted, thanks to its discipline; and by 5th January the last Israeli soldier had left Sinai.

Another chance was given, however, to attack the Gaza Strip, this time from within Israeli territory. A fresh task-force succeeded in crossing the dunes, and putting a strong wedge south of Rafah near the Israel-Egyptian border, thereby cutting the entire Strip from its rear, blocking the main road, and leaving the railroad intact but controlled from a near-by position, in the hope that this would reduce the enemy's stubbornness and encourage him to withdraw back into Egypt. At this point, the Egyptian Government agreed to enter upon armistice negotiations, provided the Israeli wedge were lifted. This was done: mistakenly, because it greatly weakened Israel's bargaining position in the subsequent negotiations for an armistice agreement, which was signed on the island of Rhodes on 24th February 1949—leaving the Gaza Strip in Egyptian hands to this day.

Once the Egyptians were out of the war, the Israelis could concentrate greater forces for the final liberation of Palestine. In a long-range movement of three brigades, the entire Southern Negev was conquered, including the Israel part of the Gulf of Akaba (16th March 1949). At the same time, Israel's part of the Dead Sea, including Massada and Ein Gedi and a part of the Judaean Desert, were liberated.

These successes, however, were offset by failures elsewhere. Owing to mistaken political considerations, certain well-planned operations to liberate the rest of the country, namely, the Hebron hills, Old Jerusalem and the Triangle—which had been on the point of being liberated in several earlier phases, especially after the Egyptian defeat—were abandoned; these territories remain still in Jordanian hands. Though the Israelis had been defeated in earlier small operations (against Jenin in the north and Bethlehem and the High Commissioner's Palace south of Jerusalem), and in spite of the lack of initiative shown in the Jerusalem area, the liberation of the rest of the country could now have been attained with less effort and greater assurance of success than in the big campaigns in the Negev and Sinai. But the chance was missed and soon afterwards armistice agreements were signed with the remaining neighbouring countries: with Lebanon on 23rd March 1949, with Transjordan on 3rd April and with Syria on 20th July. Iraq withdrew its forces from territory held by Trans-jordan without signing an agreement.

By these armistice agreements, the Israeli forces evacuated Lebanese territory south of the Litani; the Syrians evacuated their bridgehead in Upper Galilee; the surrounded Egyptian brigade was allowed to withdraw from the Faluja pocket; and Trans-jordan arrogated to herself the Samaria and Hebron areas, including the Old City of Jerusalem, and became the Kingdom of Jordan. As already indicated, Egypt continued her occupation of the Gaza Strip. All this, of course, prevented the establishment of an Arab State in Palestine as envisaged by the Partition Plan of the United Nations. The State of Israel, on its side, emerged from the war holding more extensive, and strategically more advant-ageous, territory than that originally allocated to her by the Partition Plan. This, however, was much less than it was within her military capacity to achieve; and much less, too, than was necessary for her defence against further threats from the same enemies.

From the time of the Armistice Agreements to the present day Israel has had no lasting peace. This tragic condition has effec-tively prevented the Israel defence authorities from resting on their laurels. With a view to meeting future dangers, they have been compelled to develop Israel's defence force, continually moderniz-ing it by taking into account every new advance in science, technology and tactics. But this phase of the making of Israel's Army—its growth before, during and since the Sinai Campaign—is no part of the present study, which restricts itself to the period up to and including the War of Liberation, that is, up to the emergence of Israel's defence force as a legal, regular army.

This army, it can truly be said, was made in action. Certain aspects of its development from a small group of watchmen at the turn of the century to the modern army of today were doubt-less due to imaginative leadership. But its main development, especially in size and equipment, was imposed upon it by the enemy, and at least some of its successes were due to the enemy's mistakes and weaknesses. To know how to exploit an opponent's weaknesses, however, is itself a gift. The exercise of such a gift, in turn, requires a highly organized and quick intelligence service, besides commanders and troops not only well trained and organized by usual military standards, but also specially trained, physically and mentally, for the peculiar demands of warfare directed toward national liberation and defence.

The heritage of the Haganah was multifold indeed. To begin with, the Army owed to the Haganah the very fact of its existence —that is, its man-power and arms, both on a relatively large scale. It inherited a sovereign territory as a geo-strategic base for its operations; a highly trained and dedicated cadre of commanders, from the section commander to the Chief of Staff; and a close-knit framework of units, with an *esprit* and a code of conduct as excellent as its military record. It inherited, besides, a deeply rooted purposefulness,[13] idealism, and belief in voluntary service, a spirit of comradeship and mutual responsibility, among units and ranks as well as individuals; and a peculiarly warm relationship with the nation. Indeed, though now a regular army, it remained basically a citizens' army; and was presently further confirmed in this character by the conscription of women into the appropriate branches. The freedom from obsolete Army traditions which had been so conspicuous a feature of the Haganah was retained by the new Army. As far as military forms and conventions were concerned, it adopted only the minimum necessary for securing discipline and efficiency: its attitude to these matters, in short, was (and remains) strictly functional.[14] Finally, having in mind that the Haganah had been, from its illegal underground beginnings, the creation of a popular movement for national liberation directed by democratically elected civil institutions, it is perhaps not surprising that the new Army should have inherited from it democratic values and complete loyalty to the new forms of parliamentary and social democracy: that it should become, indeed, and remain to the present day, one of the principal safeguards of democracy in Israel.

NOTES

1. Haganah (the Hebrew word for 'defence') was the name of the general illegal self-defence organization of the Jewish community in Palestine under the British Mandate. It was controlled by the elected national institutions of the Zionist movement.
2. *Kibbutz* (plural *kibbutzim*) is a form of pioneering co-operative settlement, based on collective ownership of property and a communal mode of life. It observes the principles of complete social equality, mutual responsibility and direct democracy.
3. *Moshav* (plural *moshavim*) is another form of pioneering co-operative settlement. While retaining some private ownership, it practises, like the *kibbutz*, a high degree of mutual aid on collective principles.
4. *Nehemiah*, iv. 17.
5. Although terrorism was rejected outright by the national authorities, it was adopted by two small, separatist underground groups which dissociated themselves from the elected authorities. The operations of these groups were often daring, and contributed to the overall pressure that finally led to the withdrawal of the British. But they could not have brought about the ultimate defeat of the British, chiefly because of their isolation within the Jewish community. Their contribution to the development of military conceptions as such was rather modest.
6. There were, however, cases of Arabs who co-operated with the Intelligence Service of the Haganah.
7. The single exception was Beit Ha'arava, on the northern shore of the Dead Sea. But even in this case the inhabitants were only moved to Sodom farther south on the Dead Sea which, though also isolated, was less close to the major route between Amman and Jericho than the original settlement.
8. The Arab town of Acre was liberated two days after the expiry of the Mandate; the clearing of Western Galilee was completed a few days later, on 22nd May 1948.
9. This in fact happened eleven days before the cease-fire, on 31st May 1948.
10. The Triangle covers the hilly part of east-central Palestine, and is so called because it includes the three main Arab towns of Tul-Kerem, Nablus and Jenin.
11. See particularly B. H. Liddell Hart, *Strategy: The Indirect Approach* (revised edition, London 1954).
12. According to conventional military doctrine, this plan would seem to have been quite illogical, involving as it did extended lines of communication without the support of adequate armour and

artillery. But, in a mobile war, the illogical may sometimes turn out to be the most logical—because, being least expected by the enemy, it is least prepared for and least defended.

13. This is expressed in the last of the nine principles of war adopted by Israel. These principles of war are: (i) maintenance of aim; (ii) initiative; (iii) surprise; (iv) concentration; (v) economy of force; (vi) protection; (vii) co-operation; (viii) flexibility; and (ix) consciousness of purpose or 'cause'.

14. A vivid comment on this point is to be found in Robert Henriques' *A Hundred Hours to Suez* (New York 1957). Colonel Henriques writes on page 12: 'Although Israeli units can be extremely smart on a ceremonial parade, there is very little discipline in the normal sense. Officers are often called by their first names amongst their men, as amongst their colleagues; there is very little saluting; there are a lot of unshaven chins; there are no outward signs of respect for superiors; there is no word in Hebrew for "sir". A soldier genuinely feels himself to be the equal of his officer—indeed of any officer—yet in battle he accepts military authority without question. I cannot explain, I cannot begin to understand, how or why it works. All my own military experience in the British and American Armies has taught me that first-class discipline in battle depends on good discipline in barracks. Israel's Army seems to refute that lesson.'

371

Biographical Summary

Basil Liddell Hart was born in Paris on 31st October 1895. After his parents' return to England, he went to St Paul's School and then to Corpus Christi College, Cambridge, where he took the honours course in history. In 1914 he became an officer in the King's Own Yorkshire Light Infantry. After two periods of service on the Western Front, where he was wounded and gassed, he first made a mark in the field of military theory by evolving the Battle Drill system in 1917, and other new tactical ideas subsequently adopted, particularly the 'expanding torrent' method of attack that became the basis of the Blitzkrieg technique. In 1920, at the age of twenty-four, he was given the opportunity of writing the first postwar official manual on *Infantry Training*, and subsequently edited the weapon manual *Small Arms Training*.

Invalided to the half-pay list in 1924 (and to the retired list in 1927) he was appointed Military Correspondent of the *Daily Telegraph* in 1925 as successor to the renowned Colonel Repington. Ten years later he moved to *The Times* in the same role and as its adviser on defence as a whole. Meanwhile he had also been Military Editor of the *Encyclopaedia Britannica*.

In 1937 he became personal adviser to the new War Minister, Mr Hore-Belisha, and helped to initiate a far-reaching programme for the modernization of the Army. Many of the proposed reforms were achieved, but opposition continued to delay the development of the tank and anti-aircraft forces. Feeling that progress was too slow compared with the speed at which war was approaching, Liddell Hart gave up his advisory role in the summer of 1938 in order to press the needs publicly.

Throughout the years since the first World War, he had been a leading advocate of airpower, armoured forces and amphibious strategy. Many of the foremost commanders of the second World War—including General Guderian, the creator and leader

373

of the Panzer forces—called themselves his 'disciples' and 'pupils'. The German encyclopaedia, *Der Grosse Brockhaus*, quotes Guderian as saying that Liddell Hart was 'the creator of the theory of the conduct of mechanized war', and General Chassin of France described him as 'the greatest military thinker of the twentieth century, whose ideas have revolutionized the art of war'. The late President Kennedy more recently paid tribute to his revolutionary influence on 'two generations'.

In all he has written some thirty books, and his writings have been translated into more than thirty languages. The first volume of his memoirs has recently been published and the second volume will appear simultaneously with this collection of essays.